MW01064845

4

Baseball's Good Guys

The Real Heroes of the Game

Marshall J. Cook and Jack Walsh

Sports Publishing L.L.C.
www.sportspublishingllc.com

Director of production: Susan M. Moyer
Project manager: Jim Henehan
Dust jacket design: Kerri Baker
Developmental editor: Doug Hoepker
Copy editor: Holly Birch
Photo editor: Erin Linden-Levy

Interior illustrations: Timothy Stiles

ISBN: 1-58261-722-8

Printed in the United States of America

Sports Publishing L.L.C.
www.sportspublishingllc.com

Contents

Introduction

What does it take to make the "good guys" roster? You don't need to be one of the greatest players who ever lived—although many of those included in this book surely are. Guys like Ted Williams, Hank Greenberg, Sandy Koufax, Henry Aaron, and Roberto Clemente make just about anybody's all-time all-star roster. But others, like Wilmer Mizell, Jim Eisenreich, and Ryne Duren, will never command a plaque at Cooperstown.

You don't have to be the most successful at what you do, either. Sammy Sosa came close this year but has still never appeared in a World Series. Buck O'Neill didn't even make it to the majors. Vin Scully—a good field, little hit outfielder—made it no further as a player than college ball. Ila Borders made baseball—and social—history without ever getting above Class A ball.

No, the common element that unites the men (and one woman) in this lineup isn't gaudy stats or great achievements. These folks all have what our fathers refer to as character.

In most cases they had to overcome considerable adversity—an impoverished upbringing, physical and mental disability, prejudice—to get as far as they did. And once successful, they all, in one way or another, turned around and gave a hand-up to others, in and out of the game of baseball. In many cases they transcended the world of sport to become genuine cultural heroes.

The notion of the "role model" has been pretty much beaten to death, especially by those athletes who angrily disavow any responsibility to their fans or their communities, but the folks in this book all serve in that capacity quite nicely.

What a privilege it's been for us to create a roster of baseball figures who combine baseball and inspiration into something special. Too often baseball is caught up in the world of exorbitant salaries, bad behavior, greed, and arrogance. It's easy for baseball fans to become disenchanted. We hope that these stories will remind them—and you—of just how good baseball can be and often is.

"Life is a game," Mother Theresa said. "Play it." And play it our good guys did, not only on the field, but also in how they reacted to adversity off the field. Whether it was the ravages of cancer and sickness, the numbing fear of mental illness, the scourge of racism, the hatred fueled by anti-Semitism, the anguish of a career-threatening injury, or the difficulty of facing the truth of their own sexual orientation, the 29 people depicted here rose to the occasion. Through their example, they've helped others do the same.

"If only we could transplant courage," Leonard Zakim, former executive director of the New England regional office of the Anti-Defamation League, once said. Maybe we can.

We hope that our lineup of stories will be a source of inspiration to our readers. Our good guys were all human, each with foibles just like us. Yet somehow they all transcended situations and limitations to become true role models for us all.

CHAPTER 1

Always Right on Time
Buck O'Neill

"I can honestly say I love everybody and I hate no one."
—Buck O'Neill

Full name: John Jordan O'Neill
Nickname: "Buck"
Position: First base
Negro League career: Memphis Red Sox, 1937; Kansas City
    Monarchs, 1938-43 and 1946-55
Negro League career batting average: .288

Career highlights:

- Led the Negro League in batting average in 1946 with a .353 mark.
- Played in three East-West Negro League All-Star games and two World Series.
- Hit .345 in 1940, .358 in 1947, and .330 in 1949.
- Managed Kansas City Monarchs to five pennants and two titles.

B uck O'Neill bears no grudges and has no regrets. There's no
room for such things in his heart or his head. His heart is full
up with gratitude and his head with good memories and wisdom.

Buck was one of the stars of the Negro Leagues. He led the league
with a .353 batting average in 1946 and topped that with a career-best
.358 the following year. He played with all the other greats—Satchel
Paige, Josh Gibson, Cool Papa Bell and Double Duty Ted Radcliff—and
he toured with Satch in hundreds of exhibition games in the '30s and
'40s.

He played on nine championship teams, appeared in three Negro
American League All-Star games and two Negro League World Series
and managed the Monarchs to five pennants and two Negro League
World Series titles.

Then he told us all about it in the Ken Burns baseball documentary
on PBS.

His ability and work ethic no doubt would have taken him to the
major leagues, but racial discrimination barred the way.

"It was a white man's game," Buck says. "It was pretty cut and
dried."

Folks say O'Neill, Paige, Gibson and the others came along too early
to benefit from Jackie Robinson breaking the color line in 1947. But
Buck says he was "right on time," which is also the title of his autobiography.

Although too old to join Jackie in the majors, Buck broke a few barriers of his own. When he retired from the Monarchs in 1955, he became
a scout for the Chicago Cubs, signing Hall of Famers Lou Brock and
Ernie Banks to their first pro contracts. Then he became a coach for the
Cubs in 1962—the first black coach in the majors. He became a Kansas
City Royals scout in 1988 and earned 'Midwest Scout of the Year' honors. There's nothing in the game of baseball Buck couldn't do.

Still, most of us might not know about him had he not had such a
prominent role in the Burns documentary. His wonderful narrative there
led to many interviews on national radio and television and the publication of his autobiography by Fireside Books in 1996. He became a
celebrity, to be sure, but Burns got it right when he called Buck O'Neill
"a hero ... not in the superficial sporting sense of a man who homers in
the ninth to win a game, but in the human sense of a man we all should
look to and strive to be more like."

Although the color barrier prevented Buck O'Neill, right, from playing in the major leagues and kept many Negro League stars like Satchel Paige, left, locked out of MLB until they were past their primes, Buck holds no grudges against the game.

As one of the prime movers behind the Negro Leagues Baseball Museum in Kansas City, Missouri, Buck works hard to see that other black players get recognition. He's also a member of the 18-member National Baseball Hall of Fame Veterans Committee.

He Got It from His Daddy

John Jordan O'Neill was born on November 13, 1911, in Carabelle, Florida, southwest of Tallahassee. He got his nickname and his love of baseball from his father, who played for local teams and dubbed his son "Buck" after the co-owner of the Miami Giants.

Buck signed with the Monarchs in 1938 and became player/manager of the team in 1948. He mentored Satchel Paige, Hilton Smith, Ernie Banks, and Elston Howard. He also played for the Miami Giants, Shreveport Acme Giants, and Memphis Red Sox.

For the Love of the Game

Buck O'Neill talks a lot about love. When he talks about baseball, his love for the game is evident in every syllable. Mark this passage from his autobiography:

"The first time I saw Ruth, up in St. Petersburg, it wasn't so much the sight of him that got me as the sound. When Ruth was hitting the ball, it was a distinct sound, like a small stick of dynamite going off. You could tell it was Ruth and not Gehrig and not Lazzeri.

"The next time I heard that sound was in 1938, my first year with the Monarchs. We were in Griffith Stadium in Washington to play the Homestead Grays, and I heard that sound all the way up in the clubhouse, so I ran down to the dugout in just my pants and my sweatshirt to see who was hitting the ball. And it was Josh Gibson. I thought, my land, that's a powerful man."

When he assumed a leadership role in the formation and development of the Negro Leagues Museum, he said the message he wanted to share wasn't about segregation and denial but about hope and achievement. He travels around the country spreading this message.

"I want the young people to know the wonderful changes that have happened in this country," he says. "I'm old enough to see these wonderful changes."

He uses words like "wonderful" often. He says he has no bitterness toward baseball, which has given him a great life.

"A lot of people thought we lived hand to mouth," he says, "but that wasn't the Negro Leagues. It was outstanding. They were my family.

"We were playing some of the best baseball in the country and… staying in some of the best hotels in the country. They just happened to be owned by blacks. We ate in some of the best restaurants in the country; they just happened to be owned by blacks."

He's pleased with the progress blacks have made and marvels that "a man who can hit a ball and catch a ball can make more money than the president of the United States. Only in America."

Now he wants to see black players move from the field into the front office.

"Managers don't hire or fire people," he says. "General managers have that ability…I tell young black guys that whatever they're studying in college, take at least one course in sports management. They might get a chance to be a general manager some day."

If he had any regrets, the biggest would surely be having been denied the chance to get an education. For Buck, unfairness, he says, was "[n]ot letting me attend Sarasota High School … [n]ot letting me attend the University of Florida."

Give It Up

In a long interview for the International Forgiveness Institute, Buck talked about his "Give it up" philosophy. Simply put, it is this: give love, while you let loose of anger and regret.

"[W]hen you love, when you give up anger or hatred or prejudice," he says, "it just frees you. Loving other people opens you up to receive love from others."

"Now, there are things I hate," he clarifies in his book, "but not people. I hate cancer. It killed my mother. My wife died two years ago from cancer. I hate AIDS and I hate what the Ku Klux Klan has done. I hate what the Skinheads do. But I can't hate the person. I can't hate God's creatures. You know, God never made anything ugly. We can become ugly, but God never made anything ugly."

Give love, he says, and you can turn hate around.

He credits his grandmother with helping him learn to forgive. "She took the long view," he explains. "And three years ago, you know, Sarasota High School gave me an honorary diploma. They invited every kid in Sarasota County."

His forgiveness stems, he says, from his belief in God and the assurance that he is a child of God.

And so is everybody else, he stresses, including the Klansman and the Skinhead.

"Our kids can't grow up doing evil for evil," he warns. "If you spit in my face and I spit in yours, what happens next? But if you spit in my face and I forgive you for it, you might become ashamed of what you've done. If I forgive you, I might change you."

Give love. Turn hate around. Buck O'Neill has done it all his life.

He says he thinks God might have kept him around so long to bear witness to the Negro Leagues. But he has become much more than an ambassador for the game he loves and for the great men who played in the Negro Leagues. Buck O'Neill is an ambassador for humanity.

"Waste no tears for me," he writes. "I didn't come along too early—I was right on time."

CHAPTER 2

The Iron Horse with a Lion's Heart
Lou Gehrig

"Yet today I consider myself the luckiest man on the face of the earth."
—Lou Gehrig, July 4, 1939 at Yankee Stadium

Full name: Henry Louis Gehrig (Born Ludwig Heinrich Gehrig)
Nicknames: "Columbia Lou," "The Iron Horse," "Biscuit Pants"
Position: First base
Career: New York Yankees, 1923-1939
Career batting average: .340

Career highlights:
- Led the league in batting in 1934 with a .363 mark.
- Led the league in slugging percentage in 1934 (.706) and 1936 (.696).
- Led the league in home runs in 1931 (46), 1934 (49), and 1936 (49).
- Led the league in RBI in 1927 (175), 1928 (142), 1930 (174), 1931 (184), and 1934 (165).
- Led the league in on-base percentage five times, peaking at .478 in 1936.
- Won AL Triple Crown in 1934.
- Selected as an All Star each season between 1933 and 1939.
- Selected as AL MVP in 1927 and 1936.
- Elected to the Hall of Fame.

On June 2, 2002, Lou Gehrig's farewell address once again echoed throughout the nation's baseball parks. On 14 major league diamonds, we heard his gracious speech of gratitude. James Gandolfini, Luke Perry, Chris Rock, Matt Dillon, Brook Shields, John Goodman and others recited Lou's 277-word speech, in which he pronounced himself "lucky" three times.

We remembered. We cried. We wondered. How could The Iron Horse be "lucky" while facing a prognosis of death?

Gehrig's words humbled us. We saw tragedy in a different light. His friends on the Yankees did, too. They concluded their 15-verse poetic tribute to Gehrig this way:

> *We who have known you best;*
> *Knowing the way you came through*
> *Every human test.*
> *Let this be a silent token*
> *of lasting friendship's gleam,*
> *and all that we've left unspoken.*
> *Your Pals of the Yankees Team*

Lou Spoke with His Bat

Lou Gehrig was born in New York and died in New York. He lost his body—but not his soul—to Amyotrophic Lateral Sclerosis (now called "Lou Gehrig's Disease" in his memory). This Yankee legend is alive today—in his legacy, in the game he played, and in the way he never let his disease control the way he lived.

He now lives "Up at the Hall," as Roger Angell describes Cooperstown, New York, where his Hall of Fame Plaque is brief and to the point:

HENRY LOUIS GEHRIG
NEW YORK YANKEES – 1923-1939
HOLDER OF MORE THAN A SCORE OF
MAJOR AND AMERICAN LEAGUE RECORDS,
INCLUDING THAT OF PLAYING 2130
CONSECUTIVE GAMES. WHEN HE RETIRED
IN 1939, HE HAD A LIFE TIME BATTING
AVERAGE OF .340

He was born Heinrich Ludwig Gehrig, but the name was later anglicized to Henry Louis Gehrig. His plaque couldn't hold all his nicknames:

ALS had robbed him of his baseball abilities and was soon to take his life, but "The Iron Horse" still called himself "the luckiest man on the face of this earth" while addressing fans during his farewell speech.

- "Iron Horse" for his day-to-day endurance;
- "Larrupin Lou" for his escapades with Ruth during the off season;
- "Columbia Lou" for his time at the Ivy League;
- "The Crown Prince" to the Babe's "Sultan of Swat."

His teammates called him "Biscuit Pants" and the fans "Piano Legs," references to his large buns and oversized leg muscles. The Babe called him "Buster." His wife, Eleanor, endeared him as "My Luke."

To all of us, he is "The Pride of the Yankees."

Gehrig Helped Build That House, Too

Phil Rizzuto says wearing the Yankee uniform is "the closest thing to heaven." Yankee fans had the privilege of seeing Gehrig suit up in those celestial pinstripes for 17 seasons. Yankee Stadium had just opened in 1923 when Gehrig took his first swing in the house that he would help Ruth build.

He played sparingly in 1923 and 1924, but his lusty .423 and .500 batting averages were portents of things to come.

Once he got his chance to start, he never stopped. Day after day, Gehrig showed up at first base. Beanings, fractures, colds, and an occasional bad back couldn't get him out of the lineup. From the day he pinch hit for Yankee shortstop Pee Wee Wanninger on June 1, 1925, until Ellsworth "Babe" Dahlgren replaced him at first base on May 1, 1939, Gehrig set those "scores of major and American League records."

His .632 slugging percentage is remarkable. Of his 2,721 hits, 43.7 percent were for extra bases (534 doubles, 163 triples, and 493 homers). In three seasons (1927, 1930, and 1934), Gehrig's slugging percentage exceeded .700. He placed first in on-base percentage for four consecutive years (1934-37). He knocked in close to 2,000 runs. He's runner up to the Cubs' Hack Wilson's single-season RBI record of 190. Lou drove in 184 runs in 1931, 175 in 1927, and 165 in 1934. He knocked in close to one run for each of the 2,164 games he played.

The Middle of "Murderers' Row"

Gehrig's trademark was an overwhelming strength, his specialty the homer. At the age of 15, he shocked scouts when he homered at Wrigley Field.

In 1927, when Yankee manager Miller Huggins switched Gehrig and Bob Meusel in the lineup, he created the infamous "Murderers' Row." Elevating Gehrig to cleanup was a stroke of genius. He was the guy, columnist Franklin P. Adams said, "who hit all those home runs the year Ruth broke the record."

Gehrig hit 493 in all—494 if Lyn Lary hadn't messed up.

On April 26, 1931, Gehrig homered with two outs and Lary on base. Lary thought the ball was caught when it bounced back to Washington's centerfielder Harry Rice, so he headed for the dugout. When Gehrig passed the spot he'd vacated, Lary was ruled out, and Gehrig's homer turned into a triple. Lary's blunder also cost Lou the AL homer championship. Ruth and Gehrig ended in a dead heat that season with 46 each.

The following year, on June 3, 1932, Gehrig blasted four consecutive homers against the Philadelphia Athletics. The game was a real slugfest in which the two teams hit for a record 77 total bases. The Yankees won, 20-13, and Gehrig tied two major league records.

Nobody had hit four round-trippers in one game since the Phillies' Ed Delehanty did it in 1896. "Big George" Earnshaw gave up three of the homers, and Leroy Mahaffey the fourth. Two carried into the centerfield stands, and two sailed over the rightfield fence.

Gehrig also duplicated Bobby Lowe's record for four consecutive homers. Lowe was a former Boston Nationals second basemen who hit four in a row at the old Congress Street Brotherhood Field in 1894. When Gehrig matched the feat, the 64-year-old Lowe donned his old uniform, put his arm around the grinning Gehrig, and posed for the cameras.

"It wasn't until we actually had the game salted away," Gehrig said, "that I realized that I had performed one of the rarest feats in baseball."

In the ninth inning, Lou almost connected for a fifth. Al Simmons, the Philly outfielder, made a leaping catch of Gehrig's drive at the fence.

Lou also holds the record for most career grand slams with 23. Willie McCovey, the San Francisco and San Diego star, is a distant second at 18.

The term "grand slam" wasn't coined until August 20, 1940, when the San Francisco News labeled Jim Tabor's homer a "grand slam." In Lou's day, they were called four-base clouts, homers with the bases drunk, or well-tagged blows with the sacks drugged. Ironically, Tabor, the red-headed Red Sox third baseman from Alabama, hit two grand slams in one game on Lou Gehrig's day in 1939.

One-upping the Babe and Barry

"In the fall of every year, when the leaves start to turn and World Series talk begins to crackle in the air, there comes a nostalgic moment when you're reminded of him," Jack Sher wrote of Gehrig. "You remember his thick, muscular legs, his broad back, his shy smile. And you remember not only the dynamite in his bat, the raw power of his home runs—but his rare mixture of gentleness and courage."

Barry Bonds got on base 21 times in 30 at-bats in the 2002 World Series. A record? Not quite. In the Yankees' four-game sweep of the St. Louis Cardinals in 1928, Gehrig batted .545 and reached base 12 out of his 17 plate appearances. He drove in nine runs, hit four home runs and a double, and also drew six walks.

In another four-game series, this time against the Chicago Cubs in 1932, Gehrig batted .529, hit three homers, and scored and batted in nine runs.

That series is best remembered for Ruth's "called shot" in Game 3. But according to Sher, it was actually a double shot. He says that Ruth turned to Gehrig after his historic blast and said, "You do the same thing I just done, kid." And Gehrig did. In fact, the Babe and Lou each hit two homers that day, leading the Yankees to a 7-5 win.

Gehrig played in seven World Series, batting .361. Nearly 50 percent of his hits were for extra bases. He hit 10 home runs and batted over .500 twice. The Yankees won six out of the seven Series, losing only to the 1926 St. Louis Cardinals in the seventh game when Jesse Haines edged out Waite Hoyt, 3-2.

Just a Square, Honest Guy

"The trouble started in 1938," his wife Eleanor said, "when his batting average slipped 56 points to .295."

At first she thought he was just in a slump, and the doctors thought it was a gall bladder problem.

It was neither.

Lou knew something was seriously wrong. He was shaky in the field and at bat during the 1939 spring training. After a series with the White Sox in Chicago, his wife arranged a visit to the renowned Mayo Clinic. Gehrig flew to Minneapolis and spent six days undergoing tests. The Mayo report sentenced an innocent man to death.

"The nature of this trouble," the report said, "makes it such that Mr. Gehrig will be unable to continue his active participation as a baseball player, inasmuch as it is advisable that he conserve his muscular activity."

Gehrig had Amyotrophic Lateral Sclerosis. In Greek, "Amyotrophic" means no muscle nourishment. You lose movement and strength. Your body begins to waste away, while your mind stays alert. ALS is progressive and fatal; there is no known cure.

Gehrig never complained. He dismissed the "It's not fair!" whining and "Why me?" questioning. Instead he took a position as a parole officer for the city of New York.

"He understood and had deep compassion for those, who like himself, had grown up in squalor and poverty," Jack Sher wrote. "He knew the cause of most crimes. Few men so well understood frustration and loneliness, and deprivation."

It was a way he could help the city that had given him so much joy.

"It was a fine chance," Eleanor Gehrig told Lou, "to do something good for the old hometown."

Lou Gehrig died a few weeks before his 37th birthday.

Every Gift But Length of Years

Actor Edward Hermann, who played Lou Gehrig in the 1978 television movie "A Love Affair: The Eleanor and Lou Gehrig Story," had a difficult time unlocking Gehrig's personality.

"There was no strangeness there," Hermann said, "nothing spectacular about him. As Eleanor Gehrig told me, he was just a square, honest guy."

The Iron Horse's record of 2,130 consecutive games stood from 1939 until 1995, when Cal Ripken Jr. broke it. Some worried that baseball fans would forget Gehrig, but as Ripken approached Lou's record, he revived baseball's and Gehrig's reputations. During Ripken's run at "the streak," more money was contributed to ALS research than ever before.

And one of Gehrig's records can never be broken. On July 4, 1939, he became the first baseball player to have his number retired.

"We share sentimental pain," Bruce Weber wrote. "We suffer real pain alone."

Gehrig didn't pick his battle, the battle picked him. He responded with hope, patience, and courage. By his perseverance, he served as a witness to us all.

CHAPTER 3

Keeping the Faith
Hank Greenberg

"Hank was smart, he was proud, and he was big."

—Shirley Povich

"I never put myself in Ruth's class as a hitter."

—Hank Greenberg

Full name: Henry Benjamin Greenberg
Nickname: "Hammerin' Hank"
Position: First base, Outfield
Career: Detroit Tigers, 1930, 1933-41 and 1945-46; Pittsburgh Pirates, 1947
Career batting average: .313

Career highlights:
- Led the league in slugging percentage in 1940 with a .670 mark.
- Was home run champ in 1935 (36), 1938 (58), 1940 (41), and 1946 (44).
- Topped the league in RBI in 1935 (170), 1937 (183), 1940 (150), and 1946 (127).
- Led the league in total bases in 1935 (389) and 1940 (384).
- Selected as an All Star every year between 1937-1940 and in 1945.
- Won the AL MVP in 1935 and 1940.
- Elected to the Hall of Fame.

Hank Greenberg wasn't the first Jew to play Major League Baseball, but he was the first Jewish star, and that drew the fire of bigots.

Jews were supposed to be tailors and bankers. They sold sporting goods; they didn't play professional athletics. If one of them occasionally hung around on the margins of a sport, that was okay. But a Jew who towered over other players and smashed the ball over every leftfield fence he encountered—that was a different matter.

"There was nobody in the history of the game who took more abuse than Greenberg, unless it was Jackie Robinson," according to Birdie Tebbetts, who as a young reserve catcher was Hank's teammate at Detroit. "Nobody else could have withstood the foul invectives that were directed toward Greenberg, and he had to eat them, or else he would be out of every game he played."

"He just sucked it up and went out there and hit home runs," said Aviva Kempner, who spent 13 years creating a documentary entitled *The Life and Times of Hank Greenberg*.

Unlike Jackie Robinson, Hank Greenberg was under no directive to ignore all the abuse, however. When White Sox player Joe Kuhel intentionally spiked him during the 1938 season, for example, Hank fought him, and after the game, he stormed into the White Sox clubhouse and called out the entire team.

"If you got a gut in your body," he screamed, "you'll stand up."

To a man, the Sox remained seated.

Another time, infuriated by the taunts of champion Jew-baiter Ben Chapman, Hank stomped over to the New York Yankee dugout, ready to take on the whole team.

In an interview for the documentary film on his life, he said of the insults and abuse, "It was a constant thing. I think it was a spur for me to do better. Not only were you a bum; you were a Jewish bum."

So Hank Greenberg picked up a bat and met major league pitchers and anti-Semitism head on. In the process, he came within a whisker of breaking the slugging records of Yankee greats Babe Ruth and Lou Gehrig. In 1937, he drove in 183 runs, one short of Gehrig's mark, and the next year he chased Ruth's single-season home run record, falling two short at 58.

He led the Tigers to pennants in '34, '35, '40 and '45. And like Ted Williams, he interrupted his playing career twice to serve his country in the military.

His most dramatic home run came on the final day of the 1945 season. With the Tigers and Senators dead even in a race for the pennant, Hank poked a ninth-inning grand slam to win it all.

His most dramatic personal decision came 11 years earlier, during the pennant drive of 1934, when he sat out on Yom Kippur, the Jewish Day of Atonement.

"Baseball Was Everything"

Hank Greenberg was born on New York's Lower East Side on January 1, 1911 (1/1/11), the third of four children of David and Sarah Greenberg. His parents were Rumanian Jewish immigrants who kept a kosher home, where they spoke both Yiddish and English. David Greenberg ran the Acme Textile Shrinking Works and commuted to Manhattan.

When Hank was six, the family moved to a Jewish neighborhood in the Bronx, and Hank attended the Hebrew school. By the time he was 13, he stood a towering six foot three.

He saw his first baseball game at the Polo Grounds when he was 14. He starred at James Monroe High School, where he was an All-City athlete in soccer and basketball, as well, but baseball was his passion.

"Baseball was everything," he said, "the only game that mattered."

His parents thought it was a "bum's game." They wanted him to be a professional man. He wanted to be a professional baseball player.

"Jewish women on my block…would point me out as a good-for-nothing, a loafer, and a bum who always wanted to play baseball," Hank told a reporter for the *Detroit Jewish Chronicle* in 1935. "I was Mrs. Greenberg's disgrace."

When he started pounding the ball in the Bronx Quarter League, an Irish cop named Pat McDonald told him, "You hit a ball better than Lou Gehrig." The Iron Horse became Hank's measure of success from then on.

He graduated from James Monroe High School in February of 1929 and went to New York University on an athletic scholarship. Like another famous Jewish baseball player who would come after him, Sandy Koufax, Greenberg's scholarship was for basketball, But it was difficult to make money in basketball in those days. Baseball was the only way for a star athlete to make a living.

After a year of college, Hank was ready to do just that. He was the only one of David and Sarah's children not to graduate. His parents weren't pleased.

Hank Greenberg was a giant among his peers, both for his towering home runs and his gutsy stance against anti-Semitism.

Hank played semipro ball for Bay Parkways, hitting .454 in 21 games, and moved on to the Blackstone Valley League in Massachusetts. Scouts for the Tigers and Yankees saw him there and tried to sign him. New York topped Detroit's $9,000 offer by a thousand, but Hank saw Lou Gehrig holding down first base for the Yankees and opted to sign with the Tigers.

"I never had any regrets," he said of his decision.

Still a raw 19-year-old young man, he went to Florida for spring training in March of 1930. The Tigers assigned him to Hartford of the Class A Eastern League, where he struck out 13 times in a row and batted only .214 in 12 games. They shipped him down to Raleigh in the Class C Piedmont League, and he found his stroke, hitting .314 with 19 homers.

He drew attention for another reason, too. Folks would walk up to him, he reported, and say, "I've never seen a Jew before." They said it more in curiosity than hostility initially, he said. The hostility would come soon enough.

Detroit in the 1930s seethed with anti-Semitism. Father Charles Couglin preached the virtues of Nazism on his popular radio show, and Henry Ford published a tract warning of a "vast Jewish conspiracy" to destroy Christian civilization. Hank would endure insults and taunts from his own fans; some even threw pork chops on the field.

The big club called him up at the end of the season, where he impatiently sat the bench. When he finally got to pinch hit against the Yankees' Red Ruffing, he popped up.

He started his second professional season with the Beaumont Explorers of the Class A Texas League, got sent down to Evansville of the 3-I League, and again rebounded, hitting .318 with 15 home runs.

He worked constantly, taking batting practice with anybody who would throw to him, swinging until his hands bled. A self-styled "giraffe" around first base, he worked hard on his fielding, too.

He went back to Beaumont in '32, where he was teammates with Schoolboy Rowe. Hank was ready for the Texas heat this time, belting 39 home runs and driving in 131 to capture the league MVP award.

He also took no guff, once getting into a brawl with Zeke Bonura.

The home runs, the RBIs, and the fights were all portents of things to come.

In 1933 the Tigers tried to shift him to third base in spring training, after he had worked so hard to make himself into a good first baseman. When that experiment failed, he sat the bench behind regular first baseman Harry Davis. But he started playing against lefties and got his first major league home run against the Senators on May 6, 1933, just his second hit in 14 at-bats.

He became the Tigers' regular first baseman later in the season, hitting .301 with 12 home runs and 87 RBIs in 449 official at-bats.

The same year, Adolph Hitler became Chancellor of Germany.

Hank called baseball "the most pleasant way to make a living that's ever been invented," but he still expected to be compensated fairly for his services. When the Tigers offered him $4,500 for the 1934 season, he held out for $5,500, compromising on a $5,000 base salary and a $500 bonus if the Tigers finished first, second, or third.

Greenberg earned his bonus.

The Game He Didn't Play

Hank's slugging helped propel the Tigers into a fierce pennant race with the Yankees. Knowing that he was now an integral part of the team, he agonized over whether to play on Rosh Hashanah, which fell on September 10 that year. The Tigers were up by four games on the Yankees and were playing the tough Boston Red Sox. Having had insults rained on him all year from anti-Semites, Hank now took criticism from rabbis and parishioners by deciding to play. His two home runs won the game for Detroit, 2-1.

A few days later, on Yom Kippur, the Day of Atonement and the most high holy day of the Jewish calendar, he chose praying over playing, sitting out the game and going to the Shaarey Zedek synagogue for 10:30 a.m. services. One member of the congregation was alleged to have murmured, "My God. Nobody ever saw a Jew that big."

Without him in the lineup, the Tigers lost.

His decision not to play inspired Edgar Guest to write a poem that ended:

We shall miss him in the infield and shall miss him at the bat,
But he's true to his religion, and I honor him for that!

"[H]is fine intelligence, independence of thought, courage and his driving ambition have won him the respect and admiration of his teammates, baseball writers, and the fans at large," Bud Shaver wrote in the *Detroit Times*. "He feels and acknowledges his responsibility as a representative of the Jews in the field of a great national sport, and the Jewish people could have no finer representative."

"Every Yom Kippur my father would tell us about this wonderful Detroit hitter who refused to play a crucial game on the Day of

Atonement," Aviva Kempner recalled years after, "and how he made such a statement for all Jews."

"I realize now, more than I used to, how important a part I played in the lives of a generation of Jewish kids," Hank wrote in his autobiography.

For the rest of his career, he got letters from Jewish kids exhorting him, "Don't let us down."

It was the only game he missed all year. In fact, it was the only game any member of the Tigers' starting infield missed.

Paced by Greenberg's .339 average, 26 home runs, and 139 runs batted in, Detroit captured the flag and drew over a million fans for the first time in franchise history.

Meanwhile, the St. Louis Cardinals had roared to the National League pennant behind the Dean Brothers, winning 20 of their last 25 games. Dizzy Dean won 30 games that season, with brother Paul winning an additional 19.

The Series—the first in history broadcast on the radio—went the full seven games, with the Cards prevailing. Hank hit .321 with a homer and seven RBIs but also struck out nine times and took a lot of abuse from fans and opposing players.

He worked relentlessly in the off season to improve himself, playing handball and squash to keep in shape and taking dancing lessons to improve his agility around first base. He also designed his own glove, which teammates said resembled "a lobster trap with a fishnet."

Chasing Lou

He started belting the ball from day one in 1935, sparking talk of a triple crown. By the All-Star break, he had an astonishing 110 RBIs.

Perhaps more astonishing, he wasn't selected for the All-Star game. He never forgot the slight.

He endured a 0-for-16 slump toward the end of the season but still finished with 170 RBIs, 51 more than second best, and Detroit again won the pennant en route to facing another white-hot National League team in the World Series. This time it was the Chicago Cubs, who rode a 21-game winning streak into what would turn out to be their last World Series of the 20th Century.

In the second game, Hank injured his wrist. Characteristically, he tried to play through the pain. Barely able to grip the bat, he came up in a crucial situation, with runners on first and second, and surprised everyone by laying down a perfect sacrifice bunt.

He was finished for the year. His lone hit in six at-bats against the Cubs was a home run, and it was enough. Detroit won in six games, and Hank Greenberg was a unanimous choice for league MVP, with a .328 batting average and 36 home runs to go with those 170 RBIs.

Only then did he go to the doctor for X-rays—and discovered that he had fractured his wrist.

He had the whole winter to heal, and he was an established star. He expected to be paid like one. He wanted $35,000 to sign for 1936. When the Tigers offered him $25,000, he felt "chagrin" at the disrespect shown to him by management.

He signed for the $25,000 and got ready to lead his team to another pennant. He again set a torrid early pace, driving in 16 runs in his first 12 games, but in that 12th game he recracked the bone in his wrist. He was finished for the season, and when star catcher Mickey Cochrane also suffered a season-ending injury, so were the Tigers.

Hank worked hard in the off season and signed a contract for the 1937 season for $1—with the stipulation that he'd receive a bonus of $25,000 if he demonstrated in spring training that he could play.

He could play for certain.

That year Hank made his historic run at Lou Gehrig's American League record of 184 RBIs. The record meant a lot to Hank, in part because Gehrig held it and in part because Hank considered runs batted in to be the most important measure of a hitter.

He had 181, three off the record, going into game 153 (of a 154-game season). The crowd roared when he came to the plate against Mel Harder with the bases loaded. Hank belted a towering fly ball, but it settled into the outfielder's glove just short of the fence. The runner tagged up and scored for RBI number 182, but Hank had just missed the grand slam that would have given him the record.

In the last game of the season, Hank and the Tigers faced Cleveland's Johnny Allen, a sensational 15-0 and going for an AL record 16th straight victory. Hank singled in a run in the first for RBI 183, but it was the only run of the game.

This year it would have been impossible to keep Greenberg off the All-Star roster, but he rode the bench the whole game. When he was selected as an All-Star again in 1938, he chose not to go.

Chasing the Babe

He had a good but not sensational 22 home runs in the first 69 games in 1938 when he suddenly went on a tear, belting homers in four consecutive at-bats. Suddenly he was "chasing Babe

Ruth's record," according to the press. On July 27, in the 88th game of the season, he hit home runs 32 and 33, putting himself seven games ahead of the Babe's record pace. But, as he kept reminding reporters, Ruth had had an amazing run in September. Hank would have to stay well ahead of the pace to stand a chance.

By this time, the Tigers were out of pennant contention, so Hank was free to swing for the fences. He came into September needing just 14 dingers in 32 games to catch the Babe and was still six games ahead of the pace. He hit his 50th in game 134, number 56 in game 145, and was still clinging to a three-game lead on Ruth.

Improbably, home run 57 was an inside-the-park job, the only one he ever hit. (Nobody ever mistook Hank for a gazelle on the base paths.) Hank maintained that umpire Bill McGowan gave him a break on the call at the plate.

He hit his 58th in game 149, giving him five games to hit two to tie or three to break the record.

"When I crossed the plate after hitting my 58th," Hank wrote, "I suddenly thought, 'I can do it.'"

He said he felt a special responsibility. "I was representing a couple of million Jews among 100 million gentiles," he wrote, "and I was always in the spotlight. I was big, and I wasn't the greatest player in the world." He cited his errors and strikeouts in downplaying himself as a star.

"I had to make good," he continued. "I just had to show them that a Jew could play ball. ... I came to feel that if I, a Jew, hit a home run, I was hitting one against Hitler."

He was blanked in the next two games and went into the final three-game series against Cleveland still needing two to tie, three to break.

He didn't hit any.

Many said that the Indians' staff pitched around Hank to prevent a Jew from breaking the Babe's mark. Hank called the assertion "pure baloney."

"The fact is quite the opposite," he wrote. "So far as I could tell, the players were mostly rooting for me, aside from the pitchers."

Hank had a strong if not sensational season in 1939 for a fifth-place Tigers team, hitting .312 with 33 home runs. That season Lou Gehrig, Hank's personal yardstick for achievement, sat down after a record 2,130 consecutive games.

In 1940 Tigers management faced a dilemma of its own making. They had added slugger Rudy York to the roster, and York could only play first base, Hank's position. A superstar, despite his own protestations to the contrary, Hank could have balked at the suggestion that he switch to the outfield, especially since he doubted his abilities as a fielder. And he had worked so hard to make himself into a competent first baseman.

But Hank agreed to give it a try, for the good of the team. The Tigers offered him a $10,000 bonus if he made the transition.

Hank immediately went to work, shagging flies and learning the caroms off the outfield wall.

"Hank learned to play the outfield well," Joe DiMaggio commented. "He was one of the most determined men I've ever known."

Hank was typically self-effacing about his efforts. "It's the same baseball," he told Bill Slocum of the *New York American*, "and I'm a ballplayer. I should be able to catch it in the outfield as well as anyplace else. And if I'm not a ballplayer, I'm getting old enough to find that out."

Hank Greenberg was every inch a ballplayer. He was steady in the field and sensational at the plate, hitting .340 with 41 homers and 150 RBIs—again winning the MVP in 1940. He was the first to win the award at two different positions.

With Rudy York also contributing 33 home runs and 134 RBIs, Detroit captured the flag in 1940 before losing in seven games to Cincinnati in the World Series.

The First Star to March Off to War

Then Hank Greenberg, a leader, a star, and an icon on the field, became an American hero off it.

On his way home from the Series, he registered for the military draft in Detroit. When his number came up, he made no attempt to get a deferment. When he was classified 4F anyway, because of very flat feet, many in the press accused him of bribing the doctor. Hank was reexamined and classified 1A.

"I made up my mind to go when I was called," he said. "My country comes first."

He was the only major league star drafted for service.

At age 30 he reported for active duty on May 7, 1941, three weeks into the season. When he joined the Army's 5th Division, 2nd Infantry Anti-Tank Company at Fort Custer, his salary plunged from $55,000 a year to $21 a month.

Senator Joshua Bailey of North Carolina called him a hero.

While in the service, Hank was a soldier, not a baseball player. He played exactly one game, an exhibition game against a prison team. Since they were shorthanded, Hank actually played with the prisoners, going four for four, including a long home run over the prison wall. (Many of his teammates volunteered to go get the ball.)

Hank had made sergeant by the time Congress passed a law that no one over 28 would be drafted, and he received his discharge on Friday, December 5, 1941.

Two days later, the Japanese bombed Pearl Harbor.

"I'm going back in," Hank declared immediately. "We are in trouble, and there is only one thing to do—return to service. Baseball is out the window as far as I'm concerned."

He became the first major league player to enlist, joining the Air Corps, passing Officers Candidate School as a second lieutenant, and reporting for duty in Fort Worth, Texas, where he bunked for a time with movie star William Holden.

He could have had a stateside job as an athletic instructor, but he requested overseas duty, commanding a B-29 bomber squadron in the China Burma-India Theater.

When he was discharged on June 14, 1945, he pronounced himself, "Lucky to come back in one piece."

But could he still play baseball?

The Warrior Returns to the Field

Hank represented "a symbol of hope to all the other ballplayers in the service," Associated Press reporter Whitney Martin wrote as the 34-year-old slugger attempted a comeback after his long layoff.

On July 1, Hank signed at his old salary of $55,000. In the eighth inning of his first game back, he belted a home run. It had been four years, one month, and 24 days between homers. He hit .311 in 78 games—the highest average in the league, although his 270 at-bats didn't qualify him for the batting title.

The Washington Senators finished the season 87-67. With two games left against the St. Louis Browns, the Tigers stood at 87-65. Needing a win to clinch the flag, they faced the Brownies on a rain-soaked field. Behind 3-2 in the ninth inning of the first game, Detroit loaded the bases, and up to the plate strode Greenberg. Could he come through for them in the clutch, after such a long time away from baseball?

He drove the ball deep into the left field seats for a grand slam, and the Tigers had the pennant. His teammates carried him off the field, "like I was a hero," Hank wrote.

Like?

The Series against the Cubs went the full seven games with Detroit winning the finale, 9-3. Hank injured his right wrist in that game but contributed a .304 average, with two homers and seven RBIs.

Detroit again rewarded him by asking him to make another tough adjustment. He had learned to like playing the outfield, but now the club asked him to come back to first base, where the aging star would be involved in just about every play again. Hank of course said yes.

He was hitting only .270 by the All-Star break but had 55 RBIs, and his 22 home runs were one off the league lead. Still, he wasn't selected for the American League All-Star team. Baseball was becoming hard work for him now, and when he struggled at the plate, Detroit fans actually booed their hero.

His place in baseball history was already secure. Retirement had to be tempting.

Instead, he lit up September with one of the greatest streaks of his career. He bombed six home runs in six days, to bring him to 37 for the season—more than the entire White Sox team, more than his next four teammates combined, and second only to Ted Williams in the league. He wound up with 44 dingers and 127 RBIs, leaving Williams behind (with 38 homers and 123 RBIs). Hank hit a solid .277, the first time in his career he failed to hit .300.

Grantland Rice called the late-season surge "one of baseball's greatest achievements."

Detroit management apparently wasn't so impressed. They put Hank on waivers, selling him to the Pittsburgh Pirates—dead last in the National League—for $10,000.

After 16 heroic years, Hank was no longer a Tiger. They notified him by telegraph.

"It took the heart out of me," he wrote. "I became so disillusioned overnight that I made up my mind to quit."

He had other inducements to leave the game. He had married Caral Gimbel, the department store heiress, and they had a son, Glenn. Hank wanted to be with his family and start a career in business.

Pirates management begged him to play just one year in Pittsburgh. They promised to shorten the field in left, creating a "Greenberg Gardens" for the 36-year-old slugger to hit home runs into. They told Hank he wouldn't have to endure the long train rides or put up with a roommate on the road anymore. And they said they'd pay him $100,000.

So Hank became a member of the Pirates, and Pittsburgh set a franchise attendance record. Hank led the league in walks, hustled on the field, and knocked out 25 home runs while hitting .249.

More importantly, he took a young slugger named Ralph Kiner under his big wing and taught him how to be a big leaguer, even waiving his no-roommate privilege to room with Kiner on the road.

From the Field to the Front Office

Hank finished his career with a slugging percentage of .605, hitting a home run every 6.4 at-bats (ninth best all-time). He averaged almost an RBI a game over his career.

He also figured he'd saved about $300,000 of the $447,000 he'd made; he was ready for a life outside of baseball.

But that would have to wait. Bill Veeck, whom Hank had come to admire greatly, hired him to serve as his assistant for the 1948 season at Cleveland, paying him $15,000 and expecting little more than he "learn the ropes."

Next season Hank wanted more responsibility, and Veeck put him in charge of the Indians' farm system. Hank implemented an innovative combined spring training session in Marianna, Florida (up until then, each minor league team worked out separately). He also hired Rudy York to help him, mostly because his old teammate was down and out and needed a break.

Hank's system worked. Thirteen of his 18 farm teams made their league playoffs.

The next season Veeck made Hank his general manager. Hank made several moves that were successful on the field but were unpopular with fans. He hired Al Lopez to replace the popular Lou Boudreau as manager. He brought up Al Rosen, a Jew, to play third base. ("He paved the way for people like me," Rosen said later.) Fans even complained in 1954, when the Tribe won a record 111 games (but lost the Series in four games to the Giants). The beef? He had "too many" black players on the team.

When Hank discovered next season that those black players weren't allowed to stay in the hotels with their teammates in St. Louis, Baltimore, or Washington, he immediately wrote to the hotels, telling them they were to accommodate all of the players or none of the players. They accepted all of the players.

On January 25, 1956, Hank was elected to the Hall of Fame, appearing on 164 of the 193 ballots cast. Echoing the words of songwriter Johnny Mercer, he told reporters, "It's just too wonderful for words. I'm deeply grateful and humble for this honor."

Then life took a couple of nasty turns. The Tribe released him as GM at the end of the '57 season and, since he still owned 20 percent of the team, he wasn't allowed to work for any other club. He was out of baseball.

The next year, his wife, Caral, filed for divorce.

Hank fought for custody of their three children, sons Glenn and Stephen and daughter Alva, just six years old, and wound up caring for them in an apartment in New York, so they could also be near their mother.

Bill Veeck again came looking for him. Hank sold his Cleveland stock, and he and Veeck bought a controlling interest in the Chicago White Sox in 1959. Veeck wanted Hank to run the farm system again, but Hank wanted to be team treasurer. So, Veeck handed him the purse. Hank commuted between New York and Chicago.

The rejuvenated "Go-Go" Sox, who hadn't won a pennant since the infamous "Black Sox" of 1919, drew 1.7 million fans, captured the flag, and battled the Dodgers in the World Series, losing in six games.

Veeck became sick the next year, and he and Hank sold the team. But Hank stayed on to run the club, still commuting from New York. After that final season, he quit the Sox and baseball, pronouncing it "a cold, cruel business."

After a successful 31-year career on the field and in the front office, Hank Greenberg was through with the sport he loved.

His lifetime batting average was .313. He hit 331 home runs (and another five in the World Series) and drove in 1,276 runs. He was a two-time American League MVP and led the league in home runs three times and RBIs four. His at-bat-to-RBI ratio of 4.07 ranks third behind only Babe Ruth and Lou Gehrig.

And the self-proclaimed "giraffe" in the field finished his career with a sparkling .990 fielding percentage. When he came back from the war in 1945, he played 72 games in the outfield without making a single error.

He helped redesign the baseball glove and scoreboard, changed the way baseball conducted spring training, proposed interleague play as early as 1952, helped establish player pensions, and testified for Curt Flood when he fought in court to establish a player's right to become a free agent.

He was the first Jewish owner/general manager in baseball and the first Jewish player elected into the Hall of Fame.

"When I was playing," he said, "I used to resent being singled out as a Jewish ballplayer. I wanted to be known as a great ballplayer, period. I'm not sure why or when it changed, because I'm still not a particularly religious person. Lately, though, I find myself wanting to be remembered not only as a great ballplayer, but even more as a great Jewish ballplayer."

He's remembered for that and more.

Life After Baseball

When young Glenn Greenberg, oldest of Hank and Caral Greenberg's three children, went off to college, a reporter sought him out and asked him if he was Jewish.

"I don't know," he replied.

His father had never told him.

Hank Greenberg said he wanted to "spare" his children from such awareness. He had soured on organized religion, Glenn's brother Stephen said. His father had mixed feelings about being Jewish but became in later life a kind of "militant good Jew," Stephen said. He thought organized religion was a "con game," largely responsible for wars and hatred.

Religion has "torn people apart," Hank said, "and created nothing but death and destruction."

Stephen recalled that when he was 11 and his brother Glenn was 13, their father took them to the planetarium on Yom Kippur. It was a kind of compromise, Stephen reasoned, a way of observing the Holy Day without going to a synagogue.

Stephen followed his father into baseball, playing for Yale and then signing with the Washington Senators. He topped out with three good years in Triple A before becoming a player representative.

He remembered that his father "talked about Sandy Koufax all the time."

Hank became a successful investment broker in New York City. He married Mary Jo DeCicco in 1966, and they moved to Beverly Hills, California, in 1974.

In October of 1984, Hank was diagnosed with possible peripheral neuropathy, but doctors changed their minds when they discovered cancer. At age 75, Hank had his diseased kidney removed.

His father could never accept, Stephen said, that his big, strong body had let him down. He kept his illness a secret from all but his immediate family.

On January 2, 1986, his friend and mentor, Bill Veeck, died. Later that year, Hank developed a cataract. He was in excruciating pain, and passed away on September 4, 1986.

His protégé, Ralph Kiner, was broadcasting a baseball game when he got the news bulletin.

"This is the worst day of my life," Kiner told his audience. "My dearest friend and the man who was like a father to me, Hank Greenberg, has died."

When Aviva Kempner heard the news of Hank's death on the radio, she knew instantly she would make a documentary film about him. With financial assistance from Steven Spielberg, Norman Lear, Carl Reiner, Mel Brooks, Kirk Douglas, Leonard Nimoy and others, she toiled on her labor of love for 13 years. Finally, in 1999, *The Life and Times of Hank Greenberg* premiered, starting with actor/singer Mandy Patinkin's haunting rendition of "Take Me Out to the Ballgame" in Yiddish.

At Hank's memorial service, actor Walter Matthau admitted having joined the Beverly Hills Tennis Club, even though he didn't play the game, just for the chance to talk to Hank regularly.

Dr. Rex Kennamer spoke of Hank's "gift of undemanding friendship…Hank did not shirk from the responsibilities of friendship."

Of his great fame, his friend Anne Taylor Flemming said, "he had no need to tell you about it or flaunt it."

Son Stephen said simply, "He was my mentor, my best friend."

"He gave selflessly to any number of individuals and causes," according to a *Detroit News* editorial. "If you don't believe that, just watch. Praise will flow from places you never considered: from entertainers, politicians, tennis players, celebrities, groundskeepers, restaurant owners, sportswriters, baseball fans."

The praise has flowed. Thanks in part to Aviva Kempner's documentary, Hank remains a hero to many who never met him and never saw him play but know what he stood for.

In the words of the *Detroit News* editorial, Hank "was a great man."

CHAPTER 4

Duty Calls

Ted Williams

"A man has to have goals—for a day, for a lifetime—and that was mine, to have people say, 'There goes Ted Williams, the greatest hitter who ever lived.'"

—Ted Williams

"He was a remarkable American as well as a remarkable ballplayer. His passing so close to a national holiday seems part of a divine plan, so we can always remember him not only as a great player but also as a great patriot."

—Vin Scully

"Ted was everything that was right about the game of baseball. If you really think about it, he was everything that is right about this country."

—Lloyd McClendon

Full name: Theodore Samuel Williams
Nicknames: "Ted," "Teddy," "The Kid," "The Thumper,"
"The Splendid Splinter," "Teddy Ballgame"
Career: Boston Red Sox, 1939-42, 1946-1960
Career batting average: .344

Career highlights:
• Won battle titles five times, including in 1941 when he hit .406.

- Led the league in home runs in 1941 (37), 1942 (36), 1947 (32) and 1949 (43).
- Topped the league in RBI four times, including a career-best mark of 159 in 1949.
- Led the league in bases on balls eight seasons, twice setting the mark at 162 (in 1947 and 1949).
- Was an 17-time All Star.
- Won the AL MVP in 1946 and 1949.
- Won the AL Triple Crown in 1942 and 1947.
- Elected to the Hall of Fame.

Ted Williams was not a nice man. His frequent fits of temper were sudden and severe. The few who were close to him said it was as if a demon possessed him at times.

He spoke in capital letters, lacing his speech with profanity.

His private life was a mess. He married and divorced three times and was by his own estimation "a horseshit father" to his three kids.

He spat at fans and sportswriters—literally and more than once—if always from a distance.

And he famously refused to tip his cap to the Fenway faithful until decades after he retired.

No, Theodore Samuel Williams wasn't a nice man.

But he was a good man and a great man. He was an authentic hero in an age of "superstar" celebrities.

Ted Williams was the real deal.

He was John Wayne winning the war, Robert Redford's "the Natural" knocking the lights out with a towering home run, Hemingway's Santiago battling the great fish—except that those were all fictional characters. Ted Williams was a real man. Ted Williams really did those things.

Was He the Greatest Hitter Who Ever Lived?

Ted Williams was the last big leaguer to hit over .400 for a full season—.406 in 1941. Sacrifice flies still counted as outs then, and Ted hit at least 14 of them that year. Subtract them from his official at-bats and his batting average swells to .419.

He won the Triple Crown, not once but twice, and took the batting title four other times. He lost a third Triple Crown when George Kell edged him out for the batting title by .0002. And he would have won two other titles, except that they only counted official at bats, not plate appearances, then, and Williams failed to qualify. He famously would not swing at a bad pitch, so he got a ton of unintentional walks to go with the intentional ones pitchers honored him with.

He won two MVP awards. He would have won more if he hadn't alienated most of the sportswriters in America.

He lost five seasons to military service and still hit 521 home runs to go with a lifetime .344 batting average.

He hit .327 his first year in the bigs and .316 in his last season, 21 years later. He hit 38 home runs and batted .388 at the age of 38. He hit a home run in his last at bat, at the age of 41.

No one who ever lived worked harder at and knew more about hitting than Ted Williams.

He would often visit Hillerich & Bradsby's factory in Louisville to pick out the timber for his bats. On one occasion, John "Bud" Hillerich, son of the company founder, decided to see just how acute a judge of lumber Teddy really was. He hauled out six Louisville Sluggers that varied in half-ounce increments, dumped them on the floor, and challenged Ted to arrange them in order, lightest to heaviest.

Ted did so with no errors—twice.

He consistently hit for power—topping 20 home runs in all but three of his 19 seasons. Most power hitters are free swingers, but Ted Williams refused to swing at a bad ball and wouldn't even offer at a bad strike until he had two strikes on him. He walked 2,021 times in his career while striking out only 709 times. His career on-base percentage was .482—even though he refused to bunt or slap a single to the left side of the infield against the famous "Ted Williams shift" initiated by Lou Boudreau in 1946.

He won the Triple Crown a second time in 1947 (and didn't win the MVP that year either, losing to DiMaggio again, this time by a single point). He was the league MVP twice, in '46 and '49. He won six batting titles, nine times he led the league in slugging percentage (twice topping .730), and 12 times he led the league in on-base percentage.

He hit against every team (.320 or better) and in every month (.333 or better).

He had scores of clutch hits in critical games, most famously the game-winning, ninth-inning home run against Claude Passeau at Briggs Stadium in the 1941 All-Star game. He also powered two home runs in

When duty called, "Teddy Ballgame" proved he could perform heroic feats both on and off the field. Williams lost five big league seasons due to serving his country in two wars.

the '46 All-Star game at Fenway, the second off one of Rip Sewell's looping "eephus" pitches.

In his MVP season of 1946, he led the Sox to the pennant and earned his only World Series appearance. But before the Series, Williams was plunked on the elbow by a pitch from Mickey Haefner in an exhibition game against an AL All-Star team. Red Sox management had decided to have the team play to stay sharp while the Dodgers and Cardinals battled it out in the NL playoff. Playing hurt (while telling nobody), Ted went just five for 25, and the Sox lost to the Cards in seven. Williams brooded about his "failure" and his inability to get the Sox back to the Series for the rest of his life.

When he came back from war a second time in 1953, an old man at age 35, he dispelled notions that he might be finished by slugging a home run off Mike Garcia in his first game back at Fenway. In 37 games before the end of the season, he batted .407 with 13 home runs.

He went on to hit no lower than .345 over the next four seasons, missing batting titles in 1954 and 1955 only because his huge number of free passes left him short of the necessary at-bats to be eligible.

His 1957 season was one of the best any player ever had. At age 38, Williams slammed 38 home runs and batted .388. Five leg hits would have put him at .400. But Ted Williams was 38 years old and didn't get any leg hits. Still, he hit .453 over the last half of the season, when many younger players wilted.

Tom Yawkey tried to talk him into retiring after a dismal .254 season in 1959, the only time he failed to reach .300.

"That burned my ass," Ted acknowledged in his autobiography.

He refused to quit, and Yawkey agreed to sign him at his previous year's salary, $125,000. Williams insisted he cut him back to $90,000. Then he went out and hit .316 with 29 home runs. The last homer came in his last at bat and gave him 521 for his career.

Then he was ready to retire—on his own terms.

Was he the greatest hitter who ever lived? Name a better one.

Man and Myth

Umpire Ed Hurley used to say Ted Williams could see grass grow. Teammate Jimmy Piersall said he could tell the sex of an eagle from the floor of the valley.

Not quite. Ted Williams did have 20/10 eyesight, as verified by the Marine Corps. That meant he could see at 20 feet what folks with "perfect" vision see at 10. But no, he couldn't really read the label on a spinning record. That was a myth, as was the notion that he actually saw the bat make contact with the ball when he connected.

He didn't need to do that, he explained. A carpenter doesn't need to see the hammer strike the head of the nail to know when he's hit it sweet and flush, and, if he's good enough, to keep hitting it there every time.

Another myth had it that he was a lousy fielder. He was at times an indifferent outfielder, to be sure. Early in his career, he even turned his back on home plate and practiced his swing during play, and when he did take out after the ball, he looked like the gawky kid he was. (Slapping his rump with his hand and shouting "Hi, ho, Silver!" didn't help.)

But he also fractured his elbow crashing into the wall while making a leaping catch off Ralph Kiner in the 1950 All-Star game. Typically, he stayed in the game and later had an RBI single. Two days later, doctors removed seven bone fragments from his elbow. When he came back, he hit .350 for the rest of the season.

He played through numerous other hustle injuries in his career. On the first day of spring training in 1954, he broke his collarbone diving to catch a line drive. He returned to the lineup two weeks later with a pin in his shoulder. The next day, he went eight for nine with two home runs and seven RBIs in a doubleheader against the Tigers.

Here's the biggest myth about Ted Williams, the one that might have you thinking he doesn't belong in a book on baseball's good guys. The book on Ted Williams was that he was a selfish son of a bitch who cared only about himself. The book was wrong.

"Theodore Samuel Williams will never win any popularity contest among newspapermen," a newspaperman, Joe Reichler, wrote in 1966. "Ten times as many writers hated him as liked him, but this reporter took him as he found him, and found him friendly, warm, and wonderfully cooperative.

"Faults? He had them by the bushel basket. But his virtues were many and great. He was one of the most generous of sports personalities. During the many years of our association, I found him to be a true and loyal friend. He was a thoroughly honest soul who spoke his mind. Phoniness was foreign to him. You always knew where you stood with him."

Ted could have told you how generous he was, but he never did, never would. "Why should I?" he would have said. And he didn't want the few people he allowed into his life to tell you either, which is why Richard Ben Cramer waited until after Ted's death in 2002 to talk about one of Ted's most subtle acts of charity.

For years Ted refused to tip his hat to the Boston fans, but he sure could pass the hat. He banged the drum tirelessly for the Jimmy Fund, the fundraising arm of the Dana-Farber Cancer Institute for children. But folks didn't know that he would often charter a plane to go visit sick kids. He didn't want them to know. He once flew from Washington, D.C., to Raleigh, N.C., after a night game, spent five hours with a dying youngster, and returned for an afternoon game the next day.

He often paid unannounced visits to the Jimmy Fund Clinic and dedicated many of his home runs to the kids.

And nobody knew that he would call up former ballplayers, knowing they were down on their luck, and badger them to send him a check for "a lousy 10 bucks for the kids." When the check came, Ted took the account number and used it to deposit 25 grand of his own money into the guy's account.

The Jimmy Fund actually began with a 1948 appearance of a kid they called "Jimmy" and members of the Boston Braves on Ralph Edwards's *Truth or Consequences Show*. The Fund sponsored cancer research for five years, but then the Braves hightailed it for Milwaukee, and owner Lou Perini handed the fund over to the Red Sox's Tom Yawkey.

Ted Williams grabbed it and embraced it as his own.

When he came back from service in Korea, he asked the 1,200 guests at his "Welcome Home, Ted" bash to pony up $100 each, with all the money going to the Jimmy Fund.

Thanks in large part to Ted's efforts, the fund has raised more than $170 million.

So great was Ted's personal commitment of time and energy to the charity that Boston sportswriter Dan Shaughnessy dubbed him "the guardian angel of the Jimmy Fund."

Williams was a good and generous man, who did uncounted acts of kindness, almost all of them without public recognition. He was a great man who dominated America's game like few ever have or ever will and who then became one of the greatest fishermen who ever tied a fly and cast a line. He was an authentic war hero. He lived his life precisely on his own terms.

If you made a movie of his life, not even John Wayne could have pulled it off. Who'd believe a story like his?

Believe it. Ted Williams lived it.

Growing Up Teddy

Theodore Samuel Williams—his birth certificate says "Teddy Samuel" as he was named after Teddy Roosevelt—was born in San Diego on August 30, 1918, the year the Red Sox last won the World Series. His mother, May, was a soldier in the Salvation Army. His father wasn't around much, and May eventually divorced him and raised Ted and his brother Danny alone. Ted spent a lot of time on the school grounds, playing ball.

"I used to hit tennis balls, old baseballs, balls made of rags, anything," he said. "I didn't think I'd be a particularly good hitter. I just liked to do it."

The Williams boys often had to wait on the porch of the locked house until late at night for their mother to get home.

Ted was a tornado from the get-go, constantly in motion, playing baseball for hours, shouting when he was supposed to whisper. If he were a kid today, they'd shoot him full of ritalin.

He also suffered crippling bouts of depression all his life and fought them alone.

He was a star for San Diego's Herbert Hoover High, where he majored and minored in baseball. (He even carried his bat with him to class.) He pitched and played the outfield, smoking the ball at a .586 clip his junior year and .403 as a senior. On the mound, he compiled a 16-3 record and once struck out 23 batters in a game.

The Cardinals wanted to sign him, and so did Yankee scout Bill Essick, but Ted's mother wanted him to finish high school, so Ted stuck it out, playing semi-pro ball for three bucks a week.

Then he signed with the hometown San Diego Padres of the Pacific Coast League for $150 a month. At 17, he stood six foot three but weighed just 148 pounds. He hit only .271 without a home run in 42 games, but Hall of Famer Eddie Collins liked his swing. He was actually scouting Bobby Doerr, who would become another Red Sox immortal, but after Ted hit .291 his second year, the Red Sox paid the Padres $35,000 for Ted's contract.

In spring training, the Sox decided he wasn't quite ready and optioned him to the Minneapolis Millers of the American Association. There, baseball immortal Rogers Hornsby taught him to wait for a good pitch to hit. Putting Hornsby's wisdom into practice, Ted got a base hit and five walks against Louisville. The next day he hit a line drive home run that traveled 470 feet and followed it up two innings later with a 512-foot shot.

He wound up taking the Triple Crown with a .366 average, 43 home runs, and 142 RBI. Ted was ready for Boston. But was Boston ready for Ted?

Teddy "did a lot of crazy thngs" in Minneapolis, according to teammate Wilfred "Lefty" Lefebrve, including taking joy rides on Nicollet Avenue in his 1938 Buick.

He arrived in the bigs for good in 1939, breaking in against Red Ruffing in fabled Yankee Stadium. After striking out twice, Teddy banged out a double, his first major league hit. Lou Gehrig played in that game, the only time the two great sluggers appeared in the same game.

Three days later, Ted went four for five and got his first major league home run in his Fenway Park debut. On May 4 he belted two home runs in one game for the first time. One of them cleared the right-field roof in Briggs Stadium, the first time that had ever been done.

Late that season, Ted connected for a home run off a pitcher named Thornton Lee. Twenty-one years later, Williams homered off Thornton Lee's son, Ron.

Clubhouse man Johnny Orlando probably hung the nickname "The Kid" on Ted, but others say manager Joe Cronin yelled down at "the kid" from the stands to tuck in his shirttail his first day in the majors. Whichever the source, the name stuck.

Ted was mouthy from day one but backed up his swagger by becoming the first rookie ever to lead the league in RBIs. (He collected 145.)

He had a fine sophomore season (.344 average, 23 homers, 113 RBI) and even pitched a couple of innings in a blowout loss to the Tigers. He also got knocked unconscious in the outfield when he collided with Doc Cramer chasing a ball off the bat of Jim Tabor.

And then, after two fine seasons, Ted had "The Season" in 1941. Hitting .406 made him a baseball immortal; the way he did it made him a legend.

After a late-season slump brought Ted all the way "down" to .39955 going into the final doubleheader of the season, Cronin offered to let him sit out, knowing that his average would be rounded off to an even .400.

Ted refused—and rapped out a single, a home run, and two more singles in the first game before reaching base on an error. That raised his average to .404. Again Cronin offered to let him sit, and again Ted declined. He went out and got a single and a double before flying to left, leaving him two for three in the nightcap, six for eight for the day, and .406 for the season.

"If ever a player deserved to hit .400, it's Ted," Robert Creamer quoted his manager, Joe Cronin, as saying. "He never sat down against tough pitchers. He never bunted. He didn't have the advantage of the sacrifice fly rule."

The next year, having already secured his place in baseball history and lore, he won his first Triple Crown in the majors.

Remarkably, he didn't win the league MVP award either year, losing to Joe DiMaggio (291 to 254) in '41 and to Joe Gordon by 21 votes in '42.

And then he went off to war for the first time.

When he came back from three years in the service, he hit the first pitch thrown to him in spring training for a home run. It seemed nothing could dim that batting eye or curb that determination to be the best. He hit .342 that season, with 38 home runs and 123 RBI, to lead the Sox to the pennant. One of those homers traveled 502 feet. Seat 21, Row 37, Section 42 at Fenway is painted red to mark the spot where it landed.

"I had the same desire as before," he told Bill Gilbert for the book *They Also Served*. "I always had the same desire. I wanted to be first. I didn't want anybody to beat me."

When he got called off to war a second time, the Sox threw a day for him at Fenway on April 30, 1952. They gave him a new Cadillac and a book signed by 400,000 fans. In his last at-bat, he responded with a game-winning, two-run home run off Dizzy Trout.

After serving 17 months in Korea, he played seven more years. With the exception of the 1959 season, when he was 40 years old, Ted Williams never hit below .316, and he did that in his final season, 1960, at age 41. The next player to come close to his .406 milestone set in 1941 was...Ted Williams, 16 years and two wars later, when he hit .388 in 1957.

He was elected to the Hall of Fame in 1966, his first year of eligibility, receiving 282 of a possible 302 votes. (You have to wonder about the ones who didn't vote for him.) He used the occasion of his induction to call for the inclusion at Cooperstown of Negro League stars like Satchel Paige and Josh Gibson. He was the first Hall of Famer to do so.

Ted Williams, War Hero

He received a hardship deferment as the sole support of his divorced mother but enlisted in May of 1942 anyway, first winning the Triple Crown before reporting for active duty in November. He went from $32,000 with the Red Sox to $106 a month as a cadet.

He went in with Red Sox teammate Johnny Pesky and three other big leaguers, reporting to preliminary ground school at Amherst College. A hernia put him in Chelsea Naval Hospital for two months, but then Ted trained in Chapel Hill, North Carolina; Kokomo, Indiana; and Pensacola, Florida; where he completed his advanced flight training.

The day he made second lieutenant, he married Doris Soule at the base in Pensacola.

His last stop was Jacksonville, Florida, where he learned to fly the F4U Corsair and set a student gunnery record.

V-J Day was declared while Ted was in San Francisco waiting for the boat to take him to Hawaii and then into combat. He got as far as Honolulu before receiving orders to return home.

He had served his country honorably and well, missing three seasons in the prime of his career in the process. He wasn't thrilled about inter-rupting his career a second time, but when his country called him back to active duty in the Korean War, he went, reporting to Willow Grove, Pennsylvania on May 1, 1952, as a Marine captain.

He took an eight-week refresher course in flying, learning to pilot the new F-9 fighter jet. After cold weather training in the Sierra Mountains, he arrived in Korea on February 4, 1953, as a member of the Third Marine Air Wing, 223rd Squadron.

Two weeks later, he flew in a mission against Kyomipo, North Korea, and got blasted out of the sky. He credits lieutenant Larry Harkins with saving his life by leading him back to the airstrip, where he crash landed going 225 mph, skidding for more than a mile before com-ing to rest. Williams crawled out of the burning plane and walked away.

The next day, he flew another mission.

Two months after his first crash, he had another near-miss. On April 28, 1953, on a Marine raid of Chinnampo, he was again hit by anti-air-craft fire. He considered himself lucky to get back to the base.

He left the Marines in July of 1953, having flown 39 missions.

"I was no hero," he insisted. "There were maybe 75 pilots in our two squadrons, and 99 percent of them did a better job than I did."

Ted Williams, Public Enemy

For all of his fabulous hitting and for all of his war heroics, Ted Williams was often booed by the fans and reviled by the press (whom he referred to derisively as the "Knights of the Keyboard").

He was a loner, more comfortable in the company of cabbies, bell-hops and clubhouse boys than the movers and shakers who could have promoted his image.

His career-long feud with the fans included incidents of spitting and obscene finger gestures. In 1950 he publicly apologized to the fans after making "insulting gestures" in response to getting booed after making two errors in a doubleheader against Detroit.

The Red Sox fined him $5,000 in August of 1956 for spitting at his Fenway tormentors after the crowd of 36,350 booed him for muffing Mickey Mantle's windblown fly ball in the eleventh inning of a game. He didn't just spit a little. He let loose three times, once to the left, once to the right, and once straight ahead.

It was his third spitting incident in three weeks, including spitting up at the press box after hitting his 400th home run, and the Boston press began referring to him as "The Splendid Spitter." The great Red Smith coined the term "Great Expectorations" for Teddy's antics.

In July of '58 he was fined $250 for spitting again. On September 21 of that year, at Fenway Park, Ted flung his bat into the stands after striking out. The bat struck Gladys Heffernan, Joe Cronin's housekeeper. Ted apologized profusely and sent her a $500 diamond watch.

His adversarial relationship with the press flared into open warfare when Ted accepted a military deferment in 1942. Reporters called him "Yellow" and "Unpatriotic." Ted proved them wrong, but that did little to help the relationship.

He was perhaps most reviled for his refusal to tip his cap to the fans after a home run. He started out tipping his hat, and Boston embraced him as "The Kid." But one day he muffed a base hit and heard the boos as he chased the ball to the wall. He shouted vulgarities at the fans, and the boos swelled. That started a battle that raged throughout Ted's career.

"In the dugout between innings, I swore never again to tip my hat in Fenway Park," he later said.

After Ted stopped tipping is cap, Jack Miley of the *New York Post* wrote: "…when it comes to arrogant, ungrateful athletes, this one leads the league."

A few scribes tried to be more understanding.

"Williams is a peculiar case," Arthur Daley wrote in *The New York Times*, "so tangled in his inner man that even a psychologist or psychiatrist would have trouble unraveling him."

Ted held to his convictions even on the last day of his career when, in his last at-bat, he powdered a Jack Fisher pitch 450 feet into the right-centerfield seats for his 521st and last home run. While the fans stood and cheered, Ted stoically circled the bases and disappeared into the dugout.

He never came back out. "Gods don't answer letters," author John Updike explained.

Years later, Updike put the whole hat-tipping controversy in a different light.

"We knew he never tipped his hat to the crowd when he hit a home run," he wrote, "and many of us loved him more for it, not less. He was focusing on his task. Success and failure in baseball are right there for all to see. We could read in his body language that he wanted to be the best, that this was more than a game or a livelihood for him." Updike called Ted's passion the "dangerous rage to excel."

Ted finally made his peace with the Fenway fans on May 12, 1991, during a ceremony to honor his .400 season. He put on a Red Sox cap, then doffed it and waved it to the fans.

"Today, I tip my hat to all the fans of New England, the greatest sports fans on earth," he told them.

All but the most diehard Williams haters have long since forgiven him his indiscretions. In 1984, the Red Sox retired his No. 9. In May of 1991, the Sox celebrated Ted Williams Day by renaming Lansdowne Street behind the left field wall Ted Williams Way. In 1995, Boston dedicated a $2.3 billion harbor tunnel in his name. But the greatest indication of the esteem and affection fans and players have for Ted Williams came in the All-Star game at Fenway Park on July 13, 1999.

Before that appearance, he took the time to visit the Jimmy Fund kids again, this time with the original "Jimmy," Einar Gustafson, from New Sweden, Maine. He didn't die from cancer as a boy but survived to age 65, dying of a stroke on January 23, 2001. Einar and Ted reminisced, traded stories, and mingled with the kids at Dana-Faber.

Then Ted allowed all of baseball to pay him a sincere, spontaneous tribute. The league had assembled a Major League Baseball All-Century team for the All-Star game. They were Hall of Famers all, warmly received by the fans.

Then Ted Williams rode out in a golf cart to throw out the ceremonial first pitch. As the fans rose and roared for him, an aged and infirm Williams tipped his cap.

The young All-Stars and All-Century legends gathered around Williams, to talk baseball or just be near him, lingering long after the public address announcer pleaded with them to let the game begin. Many had tears in their eyes. Many of the fans did, too. Then, with his friend Tony Gwynn supporting him, Ted threw out the first pitch, to another ovation.

"Wasn't it great!" he said later. "It didn't surprise me all that much because I know how these fans are here in Boston. They love this game as much as any players, and Boston's lucky to have the faithful Red Sox fans. They're the best."

Ted Williams died at 8:49 a.m. on July 5, 2002, at a hospital in Crystal River, Florida, of cardiac arrest. He was 83. He had suffered a series of strokes and congestive heart failure.

He was a baseball star and a war hero, an American original, a man who did great deeds of charity quietly. And Ted Williams was one more thing.

Ted Williams was the greatest hitter who ever lived.

CHAPTER 5

Baseball's Most Valuable Player
Jackie Robinson

"A life is not important except in the impact it has on other lives."
—Jackie Robinson

"When I look at my house ... I say, 'Thank God for Jackie Robinson.'"
—Joe Black

"If one can be certain of anything in baseball, it is that we shall not look upon his like again."
—Roger Kahn, writing about Jackie Robinson

Full name: Jack Roosevelt Robinson
Nickname: "Jackie"
Position: First base, second base, third base, outfield
Career: Kansas City Monarchs, 1945; Brooklyn Dodgers, 1947-1956
Career batting average: .311

Career highlights:

• Led the league in batting average in 1949, hitting .342.

• Led the league in on-base percentage with a .440 mark in 1952.

• Paced the league in stolen bases and sacrifice hits in both 1947 and 1949.

• Selected as an All-Star every year between 1949 and 1954.

• Was named NL Rookie of the Year in 1947 and NL MVP in 1949.

• Elected to the Hall of Fame.

Who's the greatest baseball player who ever lived? You'd probably need to make a list.

How can you compare the all-around excellence, grace and zest of Willie Mays, the slash and dash of Ty Cobb, or the impact of the Babe with the skill and durability of Cy Young?

But ask us to name the most significant man who ever played major league baseball, the one who made the most difference, and we won't hesitate to name Jackie Robinson.

Babe Ruth changed baseball; Jackie Robinson changed America.

His teammate, Harold "Pee Wee" Reese, called what Jackie did "the most tremendous thing I've ever seen in sports."

Jackie Robinson broke baseball's color barrier.

He was the first black man to play major league baseball in the 20th Century. He was the first black man to win the Rookie of the Year and the MVP Awards and the first black man to be elected to the Hall of Fame.

He did it with the eyes of the world constantly on him and the hopes of a race on his broad shoulders.

The burden didn't seem to weigh him down on the field. He stole home 19 times during his 10-year career with the Dodgers, the most of anyone since World War I, and in 1955, at age 36, he became one of only a dozen players ever to steal home in the World Series.

And baseball wasn't even his best sport. He just might have been the greatest all-around athlete ever to wear a major league uniform.

Dodgers general manager Branch Rickey called him the "most competitive" man he'd seen since Ty Cobb.

He had to be.

Rickey was determined to break the race barrier that had existed in major league baseball since Cap Anson refused to play on the same field with a black pitcher named George Stovey in 1884. Rickey needed the right man for the job. He couldn't simply be a great player. He had to be a great man. Rickey sent scouts out to find and sign that man, telling folks he was putting together a black team. Scott Clyde Sukeforth found Jackie playing shortstop for the Negro League Kansas City Monarchs.

When Rickey met with Robinson, he showered him with the kind of abuse he would receive the moment he stepped onto the white man's diamond.

"This is the kind of language you will hear," Rickey warned him. "And it may even be worse." He told Jackie he would have to "wear the armor of humility."

"I know you're a good ballplayer," Rickey challenged. "What I don't know is whether you have the guts."

"Mr. Rickey, are you looking for a Negro who is afraid to fight back?" Robinson thundered.

"Robinson," Rickey fired back, "I'm looking for a ballplayer with guts enough not to fight back."

"I've got two cheeks, Mr. Rickey," Jackie told him. "Is that what you want to hear?"

It was.

Jackie promised not to yell and not to fight. He would reintegrate baseball—this a year before Harry Truman desegregated the military, remember, and seven years before the Supreme Court ruled segregation in public schools to be unconstitutional—by turning the other cheek in the face of insults, beanings, spikings, and even death threats.

A Great All-around Athlete

Folks compared Jackie Robinson to Jim Thorpe, the Native American who excelled at every sport he tried. There didn't seem to be anything Jackie couldn't do well.

He was born in Cairo, Georgia, in 1919, the son of a sharecropper, the grandson of a slave. His father, Jerry, deserted the family six months later.

The story goes that Jackie's mother, Mallie, was told by her half-brother, "If you want to get closer to heaven, visit California." So she took her five kids West in 1920.

Jackie grew up in poverty in Pasadena, California, where his mother worked as a domestic to support the family.

Jackie was a gifted athlete from the beginning—marbles, dodgeball, soccer, tennis, golf, football, anything. He was a four-sport star at Pasadena Junior College and went on to become the first four-sport letterman in UCLA history. He was a slashing runner, a brilliant point guard, an NCAA champion long-jumper. He was also a brawler, ready to fight any white man who insulted him.

Sports Weekly called him "the greatest ball carrier on the gridiron today" as he averaged 11 yards per carry as a junior halfback.

With help from friend and teammate Pee Wee Reese, left, Jackie Robinson, right, successfully withstood all of the obscenities, racial slurs, and death threats opposing teams and fans could muster.

One coach called him "the best basketball player in the U.S." as he led the Pacific Coast Conference in scoring as a junior and senior.

His brother Mack—who some said was an even better athlete—placed second to Jesse Owens in the 1936 Olympic long-jump, and little brother Jackie won the 1940 NCAA long-jump title and no doubt would have gone to the 1940 Olympics had the war not intervened.

He was a semifinalist in the national Negro tennis tournament and won swimming championships at UCLA. He was also a fine golfer. Baseball was his third best sport, maybe fourth behind track. But baseball became his sport, and he became baseball's most significant player.

On March 18, 1942, long before his historic meeting with Branch Rickey, Jackie and another black man, Nate Moreland, requested a tryout with the Chicago White Sox, who were holding their spring training in Pasadena. Manager Jimmie Dykes let them work out but never called them.

After Pearl Harbor, Jackie went into the Army and became a second lieutenant in an all-black cavalry unit. In 1944 he faced a courtmartial for refusing to give up his seat at the front of an Army bus, this a dozen years before Rosa Parks took a similar stand on a public bus. Jackie was acquitted and given an honorable discharge. He went back to baseball.

On April 16, 1945, the Boston Red Sox allowed three blacks, Sam Jethroe, Marvin Williams, and Jackie, to work out at Fenway Park. None of them received a follow-up phone call.

So Jackie played shortstop for the Kansas City Monarchs of the Negro League, where Clyde Sukeforth found him.

On October 23, 1945, Jackie made baseball history when Hector Racine, president of the International League, Lt. Col. Romeo Gauvreau, vice president of the Montreal Royals, and Branch Rickey, the Dodgers GM, signed him to a contract with the Royals. (Rickey figured the racial confrontations would be less severe in Canada.) A second black man, pitcher John Wright, also signed.

When asked why he had signed a Negro now, Rickey replied, "Why not now? I want to win."

Moreover, he added, "the time is nearing fast when every professional baseball club in the state of New York will have to hire Negro players."

When he told Robinson he'd have to accept less money to play with the Royals than he was making with the Monarchs, Jackie told him, "That's OK. I have to think of the other fellows."

On March 17, 1946, the Dodgers took the field in Daytona Beach against the Royals, with Jackie in the Montreal lineup. It was the first appearance of an integrated team in "organized" (white) professional baseball in the 20th Century. Forty years later, that field would be renamed Jackie Robinson Ballpark.

When Jackie trotted out to second base in Montreal against Jersey City on April 18, he became the first black man to play in the International League in 57 years.

With the whole baseball world—and a good portion of the actual world—watching, Jackie belted a home run and three singles. He never looked back. He led the league in hitting at .349, scored 113 runs, swiped 40 bases, and made only 10 errors in 119 games. His Royals won the pennant by 19 games and then took the Little World Series. When happy fans swarmed Jackie after the last game, a black journalist wrote, "It was probably the only day in history that a black man ran from a white mob with love instead of lynching on its mind."

Montreal fans later erected a statue of Jackie.

He also made a believer out of his manager, a Southerner named Clay Hopper, who had told Rickey he'd rather die than manage a black man. He was even alleged to have wondered aloud whether "niggers" were really human. But when he saw how Jackie could play, he decided this particular human could be on his team.

Breaking the Color Line

On April 10, 1947, during the sixth inning of a Dodgers-Royals exhibition game at Ebbets Field, Robinson grounded out for the Royals. In the press box, management passed out this announcement: "The Brooklyn Dodgers today purchased the contract of Jack Roosevelt Robinson from the Montreal Royals. He will report immediately."

Rickey later said he'd reached the momentous decision just five minutes before issuing the announcement.

The baseball owners took an informal poll, voting 15-1 against bringing Jackie into the league. But Happy Chandler, who had succeeded Kenesaw Mountain Landis as Baseball Commissioner in 1945, overruled them.

"If they [Blacks] can fight and die on Okinawa, Guadalcanal [and] in the South Pacific," he said, "they can play ball in America."

Jackie was in.

"I never regretted my decision to let Robinson play," Chandler said years later, when told of Jackie's death, "but it probably cost me my job."

Then Dodger manager Leo Durocher had to put down a player rebellion, led by Hugh Casey, Dixie Walker, Bobby Bragan and Carl Furillo, who insisted they wouldn't play with a black man. Among those who stood with Robinson were Ralph Branca, Duke Snider, and his strongest supporter, the Kentucky Colonel, Pee Wee Reese.

Play with him or play someplace else, Durocher told his would-be holdouts. They played with him.

When Rickey told Dodger announcer Red Barber, a Mississippian, that Robinson would play for the Dodgers, Barber said he'd quit. His wife Lila talked him out of it.

"How should I handle him?" Red asked her.

"The same way you handle any other player," Lila told him. And that's what Barber did.

Jackie made his major league debut at age 28, on April 15, 1947.

"It was the most eagerly anticipated debut in the annals of the national pastime," according to Robert Lipsyte and Pete Levine in *Idols of the Game*. "It represented both the dream and the fear of equal opportunity, and it would change forever the complexion of the game and the attitudes of America."

Jackie didn't even play at his natural position. With Eddie Stanky established at second base, Jackie had to adjust to playing first base, where he handled 11 chances flawlessly that day. Facing Braves great Johnny Sain, he went hitless in his three official at-bats but scored the winning run.

Two days later, he got his first major league hit, a bunt single off Glenn Elliot—the first of his 19 bunt singles that year.

The next day he tagged his first major league home run, off Dave Koslo.

He endured racial slurs, taunts and threats. Fans threw black cats on the field. Jackie kept his temper but slipped into an 0-for-20 slide. One newspaper said he "would have been benched weeks ago if he were a white man."

Jackie broke the slump with a double and started hitting again.

On the road, he had to stay in a "Negro" hotel and eat at a "Negro" restaurant, away from his teammates.

On May 8, some of the St. Louis Cardinals threatened to strike to protest Robinson's presence on the field. Owner Sam Breadon came into the clubhouse carrying a message from NL president Ford Frick, who said he'd suspend any player who sat out. The Cards played—and beat Jackie and the Dodgers, 5-1—and Cardinal manager Eddie Dyer denied there had been any strike talk.

In Philadelphia, Phillie manager Ben Chapman rode Jackie so hard, Robinson later said he was "nearer to cracking up than I had ever been."

But he didn't crack up. He took it all and performed with skill, grace, and dignity. His fiery team play ignited the fans, unsettled the opposition, and won the respect of his teammates.

"Robinson could hit and bunt and steal and run," Roger Kahn wrote in *The Boys of Summer.* "He had intimidation skills, and he burned with a dark fire. He wanted passionately to win. He bore the burden of a pioneer, and the weight made him stronger."

In Cincinnati, Jackie received a death threat in the clubhouse before the game. He played anyway. Stationed at first base, he heard the waves of obscenities and threats from nearby fans. From shortstop, Dodger captain Pee Wee Reese called time, strolled over to Robinson, and put his arm around his teammate's shoulders.

The symbolism couldn't have been more obvious: He's one of us, Pee Wee was telling the crowd and the world.

"That meant so much, so much," Jackie told Maury Allen years later. "It was just a kind and incredible gesture."

"I took some heat about it when I went home to Louisville," Pee Wee remembered. "Then it was forgotten."

Speaking of his teammate, Reese said, "I grew to know and admire him a great deal. He was a great competitor in everything he did."

Jackie's play on the field and his forbearance on and off it won first tolerance, then respect, and finally admiration.

Every black person in America who cared anything about baseball—and a lot who didn't—became Dodgers fans, Jackie Robinson fans.

"As a Negro newspaper writer," A.S. "Doc" Young wrote, "I felt the natural and normal racial elation…I saw thousands of Negroes literally break down the Jim Crow section barriers to overflow among the whites to watch him play exhibition games in the South…I saw one of every five of Cleveland's Negro population turn out for a 1948 exhibition between the Dodgers and the Indians."

But Jackie wasn't a hero just to black America. He finished second only to crooner Bing Crosby in a national popularity poll that year.

He finished the season hitting at a .297 mark, with 29 stolen bases, and *The Sporting News* named him the National League's Rookie of the Year.

"That Jack Roosevelt Robinson might have had more obstacles than his first-year competitors," publisher J.G. Taylor Spink noted at the time, "and that he perhaps had a harder fight to gain even major-league status was no concern of this publication. … He was rated and examined solely as a freshman player in the big leagues on the basis of his hitting, his running, his defensive play, his team value."

Spink called Robinson "an ebony Ty Cobb."

Jackie, Spink noted, "has done it all, in his first year as a major leaguer. What more could anyone ask?"

Avoiding any hint of a "sophomore jinx," Jackie posted an almost identical .296 batting average and again hit 12 home runs the next year, and he almost doubled his RBI total, from 48 to 85.

But his first two seasons were just a prelude. In 1949, free of Branch Rickey's two-year ban on talking back and having taken the best shots racists could offer, Jackie Robinson had an MVP season. He hit .342, drove in 124 runs, scored 122, and stole 37 bases. Jackie just tore the league up.

He appeared in the All-Star Game at Ebbets Field, along with fellow Dodgers Roy Campanella and Don Newcombe. Larry Doby played for the American League. They were the first four blacks ever to play in the mid-season exhibition.

He was awarded the MVP in November, and in January of 1950 he signed a contract for $35,000, reportedly making him the highest paid Brooklyn player ever.

He played in five more All-Star games and helped the Dodgers into six World Series and their only world championship, in 1955. Through his 10 seasons with Brooklyn, he batted .311, drew 740 walks, stole 197 bases, and drove opposing pitchers and catchers crazy.

And then the Dodgers tried to trade him to the hated Giants.

On December 13, 1956, Brooklyn announced that they were swapping Jackie for oft-traded Dick Littlefield and $35,000. Three weeks later, Jackie retired.

On July 23, 1962, Jackie and fireballer Bob Feller walked into the Hall of Fame together, each in his first year of eligibility.

In 1965 Jackie established yet another baseball first, signing on to provide commentary for ABC's broadcasts of Major League Baseball, the first black to fill such a position.

Other than his stint in broadcasting, Jackie Robinson was through with baseball. But he wasn't through advocating for equality, on and off the field.

Jackie Breaks His Silence

B ranch Rickey told Jackie he had to hold his peace while people got used to the idea of a black man playing Major League Baseball. So Jackie let his bat, his glove, and his feet do his talking for him.

But once he was established as a player, Jackie began to speak out. More than just a symbol for racial equality, he became its tireless advocate. He was so visible, in fact, that he was the first witness called before the House Committee on Un-American Activities in July, 1949 "regarding Communist infiltration of minority groups." The Committee asked him to comment on statements made in Paris by singer/actor/activist Paul Robeson. Jackie characterized Robeson's apparent denunciation of America as "silly"—but then spent the rest of his testimony condemning his country's racism.

Twenty years later, in his autobiography, *I Never Had it Made*, Jackie wrote of his respect for Robeson, who "sacrificed himself, his career, and the wealth and comfort he once enjoyed because, I believe, he was sincerely trying to help his people."

The Department of Justice said that "Mr. Robinson was never the subject of an FBI investigation," but they generated a 131-page confidential file on him.

On November 30, 1952, on a local television show, Jackie charged that the Yankees were racist for not bringing up a black player. Until the end of his life, he berated baseball's owners for their failure to name a black manager.

"Let's face it," Jackie said after his retirement. "I knew there would be no place for me in baseball. There's always a place for a guy who goes along, but I've never been that way. I knew I was losing out in a personal way because of the things I fought for."

Jackie became active in the NAACP and the civil rights movement, serving as a main speaker at fundraisers and rallies. In 1956 the NAACP awarded him its medal for meritorious service to black America.

The following year, he wrote a letter to President Eisenhower, urging him to take action against Arkansas governor Orval Faubus, who was attempting to block the integration of Little Rock's public schools. Jackie was also chairman of the Freedom Fund Drive, helping to raise money for Thurgood Marshall and the NAACP Legal Defense Fund.

In 1963 he went with Martin Luther King Jr. to Birmingham, where sheriff Bull Connor was turning fire hoses on black demonstrators. Later that year, he took his family to the March on Washington and was present for King's "I Have a Dream" speech.

Jackie summed up his philosophy concisely for a white New Orleans sportswriter: "We ask for nothing special. We ask only to be permitted to live as you live and as our nation's Constitution provides."

He took his fiery competitiveness into the business world, becoming a vice-president of personnel for Chock Full O' Nuts coffee company and restaurant chain in New York. He co-founded Freedom National Bank of Harlem and was chairman of its board for eight years. In 1970 he organized the Jackie Robinson Construction Company. In both of these endeavors, he sought to improve living conditions for black Americans.

He became active in Republican politics—he was a staunch support-er of governor Nelson Rockefeller's bid for the presidential nomina-tion—and spoke out passionately on the drug problem. His son, Jackie Jr., had been a drug addict who conquered his addiction, only to die in a car accident in 1971.

"Robinson's political perspective grew increasingly pessimistic as he aged," Eric Enders wrote. "Robinson had grieved over the assassinations of John F. Kennedy, Robert Kennedy, Malcolm X, Medgar Evers, and Martin Luther King as well as the deaths of three of the people closest to him—Branch Rickey, his mother Mallie, and his son, Jackie, Jr."

But he never gave up. Ten days before his death, he was honored before the second game of the World Series in Cincinnati, accepting a plaque for his work fighting drug abuse. And on the day he died, he was scheduled to fly to Washington to speak on "The Responsibility of the Businessman in Dealing with Drug Abuse."

His Influence Grows After His Death

Jack Roosevelt Robinson died of heart disease at his home in Stamford, Connecticut, on October 24, 1972. He was only 53. He had been in failing health for a long time, racked by diabetes and arthritis. He was blind in one eye and losing his vision in the other.

More than 2,000 people packed the Riverside Church for his funer-al. A young preacher named Jesse Jackson gave the eulogy. Tens of thou-sands lined the streets of Harlem and Bedford-Stuyvesant as Jackie's funeral procession rolled by.

Jackie Robinson continues to be a force for equality in America and a presence on baseball diamonds all over the country.

His college team, the UCLA Bruins, play in Jackie Robinson Stadium, and Major League Baseball's rookies of the year receive the Jackie Robinson Award.

On January 31, 1997, the 78th anniversary of Jackie's birth, Eric Enders, a University of Texas at Austin student, founded the Jackie Robinson Society, devoted to preserving his memory and furthering his work. The Society performs community service in his name and worked with the Texas Civil Rights Project to promote the October 5, 1997 speaking appearance of Jackie and Rachael's daughter, Sharon. The Society also maintains an active website, which includes Jackie's life story, "The Athlete of the Century."

During the Jackie Robinson Ceremony at Shea Stadium on April 15, 1997, commissioner Bud Selig announced that Jackie's No. 42 would be retired by every major league team (although players like Mo Vaughn,

Jose Lima, and Kirk Rueter, who were already wearing 42, were allowed to keep it until they retired).

On February 18, 1999, the U.S. Postal Service issued a Jackie Robinson stamp as part of its "Celebrate the Century" program.

And Jackie's influence remains with the people whose lives he touched directly.

Henry Aaron was just 14 when he first saw Jackie. In the spring of 1948, "the day after Jackie changed my life by breaking baseball's color line," Aaron wrote, the Dodgers made a stop in Hank's hometown, Mobile, Alabama. They were barnstorming their way up north from spring training, the custom at the time.

"Jackie spoke to a big crowd of black folks over on Davis Avenue," Hank recalled. "I think he talked about segregation, but I didn't hear a word that came out of his mouth. Jackie Robinson was such a hero to me that I couldn't do anything but gawk at him.

"Jackie Robinson, God bless him, was bigger than all that."

Bigger than the teammates who tried to keep him off the ballclub. Bigger than the pitchers who threw at his head and the baserunners who spiked him. Bigger than the fans who mocked and threatened him.

"Robinson was not just about baseball," Maury Allen wrote in *Jackie Robinson: An American Hero*. "He was about equality, about decency, about morality, about injustice, about ending a wrong with a right after more than 60 years of America and Americans in and out of the game suggesting a kid born with a black skin could not be a big leaguer."

Doc Young summed up Robinson's significance this way:

"He was hope for the downtrodden.

"He was justification of faith for the believers.

"He was the opening door to better days, all around, in every phase of Negro life.

"He was the opening door.

"Swinging!"

"He was a fighter," Aaron concludes, "the proudest and most competitive person I've ever seen…To this day, I don't know how he withstood the things he did without lashing back…I couldn't have done what Jackie did. I don't think anybody else could have done it."

CHAPTER 6

He Was Never Really Second
Larry Doby

"I don't think about being second or first. I think about being a part of history ... a part of bringing people together."

—Larry Doby

"Baseball has come a long way. If I had something to do with it, I'm proud. My only hope is that this whole world would have come as far as baseball."

—Larry Doby

Full name: Lawrence Eugene Doby
Nickname: "Larry"
Position: Second base, outfield
Career: Newark Eagles, 1942-43 and 1946-47; Cleveland Indians, 1947-55 and 1958; Chicago White Sox, 1956-57 and 1959; Detroit Tigers, 1959

Negro League career highlights:
• Hit .458 in the 1947 Negro League World Series, leading the Newark Eagles over the Kansas City Monarchs.

Major League career batting average: .283

Major League career highlights:
• Led the league in home runs with 32 in 1952 and 1954.
• Topped the league in RBIs in 1954 with 126.

- Led hitters in slugging percentage in 1952 at .541, and on-base percentage in 1950 at .442.
- Selected as an All-Star every season between 1949-1955.
- Elected to the Hall of Fame.

Larry Doby broke into the major leagues just 11 weeks after Jackie Robinson. Doby was the second African American to play big-league baseball and the first to play in the American League.

He endured the same pressures, the same loneliness, the same taunts, the same abuse as Jackie did. He ate, slept, and even practiced separately from his teammates.

The only difference between his case and Jackie's, Larry said, was that Jackie "got all the publicity. You didn't hear much about what I was going through, because the media didn't want to repeat the same story."

But he didn't say it with bitterness. Bitterness wasn't Larry's way.

He'd had a great career in the Negro Leagues, leading the Newark Eagles to victory over the Kansas City Monarchs in the 1946 Negro Leagues World Series. He played for the Cleveland Indians for nine season, making the All-Star team six years in a row. His best year was 1952, when he led the league in home runs, slugging percentage, batting average and runs scored.

He was one of four men (with Monte Irvin, Willie Mays and Satchel Paige) ever to play in both a Negro League and a Major League World Series.

In 1978 he became the second black manager in major league history, after Frank Robinson, when he took the helm of the White Sox.

Doby Breaks the Other Color Line

Bill Veeck signed Doby to a contract with the Cleveland Indians on July 5, 1947. By some accounts, he'd been urged to do so by Branch Rickey, the man who had brought Jackie Robinson into the majors 11 weeks before. Rickey didn't want Robinson and the Dodgers to have to stand alone, the theory goes. But Veeck wouldn't have needed any persuasion to go against conventional wisdom. He was more at home drinking beer with the fans in the stands (where he was known to use his false leg as an ashtray) than sitting in the owner's box, and he wouldn't have hesitated to give a man like Larry Doby the chance he deserved.

Before the '47 season began, Veeck said he wanted a player who could help Cleveland right away.

"One afternoon when the team trots out on the field," he said, "a Negro player will be out there with it."

After Doby started off hitting .415 with 14 home runs in 41 games for the Newark Eagles, Veeck decided he was the man for the job. He dispatched Lou Jones to Newark to watch Doby in a July 4 doubleheader. "By the start of the second game," according to an account in *Sports Illustrated* commemorating Doby's life, "Doby was on a train to Chicago." Veeck announced the signing the next day.

Doby called Veeck his "godfather."

"He didn't see color," Larry told the *New York Times* 50 years later. "To me, he was in every sense color blind. And I always knew he was there for me. He always seemed to know when things were bad, if things were getting to me. He'd call up and say, 'Let's go out, let's get something to eat.'"

Veeck sat Doby down and gave him the dos and don'ts, Larry recalled. "No arguing with umpires. Don't even turn around at a bad call at the plate and no dissertations with the opposing players—either of those might start a race riot."

Before that first game, Veeck told him, "Just remember that they play with a little white ball and a stick of wood up here just like they did in your league."

The Indians' manager, Lou Boudreau, introduced Larry to his new teammates. One by one, Doby shook their hands—except for some 10 who refused his grip. Two even turned their backs on him.

"The next year, Bill Veeck eliminated about five of the guys who were discourteous to me," Larry told Art Rusk Jr. later.

When he got out on the field to loosen up, everybody suddenly got very busy throwing to somebody else, Larry remembered. But Joe Gordon, the former Yankee whose presence at second base forced Larry to learn to play the outfield, noticed him standing off to the side, threw him a ball, and asked if he wanted to have a catch.

Yankee catcher Yogi Berra also befriended Doby.

"Yogi was one of the first opposing players to talk to me," Larry recalled. "I finally had to tell the umpire, 'Please tell him to shut up. He asked me how my family was back in the first inning.'"

They would remain close friends for the rest of Larry's life.

He always spoke well of those who helped him along the way, but he would never name the people who turned their backs on him, taunted him, spiked him, or threw a baseball at his head.

The famous photo: After Larry Doby, right, slammed a dramatic home run to win the fourth game of the '48 Series, he and winning pitcher Steve Gromek, left, embraced in the clubhouse. Newspapers around the country ran the photo, which did as much to improve race relations in America as any other image of the time.

"He would say things like, 'Early Wynn, I knew if he was pitching I was O.K.,'" Larry's son, Larry Jr., told *New York Times* writer Harvey Araton, "'because if they knocked me down, then two of their guys were going down.' I believe that he and Jackie Robinson—to us it was always Mr. Robinson—would talk about the good guys and the bad guys, but to everybody else, it was only about the good guys."

"Only those for whom Doby could say something positive were spoken of," Araton wrote, "because, the way he saw it, if a man didn't learn from his experience, didn't rise above it, what, then, was the point?"

Not that the abuse didn't hurt. It hurt plenty.

"It was tough on him," teammate Bob Feller recalled. "Larry was very sensitive, more so than [Jackie] Robinson or Satchel Paige or Luke Easter."

"When I was growing up," Doby said, "my parents used to tell me, 'sticks and stones may break your bones, but names will never hurt you.' I found that to be different in real life.

"The things I was called did hurt me. They hurt me a lot. The things people did to me, spitting tobacco juice on me, sliding into me, throwing baseballs at my head. The words they called me, they do hurt. I was always taught to treat people the way you want to be treated. I was raised to respect people. I found out all people are not raised that way.

"I couldn't react to situations from a physical standpoint," he said. "My reaction was to hit the ball as far as I could."

Years later, Doby could still describe for commissioner Fay Vincent the day he slid into second base and "a guy spit on me. I felt terrible. It really got to me. I never forgot it."

Larry and Jackie Robinson talked often.

"Maybe we kept each other from giving up," Larry said later.

They would remain friends, and Larry served as a pallbearer at Jackie's funeral.

The Making of a Major Leaguer

Larry Doby was born in Camden, South Carolina, on December 13, 1924. His father, a semipro baseball player, died when Larry was eight years old. A few years later, the family moved north to Patterson, New Jersey, where Larry won 11 varsity letters—in football, track, baseball and basketball—at East Side High School and then attended Long Island University and Virginia Union University.

In 1942, still just 17 and a skinny second baseman, he signed with the Newark Eagles, playing under the name Larry Walker. He played his first professional game in Yankee Stadium.

"All I wanted to do was play ball," Larry recalled. "For a long time, I thought the only chance I had was in the Negro Leagues."

The first time he faced the Homestead Grays, Ray Brown was on the mound for the Grays, with the immortal Josh Gibson behind the plate.

"My first time up," Larry recalled, "Josh said, 'We're going to find out if you can hit a fastball.'

"I singled.

"Next time up, Josh said, 'We're going to find out if you can hit a curveball.'

"I singled.

"Next time up, Josh said, 'We're going to find out how you do after you're knocked down.' I popped up the first time they knocked me down. The second time, I singled."

When he hit against the legendary Satchel Paige, Satch called down to him, "'I'm told you're a good low fastball hitter, so I'm going to throw you low fastballs.' I singled that time, too," Larry said.

He interrupted his baseball career for two years in the Navy, serving in Guam. When he came back, he led the Eagles over the Kansas City Monarchs in the Negro League World Series. He started out on a tear the next year, and that's when Veeck and the Indians tabbed him to make history.

He spent the first six innings of that game on July 5, 1947, on the bench—under the guard of two Chicago detectives, according to an account in *Sports Illustrated*. He came to the plate as a pinch hitter in the seventh inning and struck out—a feeble beginning to a great career. The next day he started at first base and got his first major league hit.

Doby made it into just 29 games that year, showing little sign of the player he had been and would become. But in 1948, he came to spring training determined to make the club and the starting lineup. After hitting .356 in camp, he began the season as the Indians' starting right fielder. He stayed in the lineup all year, hitting .301 with 14 home runs.

He was on the field on July 13, 1948, when Satchel Paige made his much-delayed first major league start. Satch allowed just five hits in nine innings, beating the White Sox, 5-0. Doby contributed two hits and two stolen bases to the historic victory.

The Picture Seen 'Round the World

His big bat helped Cleveland get into and win the World Series that year, making Larry Doby the first black American ever to play on a world championship team. He hit a team-leading .318 in the Series, and his long home run off Braves ace Johnny Sain won the fourth game.

After that game, Doby and winning pitcher Steve Gromek embraced. The picture of their smiling faces—one white, one black—appeared in the *Cleveland Plain Dealer*—and then around the world. That photo probably did as much for race relations in America as any other image of the era.

Along with finding his stroke at the plate, Larry made a successful conversion to the outfield, convincing Tris Speaker, reputedly a former klansman, to tutor him. He became an excellent centerfielder, once playing 167 consecutive games without an error, an American League record.

He put together a string of eight straight seasons in which he hit no fewer than 20 home runs. His peak power years were 1952 and 1954, with 32 home runs each year. He also drove in a career-high 126 runs in '54, leading the league in home runs and RBIs and leading Cleveland to a record-setting 111-win season.

He appeared in the 1949 All-Star game at Ebbets Field, becoming with Jackie Robinson, Roy Campanella and Don Newcombe of the Dodgers, the first blacks to play in the mid-season classic. Larry then played in every All-Star Game through 1954 and hit a key pinch-hit home run in his last All-Star at bat.

At the end of the 1955 season, the Indians traded Doby to the White Sox for shortstop Chico Carrasquel and outfielder Jim Busby, and Larry enjoyed two more fine seasons in Chicago. In December of '57, the Sox sent him, with pitchers Jack Harshman and Russ Herman and infielder Jim Marshall, to Baltimore for pitcher Ray Moore, infielder Billy Goodman, and outfielder Tito Francona. Before even donning an Oriole uniform, Larry was shipped back to Cleveland, along with pitcher Don Ferrarese, for outfielders Gene Woodling and Dick Williams and pitcher Bud Daley. A year later the Indians traded him to Detroit, again for Francona. Doby played just 18 games for the Tigers and a final 21 back with the White Sox before retiring.

But he wasn't done playing—or making history. He and Don Newcombe signed with the Chunichi Dragons in 1962, becoming the first former major leaguers to play for a Japanese team.

Recognition Is a Long Time Coming

"Larry Doby was a remarkable player," Dodgers pitcher Joe Black told Fay Vincent. "[H]e could really do it all."

And yet, Larry waited a long time to take his rightful place next to Jackie Robinson in baseball and American history.

While he waited—with typical patience and dignity—he continued to serve the sport he loved. He coached for the Montreal Expos, Indians and White Sox, and on June 30, 1978, Bill Veeck named him to replace Bob Lemon as manager of the White Sox, making him the second black manager in major league history. Doby later served as special adviser to commissioners and league presidents.

When young Larry Jr. would ask him to talk about his playing days, his father often told him, "I do not live in the past. I live for tomorrow."

On July 3, 1994, the Indians finally retired Larry Doby's No. 14, 47 years after he joined the team and broke the color barrier in the American League.

Many felt that Doby belonged in the Hall of Fame. The Jackie Robinson Society started a letter-writing campaign to convince the Hall's Veteran's Committee, which included Yogi Berra, Monte Irvin, Stan Musial, Pee Wee Reese, Ted Williams, and Buck O'Neill. The committee voted him in on March 3, 1998.

Other monuments to his great career include a special Larry Doby wing in the Yogi Berra Museum in Little Falls, New Jersey, and a life-size bronze statue near the sandlot field at Eastside Park in Paterson, New Jersey, that bears his name.

"It was a learning lesson for baseball and the country," Larry said of his career. "If we all look back, we can see that baseball helped make this a better country for us all, a more comfortable country for us all.

"Kids are our future, and we hope baseball has given them some idea of what it is to live together and how we can get along, whether you be black or white."

"For me," Fay Vincent wrote, "the most vivid memory of Larry is his total lack of bitterness. He refused to name the players who treated him badly. He never exhibited any resentment toward the country or society that turned him away from the game he loved."

"I was never bitter, because I believed in the man upstairs," Doby told Vincent. "If I was bitter, I was only hurting me. I prefer to remember Bill Veeck and Jim Hegan and Joe Gordon, the good guys. There is no point talking about the others."

Larry Doby died Wednesday, June 18, 2003, at his home in Montclair, New Jersey, as this chapter was being written. He is survived by his five loving children—son Larry Jr., and daughters Christina Fearrington, Leslie Feggan, Kimberly Martin and Susan Robinson—and six grandchildren and five great-grandchildren.

He lost his wife, Helyn, who had been his high school sweetheart, to cancer in 2001.

"People have always given me a lot of credit for what I did," Larry once told *New York Times* columnist Dave Anderson, "but Helyn deserved just as much credit for keeping our family of five kids together."

Yogi Berra attended Larry's funeral. So did Phil Rizzuto and Ralph Branca. Fay Vincent was there. Joe Morgan escorted Rachel Robinson, Jackie's widow. Senator Frank Lautenberg, James McGreevey, the New Jersey governor, and Robert Russo, the mayor of Montclair, New Jersey, were there, too.

Larry summed up his career in an interview with the *Houston Chronicle*. "After you look back at the progress that's been made and the minorities involved in baseball, you can't think about the bad things that happened to you in '47," he said. "It was all worth it."

CHAPTER 7

The Heart and Soul of a Team
Roy Campanella

"I never want to quit playing ball. They'll have to cut this uniform off of me to get me out of it."

—Roy Campanella

Full name: Roy Campanella
Nickname: "Campy"
Position: Catcher
Career: Baltimore Elite Giants, 1938-42, 1944-45; Brooklyn Dodgers, 1948-1957

Negro League career highlights:

- Was named MVP of the East-West All-Star game in 1941 while playing for the Baltimore Elite Giants.
- While still playing for the Giants, led league in RBI in 1945, his final year in the Negro Leagues.

Major League career batting average: .276

Major League career highlights:

- Drove in a league-best 142 runs in 1953.
- Was named an All-Star every season between 1949-1956.
- Selected NL MVP in 1951, 1953, and 1955.
- Elected to the Hall of Fame.

There were many reasons for the Dodgers' miserable collapse the year they trekked from Brooklyn to Los Angeles in 1958. Just trying to find the Coliseum through the smog and the maze of freeways left many players dazed.

But the loss of Roy Campanella, the heart and soul of the Brooklyn Dodgers, had to be a major factor in the swoon.

And seeing Campy wheeled onto the field so that 93,000 fans could salute his courage had to be one of the major inspirations for the team's resurgence to win the World Series the next year.

The car crash that paralyzed his body couldn't quell Campy's mighty spirit. His playing career over, Campy, with wife Roxie, created the Roy Campanella Foundation to fund academic scholarships for students striving to become physical therapists. Campy wanted to help others the way he had been helped.

He remains an inspiration long after his death in 1993.

The Next Josh Gibson

Like many great black players, Campy's entry into the major leagues was delayed by racial prejudice. Roy Campanella was one of five black players signed by Brooklyn Dodgers owner Branch Rickey in 1946 and the first catcher to break baseball's color line. He'd proven his ability during nine great years in the Negro National League.

By the time he finally made it to the Dodgers, he had already made quite a journey.

Roy was born on November 19, 1921, in Philadelphia to a black mother and an Italian father from Sicily. When kids taunted him for being a "half-breed," he went to his mother and asked, "Is it true that my daddy is a white man?"

She told him yes, adding that it didn't matter because his father was a good man, loving and hard working.

Once when fans called him a nigger, Campy replied, "Hey, you know I'm a dago, too."

As a kid, he spent what little free time he had playing baseball and stickball, but mostly he worked to help support his family. By age 12, he was delivering milk at 3 a.m., hurrying home by 5 a.m. to help load the family truck with the vegetables his father sold. Then he cleaned up and went to school. After school, he sold newspapers and shined shoes.

In 1937, at age 14, Campy was already playing ball with men in their 20s when he caught the attention of a Negro League scout. He

A car accident ended his playing career and paralyzed his body as the Brooklyn Dodgers prepared to head west for L.A., but nothing could quell Roy Campanella's optimism or courage.

played two games with the hometown semi-pro Bacharach Giants and then signed with the Baltimore Elite Giants of the Negro League. That was as close as a black man could hope to come to the major leagues at the time. Still in school, he played only on weekends, spelling veteran catcher Biz Mackey.

The next season he quit school to join the team full time. He became the starting catcher in 1939, leading the Giants to playoff triumphs over the Newark Eagles and Homestead Grays. Soon he was challenging his idol, Josh Gibson, as the dominate Negro League catcher and was the MVP in the 1941 East-West All-Star Game. He also played winter ball in Puerto Rico and Cuba.

When Baltimore owner Tom Wilson fined him for playing in an all-star game, Campy jumped to the Mexican League for the end of the 1942 season and all of the 1943 season. He came back to the Giants in 1944 when the fine was finally rescinded. The next year he led the league in RBIs.

By the time he was 24, Campy was a 10-year veteran making $5,000 a year as one of the highest paid players in the Negro Leagues.

In October of 1945 he caught for a black all-star team in a five-game exhibition series against a team of white major leaguers managed by Charlie Dressen. The Dodgers already had their eye on the stocky five-foot-nine power-hitting catcher. Branch Rickey offered him a contract, but Campy thought it was for another Negro League team and turned it down. Talking to Jackie Robinson later, he realized that the offer was for the Brooklyn Dodgers. He signed eagerly, even though the $185 per month he'd be making was a huge cut from his salary with the Elite Giants. He was the second black player to sign a Brooklyn contract.

The club assigned him to its Class B team in Danville, Illinois, which promptly rejected him because he was black. After other teams also turned him away, he finally caught on with Class B Nashua, New Hampshire. Buzzie Bavasi ran that team, and Walter Alston was its manager. Campy roomed with pitcher Don Newcombe.

As he would do everywhere he went, Campy earned the respect of teammates, opponents and fans through his hard work and dedication—that and the fact that every team he played for greatly benefited from his presence.

Campy hit a hard .290 for Nashua and led the league in putouts and assists, winning the league MVP award. His performance earned him a promotion to AAA Montreal of the International League the next year. He had another MVP year, although a slump at the end of the season cut his average to .273.

Paul Richards, managing the Buffalo team in the I-League that year, called Campy "the best catcher in the business—major or minor leagues."

Campy was clearly ready for the big club in 1948, but Rickey wanted him to integrate the American Association first. There was no room for him behind the plate on the Dodger's American Association affiliate, so Rickey told manager Leo Durocher to play him in the outfield. As a flychaser, Campy made a great catcher, and he was demoted to AA St. Paul in May. In 35 games there, he had 40 hits and 39 RBIs.

His major league career had been delayed far too long. He came up to the Dodgers in 1948—and stayed there.

For the next 10 years, he was the quarterback of the fabled Brooklyn Dodger team that came to be known as "The Boys of Summer." Under Campy's leadership behind the plate, "da Bums" captured the flag in 1949, 1952, 1953, 1955 and 1956 and just missed it in two other seasons. They won their only world championship against the New York Yankees in 1955.

In 1949, Campy joined Jackie Robinson and Don Newcombe in the National League All-Star lineup. Along with Larry Doby of the American League, they were the first black players ever to appear in a major league all-star contest.

In a five-year stretch, Campy was the league's MVP three times. He was a superb receiver, handling a predominately white pitching staff beautifully and throwing out almost two-thirds of the runners audacious enough to try to swipe a base on him. He led NL catchers in putouts six times and belted 242 home runs in his 10-year career. In 1953, his best season, he hit 41 home runs and drove in 162, both major league records for a catcher, and scored 103 runs.

Catching is the most physically as well as mentally demanding job on a baseball field, and Campy's rugged body sustained its share of damage. His most serious injury came in 1954 when he chipped a bone in the heel of his left hand, damaging a nerve. The injury limited him to 111 games and hurt his swing. When his average slid to .167, the Dodgers benched him. The next day, May 3, he had surgery to remove bone chips from his hand.

He seemed to make a complete recovery, leading the Dodgers to a 7-5 victory over the Cardinals on June 7 with a home run and an unlikely steal of home in the 12th inning. But the hand still bothered him, and Campy played only sparingly the rest of the season.

He was back behind the plate in 1955 where, on May 5, he caught lefthander Tommy Lasorda's first major league start. Tommy uncorked three wild pitches in a single inning. After the game, he blamed his catcher for his wildness.

Johnny Podres had nothing but nice things to say about that same catcher later that season when Campy caught his 8-3 World Series win and led the Dodgers assault on Yankee pitcher Bob Turley with three hits and three RBIs.

On June 11, 1957, in the Dodgers' last season in Brooklyn and Campy's last on the field, he blasted his 237th career home run, passing the career marks of Gabby Hartnett and Yogi Berra.

Along with Gil, Pee Wee, Duke and the rest, Campy prepared at the end of the season to cross the country to inaugurate major league baseball in Los Angeles.

He never got the chance.

A Sudden End

In the early morning hours of January 29, 1958, Campy was driving home when his car hit a patch of ice and slammed into a telephone pole. His car flipped, pinning him behind the steering wheel. Still conscious, he tried to reach out to turn off the engine, realizing with horror that he couldn't move his arms or legs.

He would never move them again.

The crash broke his neck and nearly severed his spinal cord. In an instant, Roy Campanella had been transformed from a powerful major league catcher to a quadriplegic.

With courage, faith, and dignity, Roy Campanella embarked on years of painful physical therapy. His playing career over, he began a new life of community service, as a goodwill ambassador for the Dodgers and an inspiration for those whose lives he touched.

On May 7, 1959, 93,103 fans filled the Los Angeles Coliseum, where the new Los Angeles Dodgers made their home while their new ballpark was being constructed in Chavez Ravine. They came to honor the Dodger who had been unable to take his place on the field with the rest. As Campy was wheeled onto the field, the lights were extinguished, and the fans lit matches, signifying the light that Campy was for the world. In the hush, you could hear a soul sigh.

On February 23, 1960, they began tearing down storied Ebbets Field. Campy was presented with an urn filled with dirt scooped up from behind home plate.

And on January 21, 1969, Campy received baseball's highest honor, election into the Hall of Fame, along with Cardinals great Stan Musial.

In his autobiography, *It's Good to Be Alive*, he chronicled his life as a ballplayer and a quadriplegic.

"As intensely personal and vividly human a book as any ballplayer has ever written," the *New York Herald Tribune* book reviewer said. "If anybody conveys a feeling of the happiness of being alive, of the physical delight in sports, of quiet pride in having had a part in ending the racial barriers of big league ball, Roy Campanella is the man."

That book became a made-for-TV drama starring Lou Gossett Jr. and directed by Michael Landon, and Campy's can-do gospel of joy won an even greater audience.

Roy Campanella, the major league's first black catcher and one of its all-time greatest, had become far more than a ballplayer; he had become a symbol of joy in the face of sorrow and triumph over tragedy.

CHAPTER 8

The Newark Eagle Soars
Monte Irvin

"Monte Irvin is the best all-around athlete I ever saw."
—Roy Campanella

Full name: Monford Merrill Irvin
Nickname: "Monte"
Position: Outfield
Career: Newark Eagles 1939-42, 1946-48; New York Giants, 1949-
1955; Chicago Cubs, 1956

Negro League career highlights:

- Led the league in batting average in 1940 (.442), 1941 (.396), and
1946 (.441).
- Also led the league in RBI in 1946, and hit .462 in that year's Negro
League World Series.
- Played in four East-West All-Star games.

Major League career batting average: .293

Major League career highlights:

- Finished third in the NL MVP voting while leading the league in
RBIs in 1951, knocking in 121.
- Selected as an All-Star in 1952.
- Elected to the Hall of Fame.

The New Jersey Sports Writers' Association voted him the "Greatest Athlete Ever in New Jersey," and his plaque hangs in nine halls of fame in the United States, Mexico, Cuba, and Puerto Rico.

But race prejudice delayed Monte's major league debut for a decade.

He began his professional baseball career playing shortstop for the Newark Eagles in 1939, switched to the outfield, and for eight years smoked the Negro Leagues with his hitting. He played in four East-West All-Star games and led the league in hitting in 1940 (.422) and '41 (.396).

In leading the Eagles to the championship over the Kansas City Monarchs in 1946, he batted .389 for the season and then topped it with a .462 mark in the series, where he belted three home runs and scored the winning run in the seventh game.

He came close to being the first one to break the color barrier in the major leagues but didn't make it to the bigs until 1949, two years after Jackie. Once there, he helped the New York Giants to World Series championships in 1951 and 1954. In '51, he tied a World Series record with 11 hits and led all hitters with a .458 average.

After his playing days were over, he spent 16 more years in baseball, mostly working in the commissioner's office.

He was born on February 25, 1919, on a farm in Columbia, Alabama, the seventh of 10 children of Cupid Irvin and Mary Eliza Henderson. When Monte was eight, his parents moved the family north to Orange, New Jersey. Monte became a four-sport star at Orange High School, earning 16 varsity letters. He set the New Jersey state high school record for the javelin and was an All-State linebacker.

He turned down a football scholarship to the University of Michigan, instead enrolling at Lincoln University in Oxford, Pennsylvania, where he majored in political science for two years. Still just 18, he began playing for the Newark Eagles on weekends under the name "Jimmy Nelson," to protect his amateur status.

His career almost ended the next year when he scratched his hand during a basketball game. The seemingly innocent wound became infected, and Monte hovered near death for seven weeks.

Fully recovered, he signed a contract with the Eagles in 1941 for $165 a month. Despite his hitting heroics, Eagles owner Effa Manley turned him down when he asked for a $25 raise, so Monte jumped to the Mexican League. He promptly won the Triple Crown, slamming 30 home runs in just 68 games while hitting .398.

Then he put his career on hold, answering Uncle Sam's call to serve in the army for three years. That may have prevented him from being the one to break the color line in the majors.

It Might Have Been Monte

"Monte was the choice of all Negro National and American League club owners to serve as the number-one player to join a white major league team," Manley said. "We all agreed, in meetings, he was the best qualified by temperament, character, ability, sense of loyalty, morals, age, experience and physique to represent us as the first black player to enter the white majors since the Walker brothers [Moses and Weldy] back in the late 1880s."

"Monte was our best young ballplayer at the time," according to Negro League legend James "Cool Papa" Bell. "He could do anything ... [W]e wanted men who could go there and hit the ball over the fence, and Monte could do that. He could hit the long ball, he had a great arm, he could field, and he could run. Yes, he could do everything. It's not that Jackie Robinson wasn't a good ballplayer, but we wanted Monte."

But when Irvin got out of the army, he had an inner ear infection. He played in the 1945-46 Puerto Rico Winter League to get back into top shape and batted .397, capturing the league MVP award.

Meanwhile, Branch Rickey picked Jackie Robinson to shatter the color line in 1947, giving up his claim on Irvin.

Monte starred for two more seasons with Newark. The New York Giants bought his contract from the Eagles for $5,000 and assigned him to their Jersey City farm club. Monte tore up the International League, hitting .373. The Giants called him up during the pennant race in July, and Monte was a major leaguer at last. He made his debut on July 27, 1949, as a pinch hitter, as he and Hank Thompson became the first blacks ever to play for the Giants.

He started the 1950 season back with Jersey City, but this time Jersey couldn't hold him back. He hit .510 with 10 home runs in the first 18 games! He was up to stay with the Giants, hitting .299 his rookie year, playing first base and outfield. On May 18 at the Polo Grounds against the Cubs, he slammed a bases-loaded home run in the bottom of the sixth inning. Cubs catcher Rube Walker had hit a grand slam for the Cubs in the top of the inning, so Irvin's blast made history, the first time opposing teams had hit slams in the same inning.

In 1951, Monte emerged as a major league star for the "Miracle Giants." He hit .312 with 24 home runs and led the National League with 121 RBIs. He finished third in the MVP voting that year, then hit

Negro League owners and players—like legendary speedster "Cool Papa" Bell, left—agreed that Monte Irvin, right, should be the one to break baseball's color line.

.458 against the Yankees in the World Series, including a streak of seven consecutive hits over two games. He even stole home off Allie Reynolds.

Monte broke his ankle sliding into third base during an exhibition game the next spring and played in only 46 regular-season games, hitting .310 with four home runs. He came back strong in 1953 with a .329 average, 21 home runs, and 97 RBI but reinjured his leg in August and never fully regained his form. Even so, he contributed 19 home runs to the Giants' drive to the pennant in 1954.

Fifty-one games into the 1955 season, the Giants sent him down, and he spent his final big-league season in 1956 with the Cubs.

He scouted for the Mets in 1967-8 and then joined the commissioner's office as a special assistant. He spent 16 years as a public relations specialist and also served on the Veterans' Committee of the Hall of Fame.

On February 1, 1973, the Special Committee on the Negro Leagues elected Monte to the Hall.

In his autobiography, *Nice Guys Finish First*, Monte made it clear that the barrier barring blacks from the major leagues robbed him of his prime. In an interview in 2000, he pointed out that the majors had also deprived themselves of many other great players.

"They would've gotten Willie Wells, Buck Leonard, Oscar Charleston, Martin Dihigo, Satchel Paige, Ray Dandridge … Cool Papa Bell and right on down the line," he noted. "Most of those guys were over the hill when Jackie came in."

But Monte also recalled the good times and the camaraderie of the Negro Leagues. Many of the good memories center on the four All-Star games he played in.

"The game started around 2:00," he recalled, "and the stands would fill with people coming to Chicago from as far away as Texas, Mississippi, Alabama."

Lots of celebrities attended, he said, including Bill "Bojangles" Robinson.

It's a good thing the game paid big in experience.

"[A]ll we got was $50 expenses," he said. "No rings, no watches, no photos, no anything."

Still, it was a happy time, he said. "It was an occasion for people to get dressed up in their best clothes and hats and go out on the town."

Like fellow Negro League star Buck O'Neill, Monte said he has no regrets about being barred from the majors for so long. It was a case of a nice guy and incredible athlete ultimately finishing first.

CHAPTER 9

Baseball Interrupted
Jimmy Piersall

"The tower is close by the hospital and perhaps a mile in from the Worcester Turnpike, one of the main highways leading south and west from Boston. I drive over that road often in the wintertime, and whenever I pass the water tower, I say a prayer. I pray for Mary and I pray for the children and I pray for all the people who still must see the water tower only from that other angle and, most of all, I pray that it will never happen again to me."
—Jimmy Piersall, *Fear Strikes Out*

"He gets ballflys that Tris Speaker never would have reached."
—Bill McKechnie, Red Sox coach

Full name: James Anthony Piersall
Nickname: "Jimmy"
Position: Outfield, shortstop
Career: Boston Red Sox, 1950, 1952-58; Cleveland Indians, 1959-61; Washington Senators, 1962-63; New York Mets, 1963; Los Angeles/California Angels, 1963-67
Career batting average: .272

Career highlights:
- Led the league in doubles with 40 in 1956.
- Topped the league in sacrifice hits in 1953 with 19, finished ninth that year in the AL MVP voting.
- Led the league in fielding percentage in 1955, 1960, and 1961.

• Won the AL Gold Glove Award in 1958 and 1961.
• Selected as an All-Star in 1954 and 1956.

Jimmy Piersall opened the 1952 season wearing No. 2, batting fifth, and playing shortstop. By late June, he was demoted to the Sox's AA farm club in Birmingham, Alabama. Three weeks later, Jimmy was confined to a ward at Westborough State Mental Hospital, suffering from manic depression.

Throughout the early 1952 season, Jimmy exhibited puzzling and bizarre behavior. His antics came to a head on June 12 in a game against the St. Louis Browns. Browns pitcher Satchel Paige was one of the first to diagnose Jimmy. Satch was sitting in the dugout after blowing a four-run lead to the Red Sox in the ninth inning, still reeling from Piersall's unmerciful taunting.

"That man's plumb crazy," Satch said. "He's nuts altogether."

Piersall wasn't crazy; he was sick, and he needed help. He was unraveling.

In the weeks following the Paige incident, Jimmy kept flirting with disaster. The Fenway fans loved his shouting and mugging, but Sox manager Lou Boudreau saw it differently.

"I've got to consider 25 or 30 men on my team," Boudreau said. "We're trying to win, and a condition like that didn't help."

Although Lou didn't know it, Jimmy had manic depression, now also known as bipolar disorder, which affects more than 2.3 million American adults. It often runs in families, begins in adolescence or early adulthood, and can be triggered by extreme stress.

Piersall was batting 1,000 in all three departments.

His mother spent 10 years in a sanitarium. He was 22 years old and in a high-stress environment. Some believe that Lou Boudreau's insistence that he play shortstop rather than his familiar outfield position contributed to his breakdown.

His symptoms included typical signs of bipolar disorder: extreme mood swings, excessive crying, provocative, aggressive and destructive behavior, poor judgment, and overly inflated self-esteem (grandiosity).

"I don't know how many times I talked to him," coach Bill McKechnie said. "Day after day. I don't think he was even listening. Five minutes later, he'd be doing the same thing. And he'd cry and cry.

"[W]hat defensive ability he had! But he wasn't helping himself. He hurt himself as much as possible," McKechnie added. "Nobody would give him a break the way he was showing up everyone."

Jimmy Piersall overcame manic depression and confinement in a mental hospital to become one of the finest outfielders in baseball history. His candor and bravery have given hope to many others battling the disease.

Still, the fans loved him, and Piersall went on a tear starting June 6, hitting .368. So, when Boudreau and general manager Joe Cronin farmed him out to the Birmingham Barons, the fans were unhappy. Mail ran about 80 percent against the move. As one gentleman from Brookline, Massachusetts said, "I don't care how he clowned as long as he plays good ball. They can't hold him down."

But the orderlies at Westborough State Mental Hospital were ordered to do just that.

Redemption

Today, Piersall would be treated with a combination of drugs and therapy. But in the 1950s, the preferred antidote was electroshock treatment. Jimmy suffered some memory impairment, but the treatments worked. After six weeks he was able to leave the hospital.

Thanks to Cronin and Red Sox owner Tom Yawkey, Piersall and his family spent the winter recuperating in Florida. The Red Sox's generosity and support paid off. By the following April, Piersall was back in the starting lineup. He had changed numbers, position, and batting order. Jimmy was wearing No. 37, batting second, and playing rightfield.

He had a different outlook, too, battling back during the 1953 season to achieve a most remarkable comeback from the ravages and stigma of mental illness.

He was voted the "Sophomore of the Year" in the American League, besting Whitey Ford by 29 votes. He played all but three games of the 154-game season, batting a respectable .272.

On June 10, in a road game against the St. Louis Browns, Piersall went six for six. He was the 31st player to smack out six hits in a game and the first Red Sox to accomplish the feat.

But in the second game of the doubleheader, Jimmy seemed close to losing the composure he had fought so hard to achieve. He bunted foul against his old nemesis, Satchel Paige, and old Satch didn't take kindly to being bunted on. His next pitch sailed at Piersall's head. Jimmy ducked, and the ball caromed off his bat. He started toward Paige, but plate umpire Ed Rommel came between them. Piersall and Paige traded jeers, but nothing else, and Satchel proceeded to strike Jimmy out.

Lou Boudreau wisely gave Piersall the next day off—his first of the season.

"He has played every game of the series and the heat here has been terrific," Boudreau said.

"Piersall has played wonderfully. I've rested most of the players in one game or more, and I feel I should rest him."

Jimmy finished the season without incident.

The Human Highlight Reel

If ESPN's *SportsCenter* had been around in Jimmy's day, they'd be featuring him on every Web Gem segment, and we'd all watch him diving, leaping, vaulting, and bouncing off and over walls to make spectacular catches.

He was that good.

On July 19 Jimmy treated 35,000 Cleveland fans to a spectacular exhibition as the Red Sox double-dipped the Indians, 2-0 and 7-5.

In the fifth inning of the first game, he made a beautiful running catch right outside of first base, provoking a Cleveland writer to joke, "Is it legal to have Piersall playing right field and first base at the same time?"

Then in the bottom of the ninth, he made a shoestring catch off Al Rosen and doubled the runner off first. Then he finished the Indians off by robbing Bob Lemon of an extra base hit at the right field pole.

Boston Globe columnist Roger Birtwell compared him to an aroused antelope.

"[H]e went racing out there," Birtwell said. "And there was a beauty in his stride and a grace in his form as he flung his gloved hand up and out, for a one-handed stab that saved the game."

His outstanding catches—especially at critical times in the game—became almost commonplace.

Bill Lee wasn't the original Red Sox "Space Man." Boston sportswriter Harold Kease gave that honor to Piersall.

"The spaceman who defies the law of gravity is no longer a promise of the future," Kease wrote. "He has arrived. He played right field for the Red Sox yesterday."

Three catches in three separate games had Mickey Vernon of the Washington Nationals muttering to himself. On back-to-back days in August, Piersall robbed Vernon of home runs by diving into Fenway's right field stands.

The catch on August 15 came in the fifth inning. The inning before he had robbed Gil Coan, the Nats leftfielder, by gloving Coan's liner at the 380-foot marker and crashing into the visitors' bullpen wall. Then he took away Vernon's homer with a leaping catch, tumbling into the grandstand seats.

The next day, wearing a six-inch welt on his back from the Coan catch, he did it again.

"I thought I hit that one a little better than the Saturday clout," Vernon said. "When he popped out of those stands with the ball I could have shot him."

A week later in Washington's spacious Griffith Stadium, Piersall dashed to the 460-foot marker and backhanded a potential Vernon triple.

"He's a couple of steps faster, so he can play shallower," according to Jackie Jensen, the right fielder for the Nationals. "He has a great arm, and an accurate one. But most of all he is so confident in the toughest outfield in the league for my money. I've got to believe all they say about him being one of the greats of all time."

Piersall went on to play the next five years in Boston (1954-1958), covering the outfield between Ted Williams in left and Jensen (who was traded to the Sox) in right. He made the American League All-Star team in 1954 and 1956. He led the league in doubles with 40 in 1956. In 1958, he won the first-ever Golden Glove award with only five errors in 412 chances. He would have easily won Golden Gloves in 1953-1957, too, since he owned even better fielding averages during those seasons.

Turning Fear into Affirmation

After coming back from his stay in the mental hospital, Jimmy endured vicious bench riding and incessant fan insults. Piersall overcame the taunts by laughing at himself, acknowledging his "craziness" and winning the respect and admiration of his fellow players.

During his stay in Boston, Piersall spoke to mental health groups and visited hospitals. His talks and visits were therapeutic for everyone.

"It's a great help," he said, "to bring your problems out in the open and discuss them with others. The pattern in a mental illness is always the same. You feel alone. Your mind gets tired. Then your body becomes physically tired. By discussing the problem with others, yours seems small and you stop feeling sorry for yourself."

In 1955 he published his autobiography, *Fear Strikes Out*, which was made into a movie starring Anthony Perkins as Piersall and Karl Malden as his father. It was an inspirational account of his slip into the terrors and suffering of mental illness, bringing into the open what had always been a secretive affair. Jimmy's book freed many to talk about their illness rather than hide it. He gave credence to the fact that emotions such as fear can serve a purpose, and even be useful, if we learn to understand them.

He cherished the experience of hearing a stranger say, "My brother was mentally ill. Your book helped him."

In December 1958, he was traded to Cleveland for first baseman Vic Wertz and outfielder Gary Geiger. He played three years for the Indians, posting a career-high .322 batting average in 1961.

After Cleveland, he played for the Washington Senators and ended his career in 1967 with the California Angels. In all, Piersall had 17 good years in the majors.

Nearly 30 years after writing his autobiography with Al Hirshberg, he wrote a sequel called *The Truth Hurts*. This time he teamed up with Richard Whittingham to give readers an update on his roller-coaster life.

And what a bumpy ride it was. His illness tormented him. His alarm system kept going on and off, making it impossible to relax. He cycled through soaring elation and killing depression. The years took their toll: two divorces, a triple bypass surgery, multiple jobs (including baseball announcing) and multiple firings, and constant controversy.

In 1980, he spent three days in an Illinois Masonic Hospital after suffering from exhaustion.

Some days he made progress, and other days he slid back. That's the nature of the illness.

Yet through it all, Piersall endured.

"Courage is fear," one writer says, "that has said its prayers."

While at Westborough State Mental Hospital, Piersall prayed for his wife, his family, himself, and others facing the agony of mental illness. He lost a year but overcame his illness to play professional ball for 17 years. He never lost hope, and through his candor and courage, he has given hope to many others.

CHAPTER 10

Pitching in on the
Road to Capitol Hill

Jim Bunning and
Vinegar Bend Mizell

"In sports you're relying on your God-given natural ability and you're relying on yourself. In politics, you're not on your own—at all. You have to learn to count on a lot of people. It's a totally different experience."

—Jim Bunning

"It was a great victory because it belongs to the people."
—Vinegar Bend Mizell, on his 1968 Congressional win

Full name: James Paul David Bunning
Position: Right-handed pitcher
Career: Detroit Tigers, 1955-63; Philadelphia Phillies, 1964-67 and 1970-71; Pittsburgh Pirates, 1968-69; Los Angeles Dodgers, 1969
Career W-L: 224-184
Career ERA: 3.27

Career highlights:
• Threw a no-hitter in the AL in 1958 and in the NL in 1964.
• Led the league in strikeouts in 1959 (201), 1960 (201), and 1967 (253).

- Topped the league in games started with 41 in 1966 and 40 in 1967.
- Finished second in AL Cy Young voting in 1967.
- Selected as an All Star seven times: 1957, 1959, 1961, 1962, 1963, 1964, 1966.
- Elected to the Hall of Fame.

Full name: Wilmer David Mizell
Nickname: "Vinegar Bend"
Position: Left-handed pitcher
Career: St Louis Cardinals, 1952-53 and 1956-60; Pittsburgh Pirates, 1960-62; New York Mets, 1962
Career W-L: 90-88
Career ERA: 3.85

Career highlights:
- Led the league in strikeouts per nine innings pitched in 1952 (6.92) and 1953 (6.94).
- Selected as an All-Star in 1959.

July 7, 1959 was a "first of a kind" day. The 55,105 fans who jammed into Forbes Field were witnessing the start of the two game All-Star series. Never before had fans been treated to seeing their favorite players battle for league bragging rights twice in one season. Thanks to Willie Mays, the National League edged the American League, 5-4.

Also unique was the presence on the All-Star rosters of two pitchers who would later serve in the House of Representatives: Vinegar Bend Mizell for the NL and Jim Bunning for the AL.

Wilmer David "Vinegar Bend" Mizell owned the best nickname in baseball; Bunning was simply called Jim.

Both were pitchers who stood six foot. Mizell was the thick-necked southpaw; Bunning, meanwhile, was the lanky righthander.

Mizell's batterymate, Hal Smith, said Mizell could "throw a ball through a brick wall." He could, that is, if he could hit the wall. In one game against the Reds, he hurled a shutout while walking a record nine batters.

Bunning ended his career in the top 50 in most strikeouts per walk (2,855 career strikeouts and an even 1,000 walks.)

Mizell was heralded as the next Dizzy Dean. He finished his career far short of Ol' Diz at 90-88, but with a decent 3.85 ERA.

Bunning made it to the Hall of Fame with a record of 224-184 and an ERA of 3.27.

The two 1959 All-Star pitchers, Mizell and Bunning, would go on to make lasting contributions for their constituencies. Vinegar Bend became the voice for the people in the 5th District near Winston-Salem, North Carolina. Jim Bunning served the folks in Northern Kentucky, first as a Representative from the 4th district, and now as the junior Senator from Kentucky, elected in 1998.

Wasn't it Mark Twain who said, "Suppose you were an idiot...And suppose you were a member of Congress...But I repeat myself"? Political cynicism oozes these days. We've been through the bickering, the special interests, the scandals, the pork-barrel legislation, and the nasty campaigns.

But Twain never met Mizell and Bunning. These guys go the full nine innings for the home folks.

A Country Boy with a Country Nickname

In uniform or out, Mizell had that good old country way of connecting with people.

When you met him, you took a liking to him.

"I've really had a good life," he said. "It's certainly a miracle that I got to the big leagues from such a small town, and the game opened up so many doors for me.

The game is so beautiful. I would've gotten nowhere without it, or my name."

It was no miracle, just hard work, grit, and a great fastball.

Oh yeah, about that name.

Vinegar Bend, Alabama, is smaller than Congress. It's also not the town Mizell came from. He grew up 37 miles south of Mobile, Alabama, in Leaksville, Mississippi, a rural gulf town that straddles the border with Alabama. The Mississippi and Alabama Railroad hauled lumber from Vinegar Bend to Leakesville, until it was abandoned in the early 1950s. It's an area where people stay put, unless they have to leave.

But "Leaksville" Mizell just didn't sound right to Buddy Lewis, the Cardinals scout. "Vinegar Bend" would do just fine—and it sounds much better than Wilmer.

Lewis signed the 18-year-old Mizell to a minor league contract. He quickly made his way up the minor league chain from Class D in Albany, Georgia, to Winston-Salem and finally to Houston in the Texas League. And every time he went up a notch, he struck out more batters: 175 at Albany, 227 in Winston-Salem, and finally a record 257 in Houston.

Jim Bunning, left, and Wilmer Mizell, right, went from facing each other in the '59 All-Star game to the halls of Congress.

The Cardinals noticed.

By age 21, he was in the starting rotation with the Cards, along with Gerry Staley, "Baby Joe" Presko, a "kitten," Harvey Haddix, and a "cat," Harry Brecheen. In his first two years in the majors, Mizell led the league in strikeouts per game, 6.92 and 6.94. He started over 30 games in each season, going 23-19, with an ERA of 3.50. But even with Mizell and the great Stan Musial, the Cards could only manage third-place finishes, behind the league-leading Brooklyn Dodgers.

Mizell was noticeably absent from St. Louis's Sportsman's Park on April 23, 1954. Thanks to the Korean War, he was wearing a green uniform at Ft. McPherson, Georgia, when the Cards' Vic Raschi served up Hank Aaron's first of 755 homers. Mizell later made it up to Hank by issuing him Nos. 61 and 161. Appropriately, he was on hand when Congress officially honored Aaron in 1974.

He could make it up to Aaron, but not to the Cards or his record. The war years prevented him from reaching 100 wins and ultimately hurt the Cards. They plunged from third place to sixth and then seventh.

Mizell, their workhorse, spent six solid years with the St. Louis Cardinals. He started more than 30 games each season from 1952-1953 and 1956-1959.

He had pitched in nine games in 1960 with a record of 1-3 when the Cards decided to unload him, shipping him to Pittsburgh along with Dick Gray for Julian Javier and Ed Bauta. Javier became the regular St. Louis second baseman for the next 12 years, and Mizell teamed up with his former pitching mate Harvey Haddix to capture a World Series ring.

As a loyal Cardinal, Mizell was initially disappointed, but later thought his trade was providential.

"God shipped me to the team that won the World Series," Mizell said. "We beat the Dodgers when it really counted, and I won a few of those big games, and then the feared Yankees fell. Nothing could be finer. And I know I made a big contribution. I really pitched. That year made up for all the bad ones."

It was his best year at 13-5, and along with Vern Law, Bob Friend, Haddix, and the 18-1 reliever Elroy Face, he led the "Beat 'em Bucs" to the pennant. He started Game 3 of the World Series against the Yanks but exited in the first inning.

He fell to 7-10 in 1962, and the Pirates traded him to the hapless Mets, where he was released. He made one last-ditch try in the minors at Columbus, Ohio, but didn't make it back to the bigs.

"The spirit was willing," Mizell said. "But my arm wasn't."

After retirement from baseball, he journeyed back to Winston-Salem, North Carolina, where he met his future wife.

His former teammate, Jim Brosnan, thought that Mizell was headed for the pulpit.

"Vinegar Bend Mizell was a religious fanatic who I first thought might be a preacher when he got out of baseball," Brosnan said. "He was a bright guy, articulate, with plenty of dialect. He could have gone anywhere to start a congregation because of who he was, and he could charm them."

Instead, Vinegar Bend chose politics.

He started as county commissioner and then tried a run for Congress in 1968. From the onset, money and tradition ran against him. He faced Smith Bagley, a wealthy opponent whose granddaddy was none other than R. J. Reynolds. Smith spent six times more money than Mizell on the campaign. Davidson County, a democratic stronghold, hadn't sent a Republican to Congress since John Motley Morehead was elected in 1909.

Yet Mizell beat Smith Bagley, 84,905 votes to 77,112.

He was reelected in 1970 and 1972 but fell prey to the Watergate fallout in 1974. He continued in public service, working in both the Ford and Reagan administrations as assistant secretary of commerce and then assistant secretary of agriculture.

In Congress and his other governmental service, Mizell will be remembered more as an honest broker than a power broker.

"I was from an area similar to the ones I was called upon to help," Mizell said. "And there were some real success stories. I remember this place in Livingston, Alabama, that didn't have water lines for fire protection. They got an EDA loan, built an industrial park, and in no time the local high school grew from 300 students to 1,600. That was something. The school even got themselves a baseball team."

He kept in mind what every sixth grade civics teacher says about Congress. It's emblazoned high above the entrance to the House. "Here, Sir," Alexander Hamilton said, "The people govern."

It Takes Control, on the Field and in the House

For Jim Bunning, learning the ins and outs of government took time.

"Politics is just like baseball; it's one on one," Bunning said. "In committee meetings, you have to convince people you have a legitimate point.

"Baseball was also a control thing for me. I had to dominate the batter. It didn't matter what the score was, if I handled the guy at the plate, I thought I had won. It took me a long time ... to control my emotions. I finally did become a much better person to live with. That's when baseball became a lot more fun. Now I'm learning to apply these lessons in the political world. I'm learning how to listen to people."

But then again, nothing came easy for Bunning.

He threw more than 1,000 innings in the minors before firing his first major league pitch. He managed for the Phillies for five years and then was fired. He missed becoming a 20-game winner by one game in four seasons (1962, 1964, 1965, and 1966). He waited 20 years to be elected to the Hall of Fame.

Even his delivery took extra effort.

Warren Spahn and Juan Marchial had the high leg kick. Luis Tiant and Hideo Nomo did the twist. Jim Bunning scraped his knuckles when he pitched.

"The thing about Bunning on the mound," Larry Merchant said, "is that there is nothing classic about him. He does what he has to do the best way he can. That is to throw himself and the ball at the same time. He literally flings himself off the rubber, falling toward an imaginary spot somewhere between first and home, like a toppled statue."

Each time he fell, the determined Bunning got up.

After an unremarkable 33-41 record in the minors, Bunning caught fire in the bigs. In his first full year as a Tiger in 1957, he went 20-7 with an ERA of 2.69. He dropped to 14-12 the following year but reached an important milestone on July 28, 1958. Three years to the day after Bunning debuted as a Tiger pitcher, he became the fourth pitcher to throw a no-hitter at Fenway Park in Boston.

Even before the "pitch counts" era, Detroit coach Don Lund was keeping tabs on Bunning. After throwing 51 fastballs, 49 sliders, 25 curves, and seven change-ups, he ended up with a slice of baseball immortality and 100 quarts of fresh Vermont milk. (It was State of Vermont Day at the ballpark.)

His first pitch of the game was a fastball that Gene Stephens drove 375 feet deep to right field. Al Kaline went back to the warning track and hauled it in. The second batter, Pete Runnels, smashed a grounder to third baseman Ossie Virgil, who knocked the ball down and just nipped Runnels at first.

After that it was clear sailing for the sidearmer.

"As far as I am concerned," Bunning later reflected, "pitching a no-hitter is a lot like participating in an automobile accident that almost happened. If you have ever been in a car during a near miss, you know the feeling."

Six years later, Bunning avoided another "accident."

This time it was Father's Day, he was wearing a different uniform, and the game was perfection. Bunning mowed down 27 straight Mets.

Jim ended up in Philly because Detroit manager Charlie Dressen thought Bunning had seen brighter days. The Tigers dealt him to the Phils, along with batterymate Gus Triandos, for outfielder Don Demeter and pitcher Jack Hamilton.

Boy, was Charlie wrong.

On June 21, 1964, 17 days after Sandy Koufax's no-hitter against the Phillies, Bunning no-hit the Mets.

"I knew I had a no-hitter after the fifth inning," Bunning said. "You hate to blow one of those things. I was just trying to get them out any way I could in the last two innings."

In the Mets' half of the eighth inning, right fielder Joe Christopher struck out. Next up was Jesse Gonder who was robbed earlier by Tony Taylor's lunging dive in the fifth. First-ball hitting, he easily grounded out this time to Taylor. Bob Taylor then ran the count to 3 and 2, before taking a called third strike.

Bunning led off the top of the ninth to a standing ovation. He then calmly set New York down easily in the home half. Charles Smith fouled out. George Altman fanned, and then, on a 2-2 pitch, John Stephenson swung and missed.

After Stephenson's swing, Bunning joined hands with Cy Young in the record books. He became only the second pitcher to hurl no-hitters in both leagues. Young pitched a no-hitter with the Cleveland Spiders (then in the National League) in 1897 and with the Red Sox in 1904 and 1907.

Even Bunning's two-year-old son was impressed.

"That's my daddy!" he cried when he saw his father on television.

In his 17 years, Bunning put up Cal Ripken-type numbers on the mound. From 1957 through 1967, he never missed a start (240 with the Tigers and 159 with the Phillies).

Bunning reached his final plateau on August 11, 1970, when he beat the Astros, 6-5, becoming the second pitcher in history to win 100 games in both leagues. The first was the old Cyclone himself, Denton True Young.

Bunning retired after the 1971 season and returned home to Fort Thomas, Kentucky. Jim was never one to hang his baseball hat on only one peg. So, when he was fired as manager at AAA Oklahoma City, he tried politics.

He began as a Fort Thomas city councilman, then served Kentucky's 11th district as state senator. After an unsuccessful shot at running for governor, he became a six-term congressman (1986-98) from the 4th District. He's currently a U.S. senator from Kentucky.

For the past 16 years, he has brought to Congress a rich understanding of leadership, ethics, and family issues. Just as he made a difference on the mound, Jim is making a deliberate and positive impact on our country, especially in the areas of social security and adoption.

"Baseball gave me a great image," Bunning said. "People knew that I play the game by the rules, that I have ethics. They also know I'm a competitor. And I'm grateful for that."

Sportswriter Harold Kaese called Bunning a "vinegary competitor." Even the Buddha-like Don Zimmer said, "This guy's got a little mean spot in him."

Bitter? Naw. Disagreeable? Sometimes. Irascible? Could be. Intimidating—yes!

"Pitch him inside, go away with another pitch, and then come back inside, and sometimes that looks like a knockdown pitch," Bunning said of his reputation for keeping hitters "loose."

He brings that same intensity to Congress.

"Over the long haul in public life," former White House adviser Roger Porter wrote, "honesty and decency are recognized and rewarded... The strength of our democracy depends on an underlying set of values that includes fairness, respect for others, and intellectual integrity in the marketplace of ideas."

Mizell and Bunning chose public service, believing that ordinary people count, that people need help. It's not the resume that's important—it's what lies behind it. Vinegar Bend and Jim pitched in both on and off the field.

CHAPTER 11

Life Begins After Baseball
Ryne Duren

"There are two kinds of alcoholics, the ones who are drinking and the ones who aren't."

—Ryne Duren

Full name: Rinold George Duren
Nickname: "Ryne," "Blind Ryne"
Position: Right-handed pitcher
Career: Baltimore Orioles, 1954; Kansas City Athletics, 1957; New York Yankees, 1958-61; Los Angeles Angels, 1961-62; Philadelphia Phillies, 1963-64 and 1965; Cincinnati Reds, 1964; Washington Senators, 1965
Career W-L: 27-44
Career ERA: 3.83
Career saves: 57

Career highlights:
- Led the league in saves in 1958 with 20, and finished second the following year with 14.
- Selected to the All-Star team in 1958, 1959, and 1961.

Imagine you're standing in the on-deck circle, waiting for your turn at bat.

You've heard stories about the pitcher you're about to face. He was so fast and so wild in high school, they say, his coach wouldn't let him pitch for fear he'd kill somebody. He's hit lots of guys, including one in the minors who was still kneeling in the on-deck circle, right about where you are.

That's what folks say. They also say odds are good he's been out drinking last night, and he's probably hungover now.

They also say those bottle-bottom thick glasses aren't for show. Without them, he's blind as a bat, and with them he still can't see all that well.

You don't need anybody to tell you that the guy is flat-out throwing gas. And the fact that his last pitch just whistled over the catcher's head does nothing for your state of mind.

Ready to stand in the batter's box and hit now?

Ready to face Ryne Duren?

He was one of baseball's first great firemen and was as feared as any man who ever toed the rubber. When "Blind Ryne" peered in at home plate for his sign, he literally had trouble seeing the catcher's hand. Uncorrected, he was 20/70 in one eye, 20/200 in the other.

Often his first warm-up toss would sail over the catcher's head and hit the screen. Then Duren would carefully take off those thick glasses and clean them with his shirt flap before throwing again.

He was baseball's original "Wild Thing." The sight of Duren coming in from the bullpen with a baseball in his hand was enough to make a man remember that he had better things to do than stand 60 feet, six inches away from the mound with nothing but a skinny baseball bat for protection.

Small Town Saturday Night

Ryne Duren was born in the dead of a Wisconsin winter on February 22, 1929, in the tiny town of Cazenovia. If you've never been there, it's right down the road from Iola. And it isn't a very big road.

There wasn't much for a kid to do in Cazenovia. He played sports, of course, being a big, strong kid. But when he went out for the baseball team, one of his first pitches broke a teammate's ribs and scared his coach out of letting him pitch again.

As a major league pitcher, "Blind Ryne" intimidated hitters with both his blazing fastball and erratic control. Now, baseball's original "Wild Thing" helps recovering alcoholics control their addictions one day at a time.

Like a lot of small-town Wisconsin kids, Duren started drinking early. He had that genetic twist in him that makes one drink too many and 100 not enough. Ryne Duren was an alcoholic, maybe even from the first beer he ever knocked back on a small-town Saturday night.

But he'd been given an incredible right arm capable of launching rockets, and that right arm carried Ryne Duren all the way to the major leagues and stardom.

After a two-inning tune-up in 1954 with the Baltimore Orioles, Ryne broke into the majors for real in 1957, at the age of 28, with the old Kansas City Athletics. He appeared in 14 games, eight of them in relief, struck out nearly a batter per inning but walked almost as many, went 0-3 and picked up his first major league save.

The next year he was a star for the world champion New York Yankees as the Bronx Bombers got revenge on the Milwaukee Braves.

Duren was one of the beneficiaries of an unspoken agreement that saw Kansas City ship most of its best players to the Yankees, often receiving little in return. The Athletics in those days were known as the Yankees' top farm team.

Duren escaped the A's with outfielders Jim Pisoni and Harry Simpson (who was traded so often he earned the nickname "Suitcase") for outfielder Bob Martyn, infielders Woodie Held and Billy Martin, and pitcher Ralph Terry.

Given the course of Duren's career after that, the story behind the trade is more than a little ironic. The Yankees wanted to get rid of "Billy the Kid" Martin in part because of an ugly incident at the Copacabana, the high-toned New York nightclub. It wasn't the first time Martin and drinking buddy Mickey Mantle had gotten into trouble. The Yankees wanted to hang onto Mantle but figured Martin was expendable.

Whatever got him there, Ryne hit it big in the Big Apple. He came out of the bullpen 43 times that year, going 6-4 with a 2.02 ERA, a league-high 20 saves and 87 strikeouts in 75 and two-thirds innings. He made another three appearances in the World Series, notching a win and a save and posting a 1.93 ERA with 14 strikeouts in nine and one-third innings.

On October 4 he combined with starter Don Larsen to shut out the Braves, 4-0, with Hank Bauer accounting for all four runs. The same day, *The Sporting News* named him its American League pitching Rookie of the Year. (Senators outfielder Albie Pearson was the top AL rookie position player.)

Duren was on top of the baseball world, right up there with Mickey, Whitey and Yogi.

Although the Yanks lost the flag to the Go-Go White Sox in 1959, Duren was again brilliant with a glittering 1.88 ERA, 14 saves, and 96 punchouts in 76 and two-thirds innings. He went 36 innings over an 18-game stretch without allowing a run. Leave out the grand slam he served up to pinch-hitter Vic Wertz in an 11-6 Yankee loss to the Red Sox, and his ERA practically disappears.

Over that two-season stretch, he gave up only 89 hits and fanned 183 in 151 innings.

And then—although he toiled for six more years in the majors—he was pretty much washed up.

Free Fall After a Short Season in the Sun

He worked only 49 innings for the Yankees in 1960. His saves shrunk to nine while his ERA swelled to 4.96. He got into a couple of games against the upstart Pittsburgh Pirates in the World Series, working four innings without a win or a save, and watched Bill Mazeroski's classic series-winning home run from the bullpen.

After four games in 1961, New York cut him loose, sending Duren, pitcher Johnny James, and outfielder Lee Thomas to the expansion Los Angeles Angels for pitcher Tex Clevenger and outfielder Bob Cerv. Trading for Cerv had become a Yankee tradition; this would be Bob's third hitch in pinstripes.

At age 32, Duren found himself on a team so strapped for pitching that they stuck him in the starting rotation with the vowel-deprived Eli Grba, Ken McBride, and Ted Bowsfield, the ace of the staff at 11-8 with a 3.73 ERA. Position players included Duren's fellow Rookie of the Year, Pearson, a flashy outfielder named Leon "Daddy Wags" Wagner, former Cincinnati strongman Ted Kluzewski, and a legendary minor league slugger named Steve Bilko. "Big Steve" had torched "little Wrigley Field" in Los Angeles for 55 and 56 home runs in consecutive seasons when the Angels played in the AAA Pacific Coast League. Bilko managed only 20 for a team that had to fight hard to avoid beating the Senators and Athletics to the bottom of the league.

Duren went 6-13, with two saves and a 5.19 ERA, but he set a personal season high with 115 strikeouts in 104 innings.

Four of those strikeouts came in one record-tying inning. Just 10 days after joining the Angels, he came out of the bullpen in the seventh inning to face the White Sox and struck out Minnie Minoso, Roy Sievers, J.C. Martin, and Sammy Esposito. One of Duren's third-strike flames got past catcher Del Rice, allowing the runner to reach first base and the winning run to score. It was that kind of year for Duren and the Angels.

Season highlights included a shutout, his only complete game of the year, and a 5-1 win over the Red Sox, in which he set an American League record with seven straight strikeouts and wound up with 11 for the game.

Duren went 2-9 with a 4.42 ERA and eight saves in 1962. The Angels were beginning to put together one of the more flashy starting rotations in baseball around Dean Chance and Bo Belinsky. So they sent Duren to the Phillies, where in '63, at 34, he had a solid 6-2 season with a 3.30 ERA and two saves.

But he would save only one more game in his career, with the Reds in '64, and notch only one more win, with the Senators in '65.

He was finished.

His career numbers were far from Hall-of-Fame caliber: 27-44, 3.83 ERA, and 57 saves. He did strike out 630 in 589 and one-third innings, though, with a heater as good as any, which was enough to make you wonder why he didn't have more good years and a longer stay in baseball's midsummer sunshine.

Drinking did Ryne Duren in. He'll be the first one to tell you.

Life Begins After Baseball

He's still an alcoholic, just ask him. There are two kinds of alcoholics, he'll tell you, the ones who are drinking and the ones who aren't—right now, today, one day at a time.

Alcoholics can be "recovering," but they're never "recovered." You don't get over this disease, but you can fight it to a draw.

Ryne Duren has done that, does it every day. It's a lot tougher than facing Hank Aaron, Eddie Mathews, and Joe Adcock with the World Series on the line.

His old teammate, Mickey Mantle, waited a lot longer to get dry and paid a higher price for his drinking. But with his honesty and his example, he undoubtedly helped a lot of other drunks find their way out of the bottle. And for every one Mantle might have touched at the end of his life, Duren has reached many more through years of one-on-one counseling and public speaking.

Ryne Duren's hall-of-fame work began after his baseball career ended. From 1968 to 1972 he served as counselor supervisor at the Norris Foundation in Mukwanago, Wisconsin, then developed and headed the Stoughton Community Hospital Alcohol Rehabilitation and Education Program in Stoughton, Wisconsin.

He remained there until 1980 and then became a consultant on alcohol and other drug abuse for many agencies, associations, and professional sports organizations. He also served on the Wisconsin Governor's Citizen Advisory Committee on Alcohol Abuse and the Wisconsin Drinking and Driving Council.

He's a charter member of the American College of Sports Medicine's Alcohol Use and Abuse Standing Committee and on the Board of Directors of Winning Beyond Winning.

With baseball fame far behind him, he still turns up for signings on occasion. You might find him at Madison, Wisconsin's Warner Park, where he's happy to chat with fans. If you don't have a card or picture for him to sign, he'll hand you one of his own. But it's not an old Yankee or Athletics or Angels card. One side features a pen and ink drawing of Ryne on the mound, but on the other, instead of his strikeouts and saves, Duren lists some phone numbers to call if alcohol or other drugs are controlling your life.

That's Duren's game these days, and his control is letter perfect, every pitch a strike.

CHAPTER 12

Grace Under Pressure
Henry Aaron

"You will discover in time that the challenge comes not nearly so much from without as it does from within. There comes a time when those who know better must always do better."

—Henry Aaron

Full name: Henry Louis Aaron
Nicknames: "Hammerin' Hank," "The Hammer," "Bad Henry"
Position: Outfield
Career: Indianapolis Clowns, 1952; Milwaukee/Atlanta Braves 1954-74, Milwaukee Brewers, 1975-76

Negro League career highlight:
• Hit .400 with five home runs in 1952 Negro League World Series.

Major League career batting average: .305

Major League career highlights:
• Won batting titles in 1956 (.328) and 1959 (.355).
• Crowned home run champ four times, three of those times hitting 44 homers.
• Led the league in RBIs in 1957 (132), 1960 (126), 1963 (130), and 1966 (127).
• Selected as an All-Star 21 consecutive seasons between 1955 and 1975.

- Won the NL MVP in 1957.
- Won the NL Gold Glove Award in 1958, 1959, and 1960.
- Elected to the Hall of Fame.

Major League career records:
- Home runs: 755
- RBIs: 2,297
- Extra base hits: 1,477
- Total bases: 6,856

On June 14, 1952, 18-year-old Henry Aaron, rail thin and, by his own admission, "scared as hell," climbed into the batter's box to face a pitcher named Art Rosser, who was unlike any he had ever faced.

Young Henry knew he could hit, having starred for the Mobile Black Bears and the Indianapolis Clowns of the Negro Leagues.

But he didn't know if he could hit a white man.

He'd never tried it before, never had the chance. Maybe what his society had told him all his life was true—that whites were better than blacks in every possible way.

This was 1952, remember. True, there had been no reported lynchings in America that year, but it was the first lynch-free year in the last 71. True, Jackie Robinson had finally broken the color line in major league baseball five years before, but 10 of the 16 major league teams still had no black players.

Jim Crow was alive and well in America.

So Henry was unsure of himself as he played his first professional (meaning against whites and for a paycheck) game for the Class C Eau Claire Bears against the St. Cloud Rox.

But he didn't have to doubt himself for long. Rosser went into his stretch, came to the plate, and young Hank roped an RBI single to left, getting thrown out trying to stretch it into a double. His next time up, he hit an almost identical RBI base hit.

Henry Aaron could hit white men. He could hit white men and black men, brown men and any other color you threw at him. Henry Aaron could hit anybody.

He didn't hit many out of the park yet, though. At six foot one and 160 pounds, baseball's future home run king was downright scrawny. He did hit his first professional home run a week later, on June 22 off

Reuben Stohs in an 8-4 win over Fargo-Moorhead in Fargo, North Dakota. But he hit only eight more all year.

He never did get big—not Mark McGwire, Sammy Sosa or Barry Bonds big. Henry played at 180 pounds most of his career. But with his massive wrists he generated incredible bat speed, and by the time he got to the major leagues, a lot of his line drives started clearing the fences.

He didn't hit homers in huge bunches—never more than 47 in a season. He just kept hitting them, year after year, quietly creeping up on the most sacred record in baseball, Babe Ruth's career home run mark.

He wasn't showy, and he labored in relatively small cities. He's a shy, quiet man. And he's black. Maybe that's why folks hardly noticed him closing in on the Babe. When they finally did notice, some sent him hate mail. Some even threatened to kill him.

Through it all, Hammerin' Hank kept hitting home runs. He also hit for high average and played right field with skill and grace, first for the Milwaukee and then the Atlanta Braves. Henry Aaron did it all. He was relentlessly consistent at an extremely high level of excellence.

Few call him the greatest player who ever lived, but it's awfully hard to find one to match him.

He ended up quietly hitting 755 home runs, 41 more than the mighty Babe Ruth.

The Making of a Home Run King

Henry Louis Aaron was born on February 5, 1934, the day after Babe Ruth's 39th birthday, in Mobile, Alabama, which also gave baseball Satchel Paige and Willie McCovey. Henry was the third child of Estella and Herbert Aaron, a boilermaker's helper and shipyard rivet-bucker who put three of his eight kids through college on $75 a week.

As a kid Henry played baseball with one of his mother's broomsticks and a ball made out of tightly wrapped rags. He went to an all-black grammar school and then to Mobile's Central High. They didn't have a baseball team at Central, or at Josephine Allen, a private school where he finished his education. So he played football instead and joined a fast-pitch softball team. He also played for a local sandlot team. Baseball was his passion, and Jackie Robinson was his hero.

"I never thought about anything but playing baseball," Henry says. "My mother and father wanted me to go on to college after I got out of high school, but I wanted to play major league ball. And after Jackie broke in, I thought blacks had as good a chance as anybody, if they could show they had major-league skills."

"Hammerin' Hank" Aaron was in a class all by himself after parking an Al Downing fastball over the left-centerfield fence to pass the Babe as baseball's all-time home run leader.

Ed Scott, a scout for the Mobile Black Bears, spotted Henry playing softball when he was 15 and signed him to play shortstop for $10 a game. When he turned 18, Henry signed with the Indianapolis Clowns of the Negro American League. The door had finally been pried open for Blacks to play in the major leagues, so the Black National League had already shut down, and the American was on its last legs. Hank got $200 a month and $2 per day meal money, which meant he often got by with a big jar of peanut butter on the road. But he stung the ball, leading the Clowns to the World Series against the Birmingham Black Barons, where he hit .400 with five home runs.

And then the young hero "went right back to a segregated society, right back into the same old thing," he says.

While playing for the Clowns, Henry made a lasting impression on team GM Ed Hamman.

"I think Hank Aaron is one of the greatest men in sports," Hamman told Bill Heward for Heward's book on the team, *Some Are Called Clowns*. "He never lets anything go to his head. He's the same Hank who used to wear a Clown uniform."

But Hank didn't even last a full season with Hamman and the Clowns. Milwaukee Braves scout Dewey Griggs paid the Clowns $10,000 for the rights to Aaron and signed him to a no-bonus contract. When Henry got on a North Central Airlines flight in Mobile, it was the first time he'd ever been on an airplane. He landed in Eau Claire, Wisconsin, a peaceful town of 35,000, maybe as many as a half dozen of them black, in the heart of America's dairyland. He might as well have landed on the moon.

He got a room at the downtown YMCA and tried to prepare himself to be a professional baseball player. He wasn't all alone. Billy Bruton had integrated the Eau Claire Bears two years before, and Hank had two black teammates, Wes Covington and Julie Bowers. And many of the white people welcomed him wholeheartedly. Buzz Buzzell and his wife, Joyce, befriended Henry, and he struck up a friendship with Susan Hauck, becoming a regular at the home of her parents, Butch and Blanche Hauck.

He made his debut at Carson Park, a beautiful old Works Progress Administration yard built in 1937 and set among the tall pines next to Half Moon Lake. He played shortstop, wore No. 6, and batted seventh. With 1,250 white folks watching, he lined those two pretty singles off Art Rosser, and he was on his way.

His career almost ended a week later, though. While trying to turn a double play, he hit a base runner, Chuck Wiles, with his throw at point-blank range. Wiles never played again, and Henry wanted to quit right there. But he pulled himself together and kept hitting ropes, leading the league at the All-Star break with a .374 average.

On the road, the Bears traveled in two nine-passenger Chrysler airport limos, hand-me-downs from Class A Hartford of the Eastern League. While grinding out road trips to places like Grand Forks, 416 miles away, Henry became known for his ability to sleep sitting up.

Aaron, Covington and Bowers were refused a room at the team hotel in Aberdeen, so player/manager Billy Adair pulled the whole team and found a place outside town that would take them all, a gesture Henry never forgot.

At the cozy little park in Aberdeen, the fences were just 291 feet away from home down both foul lines, but Henry didn't hit a home run in his six games there.

He got lots of other hits, 116 of them in just 87 games with the Bears. He had 61 RBIs, swiped 25 bases, scored 89 runs and struck out just 19 times in 345 at bats. His .336 average led the team, followed by Covington at .330 and Bowers at .312.

Henry was the unanimous choice for Northern League Rookie of the Year.

The Aaron-Maris Connection

The year after Henry played for the Bears, a Fargo boy named Roger Maras (his father changed the spelling later because of the taunts of fans intentionally mispronouncing the name) played for Fargo-Moorhead, where Aaron hit his first professional home run. Like Aaron, Maris hit nine home runs in his first professional season. Both wound up playing right field. Both were shy and soft-spoken. Both were born in 1934. Both were Rookies of the Year for the league. And both, of course, went on to break a home run record held by Babe Ruth—Maris for a single season, Aaron for a career.

Coincidence? Well, sure, but it's kind of fun, isn't it?

The next year Henry helped integrate the Class A South Atlantic (Sally) League, where he played second base for the Jacksonville Tars. He tore up the league, leading all hitters with a .362 average, 208 hits, 125 RBIs, and 115 runs scored. He was second in home runs with 22. The Tars won the pennant, and Henry was the League MVP.

"[T]he league was highly segregated," he says, "and Jacksonville wasn't one of your liberal cities; the fans didn't want us playing there."

But one fan didn't mind. Barbara Lucas lived near the ballpark and went to a lot of games. She and Henry began dating and within a few months became engaged. They were married on October 13, shortly after the season ended.

Aaron went to spring training with the Milwaukee Braves in 1954 with a shot at making the big club. When Bobby Thomson (of "home run heard 'round the world" fame in 1951) broke his ankle, opening up an outfield spot, Henry had his chance, and he didn't blow it.

He hit his first major league home run on April 23 at Sportsman's Park in St. Louis off a Vic Raschi fastball. He was hitting a respectable .280 with 13 home runs when, ironically, he too broke an ankle.

Little would slow him down from then on.

The Braves first assigned him No. 5, but after two years, he switched to No. 44, which he wore for the rest of his career. Teammates joked that he was too skinny to wear a double-digit number.

In 1957, his MVP season and the year the "Miracle Braves" beat the Yankees in the World Series, Topps printed Henry's baseball card backwards, the '44' clearly showing as Henry appeared to bat left-handed. That didn't shake him. Nothing did. Not when he had a bat in his hands.

Curt Simmons said that trying to get a fastball past him was "like trying to sneak a sunrise past a rooster." Another frustrated opposing pitcher said that trying to fool him was like trying to slap a rattlesnake.

He seemed so relaxed when he went up to the plate, folks said he appeared to be looking for a place to sit down. Robin Roberts said Aaron was the only batter he knew who could "fall asleep between pitches and still wake up in time to hit the next one." But that was just Henry's way of handling the pressure.

"I think every black person is prepared to deal with pressure," he says, "because they're born under adversity, and they live under pressure every day of their lives. They know damn well that they've gotta go out there and do better than the average person in order to keep the job."

His parents might have initially hoped their son would choose a career other than baseball, but they soon became avid supporters.

"My boy has a chance to do it," Estella Aaron said early in son Henry's career. "He takes care of himself and nothing comes in front of baseball for Henry. Nothing. On days when he is feeling good, it's just too bad for the pitchers."

"When Henry came up," his father said, "I heard fans yell, 'Hit that nigger. Hit that nigger.' Henry hit the ball [over the fence]. The next time he came up, they said, 'Walk him, walk him!'"

What the Numbers Tell Us

Quietly, almost methodically, game after game, season after season, Hank Aaron put up the numbers.

His home run records fill pages. First, of course, is the career mark of 755. He's also first all-time in the National League with 733. He and brother Tommy combined for 768, a record for a brother act. Henry and teammate Eddie Mathews combined for 863 homers while with the Braves (1,267 overall between them), a record Henry says is dear to him because "this particular record happened to be broken by a black player and a white player." He and Mathews are also the only players to have hit 400 homers apiece while teammates, 442 for Henry, 421 for Eddie.

Only one of his dingers was an inside-the-park job, hit against Jim Bunning. The other 754 cleared the fences.

His favorite victim was fearsome Dodger righthander Don Drysdale, who gave up 17 long balls to Henry.

Aaron hit 16 grand slams, smacked two homers in a game 61 times, and drilled three homers in a game only once, on June 21, 1959, against the San Francisco Giants. He never hit four home runs in a game or 50 in a season. But he hit 20 or more per season for a record 20 seasons in a row.

Henry was the third player to enter baseball's 30/30 club (30 or more home runs and stolen bases in the same season), with 44 homers and 31 steals in 1963. He was the first player to enter the 500 home run/3,000 hit club. He wound up with 3,771 hits, third only to Pete Rose and Ty Cobb.

He captured three home run titles and tied for a fourth. He also won two batting crowns, the first in 1956 in only his third big-league season. That season he played in his first of 21 All-Star games.

In his 1957 MVP season, he almost nailed the Triple Crown, leading the league with 44 home runs and 132 RBIs. He made another strong bid for the Triple Crown in 1963, again leading the league in home runs (44) and RBIs (130), but his .319 average was third best to Tommy Davis (.326) and Roberto Clemente (.320).

The biggest home run of his career? The one he hit off Cardinal Billy Muffet—he says without hesitation—on September 23, 1957, in the 11th inning, which clinched the National League pennant for the Braves, their first in Milwaukee.

He also cherishes the first home run he hit in an All-Star game. It came in 1971, "rather late," he says. "I thought I was never gonna do it."

Almost forgotten among all his hitting records are Aaron's three Gold Gloves. Henry simply did everything well.

Passing the Babe

He belted a career-best 47 home runs in 1971, climbing into third place behind the Babe and Willie Mays with 639. The 34 he hit the next year lifted him into second place ahead of Mays. And in 1973, at the age of 39, Henry hit 40 more, the most ever by a player his age. He ended the season just one behind Ruth.

He didn't have to wait long to make history. On opening day, April 4, 1974, in Cincinnati, on a 3-1 pitch from Jack Billingham, Henry hit No. 714 on his first swing of the season. So much for suspense.

Four days later, before the largest crowd ever at Atlanta Fulton County Stadium—53,775 fans—Aaron faced Dodger pitcher Al Downing in the bottom of the fourth inning, still dead even with Ruth.

Henry's first time up, Downing had walked him on five pitches, one a called strike, as the fans booed loudly. Nobody seemed to notice that as he scored a few minutes later, the 2,063rd run of his career, he passed Willie Mays for the National League record, behind only Ty Cobb and Ruth overall.

Henry batted in the fourth inning with nobody out and Darrell Evans on first. It was raining. Downing, who also wore No. 44, started him off with a ball, low and away. His second pitch, a fastball, came in right over the plate, belt high.

"I was trying to get it down to him," Downing said after the game, "but I didn't, and he hit it good—as he would."

The ball cleared the left-centerfield fence 385 feet from home plate, just over the outstretched glove of Billy Buckner. Reliever Tom House caught the ball in the bullpen and brought it back to Henry.

Baseball had a new magic number: 715.

Second baseman Davey Lopes and shortstop Bill Russell shook Aaron's hand as he rounded the bases. Two kids, Britt Gaston and Cliff Courtney, jumped out of the stands and somehow made it out onto the field, where they escorted Henry between second and third, patting him on the back. Aaron kept his head down, showing no emotion. His teammates mobbed him at home plate.

The game stopped for 11 minutes while the fans cheered, his teammates took turns thumping the new home run king, and his parents hugged him. Monte Irvin presented him with a diamond watch from the commissioner's office (commissioner Bowie Kuhn wasn't there). Two innings later, president Richard Nixon called Henry in the clubhouse to congratulate him.

"I have never gone out on a ballfield and given less than my level best," Henry said after the game. "When I hit it tonight, all I thought about was that I wanted to touch all the bases.

"I'm thankful to God it's all over."

Later he would say he never wanted people to forget Babe Ruth. "I just want them to remember me!"

He says he isn't worried about someone breaking his record. In fact, he says, "I'm hoping someday that some kid, black or white, will hit more home runs than myself. Whoever it is, I'd be pulling for him."

After that record-busting season, Aaron faced Sadaharu Oh, the all-time leading home run hitter in Japan, in a home run-hitting contest at Korakuen Stadium. Henry won the duel, 10-9.

On January 13, 1982, Aaron and Frank Robinson became just the 12th and 13th players elected to the Hall of Fame in their first year of eligibility. Aaron fell nine votes short of becoming the first-ever unanimous selection. His 97.8 selection percentage is second all-time only to Ty Cobb's 98.2.

Perhaps the most significant statistic of Henry's career is the one that doesn't exist. Many rating services categorize players of like ability—but they all put Henry literally in a class by himself. There simply isn't another player like him.

What the Numbers Can't Tell Us

As when Roger Maris chased the Babe's single-season home run mark in 1961, Henry Aaron was under tremendous pressure—from fans, the media, and opposing players—as he stalked Ruth's career mark. He received almost a million pieces of mail, most of it encouraging, but some of it openly threatening. The Braves took threats on his life seriously and hired bodyguards to protect him.

He was an authentic hero to millions of Americans—black and white. Many can still tell you exactly where they were when they heard the news.

And yet, Henry says he "never felt pressured…The only way I could play baseball was to relax…I couldn't play under pressure."

He stayed calm, he says, by taking his mother's advice: "If you have no control over it, don't worry about it."

"When I was in a ballpark," he says, "I felt there was nothing that could bother me. I felt like I was surrounded by angels and I had God's hand on my shoulder."

That faith and his mother's philosophy have kept him from being bitter about the racism and the slights over the years.

But that doesn't mean he's kept quiet about it.

"I've always spoken out," he insists to those who accuse him of having been silent about racial inequality in his early playing days. "But before, when I said something, nobody listened. It's just like a high school student versus a guy with a master's degree. I've got my master's degree now, in baseball, and I paid my dues...I've said the same thing over and over again—that I think there's injustice in baseball."

His silence spoke loudly on January 28, 1980, when he refused an award from commissioner Bowie Kuhn, saying that baseball's treatment of retired black players was completely inadequate.

He says he's never had any interest in managing, but he thinks baseball needs a lot more black managers and black people in the front office. "There haven't been too many real opportunities for blacks after they stop playing," he notes, "other than coaching first base."

Aaron made the climb into the front office, becoming director of player development and then a senior vice-president for the Braves.

Right Back Where He Started

During the player strike of 1994, Henry Aaron returned to Eau Claire, Wisconsin, and Carson Park, now home field for the semi-pro Eau Claire Cavaliers.

He had been back at least twice before. In 1962 he and Joe Torre attended an Eau Claire Braves kickoff dinner. They first stopped in to visit a bedridden fan, Emma Brion, in the small town of Durand, giving her what she called the "highlight of my life."

And 20 years later, two weeks before his election into the Hall of Fame, Henry gave a talk at the University of Wisconsin campus at Eau Claire. He spoke to a crowd of more than 1,000 people on "the courage to succeed," quoting Martin Luther King, Shakespeare and Socrates in his 18-minute speech.

Soon after, UW-EC created a scholarship fund in Aaron's name for minority students.

Henry became a tireless advocate for Big Brothers and Big Sisters, and in 1994 he created the National Chasing the Dream Foundation, to foster arts instruction for kids aged nine to 12.

Then he came "back home" to Eau Claire.

More than 5,000 were on hand to witness the unveiling on August 17 of a bust of Aaron that sits in a special courtyard in front of the park where he launched his career. Henry told the crowd that education was a lot more important than home runs.

He later helped dedicate Henry Aaron Stadium in his hometown of Mobile, and on April 5, 2001, the Milwaukee Brewers dedicated a seven foot bronze statue of Hammerin' Hank at their new ballpark, just a few yards from the site of old County Stadium, where Hank did most of his hammering.

In 2002, Henry Aaron received the Presidential Medal of Freedom.

"The greatest thing I want to be remembered for," he says, "is the fact that I've worked for many years for Big Brothers and Big Sisters. ... The greatest thing we do in order to show our appreciation is to pave the way for the young people we care about."

CHAPTER 13

The Greatest Moment in Baseball History
Sandy Koufax

"Either he throws the fastest ball I've ever seen, or I'm going blind."
—Richie Ashburn

"Trying to hit him was like trying to drink coffee with a fork."
—Willie Stargell

Full Name: Sanford Koufax
Nickname: "Sandy," "Koofoo," "Super Jew"
Position: Left-handed pitcher
Career: Brooklyn/Los Angeles Dodgers, 1955-1966
Career W-L: 165-87
Career ERA: 2.76

Career highlights:

- Led the league in ERA every year between 1962-1965, topping out with a 1.74 ERA in 1964.

- Led the league in wins with 25 in 1963, 26 in 1965, and 27 in 1966.

- Was the strikeout king in 1961 (269), 1963 (306), 1965 (382), and 1966 (317).

- Pitched one perfect game, three additional no-hitters in the NL and led the league in shutouts from 1963-65.

- Chosen as an All Star each year between 1961-66.
- Won the Cy Young Award in 1963, 1965, and 1966.
- Also won the NL MVP in 1963.
- Was named the World Series MVP in 1963 and 1965.
- Elected to the Hall of Fame.

What's the Greatest Single Moment in Baseball History?

A nearly impossible choice, of course. Still, Major League Baseball asked us to make it in the months leading up to the 2002 World Series, and lots of folks voted.

Given the choices they offered, I would have gone with Jackie Robinson first setting foot on a major league baseball diamond, but I have no complaint with the selection of Cal Ripken Jr. passing the Iron Horse to become the most dependable laborer in baseball's vineyard.

But I've got another nominee, one that wasn't on Major League Baseball's ballot. For me, the greatest moment in baseball history occurred at Dodger Stadium in Los Angeles at 9:46 p.m., Pacific Daylight Time, September 9, 1965.

On a two ball-two strike pitch, Harvey Kuenn struck out swinging. Sandy Koufax had pitched a perfect game, winning a tense 1-0 duel with the Chicago Cub's Bob Hendley.

It was the fourth no-hitter in four years for the Dodger lefty and only the ninth perfect game in major league history.

Anyone who saw Sandy pitch that night might have wondered how any human being could pitch so well.

Anyone who knew what kind of pain he was in when he did it must have wondered how he could pitch at all. He had to soak his arm in ice (the only treatment of the time) after each game and take cortisone injections before every other start in addition to pain medication that could literally kill a horse. The trainer had to put on rubber gloves to rub Sandy's arm with a jelled flame called Capsolin.

And yet Sandy threw 335 and two-thirds innings that season. He never missed a start and finished most of them. When his team needed him, he threw on two days' rest, carrying a weak-hitting team to a pennant.

And then he did miss a start—the biggest start in baseball, the first game of the World Series—and in the process became a cultural as well as baseball hero.

Sometimes All He Had Was Heat

The pitch that struck out Harvey Kuenn was a fastball. It probably traveled over 100 mph, although we'll never know, since the radar gun hadn't been invented yet.

Sandy had only one other pitch, a devastating 12-to-6 curveball that came off the same sweeping overhand motion.

Two were all he needed.

Many claimed he tipped his pitches by the way he held his glove. It didn't matter. Even if you knew what was coming, you couldn't hit it.

Sometimes his arm hurt too much for him to throw the curve. Then he just went with the heat. They still couldn't hit it.

People said they never heard a baseball make the kind of sound it did when Sandy threw it. In the words of one of his biographers, Jane Leavy, when Sandy threw it, the ball made the air cry.

It's probably a good thing it did. If you couldn't see it, at least you could hear it coming.

"It sounded like a little tornado," slugger Orlando Cepeda once said—and he was talking about the curveball. Jimmy Wynn called it "a mystic waterfall." Gene Mauch called the heater a "'radio ball,' a pitch you hear but you don't see."

"He was Michelangelo and Picasso rolled into one," Sweet Lou Johnson said.

Sandy won the ERA crown five years in a row. (His ERA was 1.5 runs lower than the rest of the league.) He won the Cy Young Award three of those five years, back when they only gave out one for both leagues.

He carried the Dodgers to a pennant and a world championship in 1965 and then brought them back to the Series the next year, winning 27 games for a team for which one run was a rally.

And then he retired. He walked away from the game in a prime so far above mere mortal standards that many refused to believe his arm could possibly hurt at all, let alone force his retirement.

From a Baseball Hero to a Cultural Icon

For the last three innings of his perfect game, Sandy pitched as well as a human being ever has, perhaps as well as a human being can.

With the Cubs just playing out the string and the Dodgers locked in a three-way pennant race with the Pirates and Giants, the two teams

Anyone who saw Sandy Koufax pitch his perfect game against the Cubs in 1965 might have wondered how a human could pitch so well. Anyone who knew what kind of pain he was in at the time would have wondered how he could pitch at all.

amassed a grand total of one hit and two base runners—both of them Dodger leftfielder Lou Johnson, who was playing only because batting champ Tommy Davis was injured. Johnson scored the game's only run on a walk. A bunt got him to second, and when he took off to steal third, catcher Chris Krug's throw sailed into leftfield.

That's all journeyman Cub pitcher Bob Hendley gave up all night. Against Koufax, it was too much. Koufax gave up nothing.

A month later, having brought his team to the World Series, Sandy turned down the assignment to pitch the first game against the Minnesota Twins, because it fell on Yom Kippur, the Day of Atonement, the most holy day in the Jewish year.

Thirty-five years later, people still talk about the influence Sandy's decision had on their lives.

He did pitch the second game, and the fifth, and then the seventh, on two day's rest. When he fanned Bob Allison for the final out of a 2-0 three-hitter, it was his 360th inning of the season. If the perfect game isn't baseball's best moment, then maybe that seventh game is. Both perfectly demonstrate the triumph of courage over adversity, and both display the game played as well as it can be played.

Baseball Wasn't Even His Game

Early on, folks figured Sandy would be a great athlete, but most thought he'd make his mark in basketball.

He was born on December 30, 1935, in Brooklyn to Evelyn and Jack Braun. His father left the family when Sandy was three, and his mother supported them as a CPA. Sandy spent a lot of time with his grandparents, Max and Dora.

When he was nine, his mother remarried. Although Irving Koufax never legally adopted Sandy, he became his father in every other sense.

"When I speak of my father," Sandy wrote in his 1966 autobiography, "I speak of Irving Koufax, for he has been to me everything a father should be."

Sandy was a natural athlete, with his mother's broad shoulders and strong back. In 1951 he played on the National Jewish Welfare Board championship basketball team and was captain of his Lafayette High School basketball squad in 1953.

He also played on the baseball team—but not as a pitcher. One day, a man named Milt Laurie watched while first baseman Koufax threw infield between innings. Impressed with the snap the lefty put on the ball, Laurie got his sons, Wally and Larry, to recruit him for his sandlot team, The Parkviews, of the Coney Island Sports League. Wally Laurie became Sandy's first catcher.

Basketball was still Sandy's main game, though, and he went to the University of Cincinnati in the fall of 1953 on a basketball scholarship. He enrolled in the school of liberal arts, thinking he might transfer to the school of architecture later. He went out for baseball that spring and posted a 3-1 record with a solid 2.82 ERA. Showing signs of things to come, he struck out 51 in just 32 innings—but also issued 30 walks.

On the strength of Dodger scout Bill Zinser's evaluation (Arm: A+), Al Campanis offered Sandy a contract. Irving Koufax negotiated for his 19-year-old son, getting a $6,000 salary and a $14,000 signing bonus. (The payroll for the entire team that year was $500,000.)

Under MLB rules at the time, the Dodgers had to keep their "bonus baby" on the major league roster or risk losing him to another team. They had already lost a prospect named Roberto Clemente to the Pirates and weren't keen to risk another theft.

When Sandy reported to Dodgertown in Vero Beach, Florida, on March 1, 1955, he was the only bonus baby in camp. He was also the only Jew.

He made his major league debut on June 24, in the fifth inning against the Milwaukee Braves, with the Dodgers trailing, 7-1. Johnny Logan blooped a single, and when Eddie Matthews crossed the Dodgers up by bunting, Koufax threw the ball into centerfield, putting runners at second and third. Sandy then walked Henry Aaron on four pitches to load the bases.

The kid now had to face Bobby Thompson, the man who had hit the "Shot heard 'round the world" to give the Giants the pennant over the Dodgers in 1951. On a 3-2 pitch, he struck Thompson out. Bobby would have a lot of company.

Two weeks later, Sandy made his first start, against Pittsburgh, and walked eight in four and two-thirds innings before manager Walt Alston yanked him.

He didn't get another start for seven weeks. When he did, on August 27, 1955, at Ebbets Field before 7,204, he struck out 14 Cincinnati Reds and notched a two-hit, 7-0 shutout for his first major league victory.

Which Came First, Wildness or Inactivity?

That would be the pattern for the next five years. Alston used Koufax infrequently. When he was bad, he was very, very wild. When he was good, he was almost unhittable.

Alston said he didn't use Sandy much because he was inconsistent. Sandy said he was inconsistent because Alston didn't use him much.

He made only 12 appearances that rookie season. Without much help from him, the Dodgers went on to become world champions, finally whipping the hated Yankees.

After the seventh game sent Brooklyn into delirium, Sandy went directly from Yankee Stadium to Columbia University to attend his architecture class. He wasn't at all sure baseball would be his future.

Nothing that happened the next season would make him feel any more secure. He pitched just 58 and two-thirds innings, striking out 30 but walking 29 in struggling to a 4.91 ERA.

In 1957, as the "Miracle Braves" took the pennant and beat the Yankees, Sandy made the starting rotation for two weeks. He carried a no-hitter into the sixth inning of one game but didn't make another start for 45 days. He fanned 59 in his 49 and two-thirds innings of work that season and posted a fine 2.90 ERA.

He also gained the distinction of being the last man ever to pitch at Ebbets Field and the last to pitch for the Brooklyn Dodgers. After Sandy pitched an inning of relief in a losing cause before just over 7,000 inconsolable fans, he moved west with the rest of Brooklyn's beloved Bums to Los Angeles.

His record after three years in Brooklyn was 9-10, hardly the stuff of legend.

Pitching in the lopsided Los Angeles Coliseum and its juryrigged diamond, with the leftfield fence just 251 feet away down the line, Sandy reeled off four straight wins and was 7-3 in 1958 before a sprained ankle forced him to the sidelines. He finished just 11-11 for an awful team and led the league in wild pitches.

Wildness again plagued him in 1959, but he showed flashes of absolute brilliance. On June 22, he fanned 16 Phillies in a 6-2 win. On August 31 he struck out 18 San Francisco Giants. On September 6 he finished a streak of 41 strikeouts in three games. Still, he went just 8-6, 4.05 for a team that beat the White Sox in the World Series.

The next year he worked 175 innings and responded by striking out 197, but his record was only 8-13.

Discovering How Good He Could Be

He was ready to quit baseball. He even tossed his glove and spikes into a trash bin after the last game of the season. Fortunately, the clubhouse man fished them out and brought them to spring training for him the next year.

That winter, Sandy started working out much more seriously. Instead of blaming Alston for his inconsistency, he began to take responsibility for his own career.

"I decided," he told his friend Kevin Kennedy, "I was really going to find out how good I could be."

He did, and so did everybody else.

After Sandy walked the bases loaded in an exhibition game, catcher Norm Sherry came out to the mound and told him, "You've got to throw the ball over the plate or we'll be here all day." In his autobiography, Sandy remembered his batterymate telling him to "take the grunt out of the fastball."

Whatever the exact words Sherry used, Sandy heard them. Instead of trying to throw the ball through the backstop, he just tried throwing it into Sherry's glove. Taking something off the fastball, he struck out the side, leaving the bases loaded, and went on to throw seven innings of no-hit ball, striking out nine. The small crowd in the stands that day saw the pitcher Sandy Koufax was at last ready to become.

Going into the 1961 season, his career record was a lousy 36-40. By July, he was an All-Star. Despite pain that would have sent most of us to the hospital or the psych ward, Sandy became the best pitcher in baseball over the next six years and as good as any who ever lived.

"I became a good pitcher," Sandy would later comment, "when I stopped trying to make them miss the ball and started trying to make them hit it…If there was any magic formula, it was getting to pitch every fourth day."

He won 19 games against 13 losses in '61. His 269 strikeouts in 256 innings broke Christy Mathewson's single-season record, which had stood for 58 years. He completed 15 of his 35 starts, throwing 205 pitches in a single game. There were no long relievers and set-up men then. You were supposed to finish what you started.

He began the next season brilliantly, striking out 18 Cubs in nine innings on April 24. On June 30 he no-hit the Mets, 5-0. Sandy had finally arrived.

But when he tried to bat left-handed against Pittsburgh pitcher Earl Francis (Sandy had been strictly a right-handed non-hitter until then), Francis jammed him with a fastball. The heel of the bat dug into the palm of Sandy's left hand. Soon his index finger turned numb. He didn't know it, but he had crushed an artery.

Typically, he tried to gut it out and pitch through the injury, but on July 17, he had to leave the game against Cincinnati after one inning with no feeling in the finger.

The hand recovered. Sandy came back. Oh, how he came back! For the next five years, he was beyond dominant. He was often unhittable.

"As far as I'm concerned," Cardinal flamethrower Bob Gibson wrote in his autobiography, "no other pitcher in the history of baseball ever put together five years like Koufax did from 1962-1966."

He threw his second no-hitter, blanking the Giants on May 11, 1963. He carried a perfect game into the eighth inning before walking Ed Bailey.

On August 2 his determined face peered out from the cover of *Life* magazine as he led the Dodgers into the World Series against the inevitable Yankees. In baseball's showcase series, Sandy fanned the first five Yankees he faced on his way to a World Series-record 15 strikeouts in his first start. Then he beat Whitey Ford, 2-1, to complete a stunning Dodger sweep.

Eighteen days later, on October 24, he was the unanimous choice for the Cy Young Award. Five days later, he captured the Most Valuable Player Award in the National League, beating out Pirate shortstop Dick Groat, 237 votes to 190. He also won the Hickok Belt, signifying the professional athlete of the year, and was the Associated Press male athlete of the year, the United Press International player of the year, and the winner of the B'nai B'rith Sports Lodge Award.

But all those blazing fastballs and knee-buckling curves were already taking their toll on Sandy's arm. It hurt all through spring training of 1964, and he took a cortisone shot in his inflamed left elbow. He struggled, winning only five of his first nine decisions. But before his turn against the Phils at Connie Mack Stadium on June 4, Sandy compared a recent picture of his pitching motion to an old *Sports Illustrated* photo and thought he detected a flaw in his delivery. Phil's manager Gene Mauch swore Sandy threw 114 warmup pitches on the sidelines that day, trying to find his rhythm.

He found it. Sandy no-hit the Phils, 3-0, becoming the fourth pitcher in big-league history to throw three no-hitters.

On August 8 he won his 17th game of the season. Ironically, his single touched off the winning rally. He hurt his elbow sliding back into second and missed most of the rest of the season, winning just two more games.

Dr. Robert Kerlan gave him the bad news. The injury had triggered traumatic arthritis in the elbow. The pain would be constant, the damage irreversible.

Sandy began getting regular cortisone shots. He took Empirin with codeine for pain, and when that no longer cut it, he took Butazolidin, a drug often prescribed for race horses. Sandy had to take drug tests to make sure the drug wasn't reaching potentially toxic levels in his blood. The liquid flame arm rubdowns became a pregame ritual.

The game plan called for him to start only every fifth day and not throw at all between starts. Yet for the next two years, Sandy never missed a start and often started on two days' rest. He threw 335 and two-thirds innings in '65. (If someone throws 200 in a season now, we call him a workhorse.) He also struck out 382 (10.25 per game) while keeping the Dodgers in the pennant chase.

On August 14, with smoke billowing from fires a few miles from Dodger Stadium from what was being called the Watts Riots, Sandy won his 21st game in his 29th start.

He would go three weeks before winning another game. At some point during that long, hot August, fighting relentless pain, Sandy decided that the next season would be his last. He told only one trusted sports writer, who agreed to keep his secret.

On August 22 he was on the mound when Giant pitcher Juan Marichal, enraged at what he perceived as Dodger catcher Johnny Roseboro's attempt to hit him with a throw back to Koufax, spun and cracked Roseboro's head with a bat, touching off a 14-minute brawl. Sandy sprinted down off the mound to try to play peacemaker.

He took a 21-7 record to the mound on September 9 against the Cubs and Bob Hendley, who had a sore left arm of his own and had just been recalled from AAA. Many of the 29,139 who paid to get into Dodger Stadium that night listened tensely to announcer Vin Scully on their transistor radios as Sandy set the Cubs down in order inning after inning. Hendley nearly matched him pitch for pitch.

As he took the field for the ninth inning, leading 1-0 and still perfect, Sandy received a long standing ovation. "Sandy Koufax is slowly walking out to the mound for a meeting with destiny," Dodger announcer Vin Scully told his listeners.

Sandy fanned catcher Chris Krug on a 2-2 fastball for his 12th strikeout. Joey Amalfitano, pinch hitting for shortstop Don Kessinger, struck out swinging on an 0-2 pitch. Then Harvey Kuenn, a former batting champion and lifetime .300 hitter, settled into the batter's box to bat for Hendley.

Incredibly, it was the second time Amalfitano and Kuenn were all that stood between Koufax and a no-hitter. The first time, the previous season, Sandy had gotten his no-hitter. This time he sought perfection.

He missed very high with a fastball. He overthrew the next pitch, too, his follow-through so violent, his cap fell off. Then he got two quick strikes.

On a 2-2 fastball—Sandy's 113th pitch of the game—Kuenn went down swinging, and Sandy climbed another notch among baseball's immortals.

As Sandy was attaining perfection, Major League Baseball announced that the 1965 World Series would open on October 6. Yom Kippur also fell on October 6 that year.

On September 18, Sandy shut out the Cardinals, 1-0, and then shut them out again a week later, 2-0. In the process he broke Bob Feller's single-season MLB strikeout record. Mike Shannon was victim number 349. Bob Uecker was number 350.

Sandy led the league in wins (26), ERA (2.04), complete games (27), innings pitched (335 and two-thirds), guts and grace under pressure.

Then he refused to pitch the first game of the World Series.

A Pitcher Becomes a Symbol

Sandy was neither a devout nor a practicing Jew when he turned down that starting assignment. He in fact didn't attend services that day—although it was widely reported that he did. But he was a Jew, and a Jew doesn't pitch on Yom Kippur. On that point, Sandy was apparently never in doubt.

He became a symbol that day, to Jews worldwide and to all people for whom religion means more than money or fame. Although decades have gone by, folks haven't forgotten his brilliance or his decision to put religious observance first. In the 1990s movie *The Big Lebowski*, actor John Goodman uttered the line, "Three thousand years of beautiful tradition: from Moses to Sandy Koufax." When senator Joe Lieberman ran for vice president in 2000, the first Jew on a presidential ticket, pundits called him "The Sandy Koufax of politics."

In an article in the SF Jewish Community bulletin published September 20, 1996, rabbi Lee Bycel wrote that Koufax "taught pride to a generation of young Jews," helping them realize that "no one should ever be embarrassed when practicing one's religion or identifying with one's ancestral culture."

Sandy's courageous act, Bycel wrote, inspired a generation "to take responsibility for our own actions and to work for a world where freedom, justice and peace are a living reality for all people."

Taking Sandy's turn in the rotation against the Minnesota Twins in Metropolitan Stadium, Don Drysdale, the right-handed ace of the Dodger staff, got drubbed. When manager Alston came out to get him, Big D reportedly said, "I'll bet you wish I was Jewish, too."

Koufax started the second game, and the Twins' stylist lefty, Jim Kaat, beat him, 5-1, putting the Dodgers in a two-nothing hole with the series shifting to Los Angeles. But Clyde Osteen and Drysdale got the Dodgers even, and Sandy threw a four-hit shutout, 7-0, to give the Dodgers a 3-2 edge.

When the Twins won Game 6, setting up a climactic seventh game, Alston faced a tough decision. Logic dictated that he start Drysdale on three days' rest rather than Koufax, who had had only two days off. He kept his decision to himself until game time, announcing simply, "We're going to start the left-hander."

So Sandy took the hill with the world championship on the line. He'd pitched 351 innings, and he was exhausted. His arm raged with pain, and he couldn't throw the curve for a strike. He walked the first two batters he faced, and Drysdale got up in the bullpen behind him.

But, with only his courage and his fastball, Sandy shut the Twins down, 2-0, a Lou Johnson home run giving him all the support he needed. It was a remarkable performance.

He was a unanimous choice for the Cy Young and barely lost a second Most Valuable Player Award, trailing Willie Mays in the voting, 224-177.

The First Organized Labor Movement in Baseball

Sandy put himself in the record book of baseball and American culture again in the off season by staging a holdout with Drysdale. They united to ask for a three-year, $1.05 million contract, the money to be split evenly, $167,000 per year for each of them.

It was an audacious move. Players had never joined forces in salary negotiations and had in fact often been played off against each other. No player made more than $100,000—at least not officially.

When the team plane left for Vero Beach on February 26, Sandy and Big D weren't on it.

On March 17, the pair signed contracts to appear with David Janssen in the movie *Warning Shot*. They seemed prepared to skip the season if need be.

But on March 30 they came to terms, ending their 32-day holdout. Sandy signed for $125,000 for one year, Don for $110,000.

The extended holdout seemed to hurt Drysdale, who struggled all season. But Sandy, aching arm and all, picked up right where he left off in 1965, fanning seven Braves in a row on June 26 to tie his own National League record. He started the All-Star game in St. Louis on two days' rest and went three fine innings.

When he faced Jim Bunning at Dodger Stadium before 45,000 fans on July 27, it marked the first time that perfect game pitchers had ever faced each other. (It didn't happen again until 1991, when Tom Browning started against Dennis Martinez.)

With Sandy again leading the way, the Dodgers battled the Pirates and Giants for the flag all summer. On the final day of the season, October 2, again pitching on two days' rest, Sandy took the hill with the pennant on the line—a year to the day after he had clinched the '65 flag. Again he faced the great Bunning.

In the second inning, his curve ball again deserted him. In the fifth, he felt something pop in his back, and trainers struggled to pop it back between innings. Still, he shut the Phils out for the first eight innings. Running on fumes, he gave up three runs in the ninth, which sliced the Dodger lead in half, without getting an out. Now Alston, who once made Sandy wait weeks between starts and then yanked him at the first sign of trouble, was afraid to take his star out of the game. It was Sandy's game to win or lose.

He struck out Bob Uecker for the first out, got Bobby Wine for the second, and fanned Jackie Brandt on three pitches to win it. It was his 27th victory of the season against only nine loses, and the Dodgers had needed every win.

The World Series was an anticlimax, the Baltimore Orioles sweeping the Dodgers. The key to the series may have been the fifth inning of the first game when, with Sandy on the mound, Dodger centerfielder Willie Davis dropped two fly balls and then heaved the second muff into the dugout. Willie got an unwanted World Series record, and the Phils got three unearned runs.

The Dodgers never recovered.

After that disastrous inning, Sandy approached Davis in the dugout, and teammates tensed. They should have known Sandy better than that. He put his arm around the outfielder's shoulders and told him not to worry about it.

On November 1, 1966, Sandy became the first three-time Cy Young Award winner in baseball history, again a unanimous choice. Perhaps fearing that no one else would ever win it unless they changed the rules, the following year MLB decided to give a separate award for each league.

Sandy's record over the last six years had been phenomenal. He led the league in wins in '63, '65, and '66, in ERA from '62 through '66, and in strikeouts in '61, '63, '65 and '66.

He was an All-Star all six of those seasons. He pitched no-hitters in '62, '63, '64 and '65, the last one the perfect game. He led the Dodgers to pennants in '63, '65, and '66 and was the league's Most Valuable Player, a rare honor for a pitcher, in '63.

And then, at age 31, he walked away.

On November 18, 1966, Sandy held a press conference to announce his retirement. No Dodger officials attended.

"If there was a man who did not have the use of one of his arms," Koufax told reporters, "and you told him it would cost a lot of money if he could buy back that use, he'd give every dime he had, I believe."

He said he didn't regret one minute of his 12 years in baseball, "but I think I would regret one year that was too many."

Life Off the Mountain Top

Some say Sandy became a recluse after retiring. They wondered out loud what he did all day, how he managed without the cheers, without the rush.

His friends knew better.

Sandy is no hermit, but he has tried to live outside the limelight since he stopped throwing a baseball for a living.

In 1969 he married Anne Widmark, daughter of actor Richard. She didn't even know he was famous. The two bought an old farmhouse to renovate in Ellsworth, Maine.

Sandy surfaced to sign a 10-year, $1 million contract with NBC to do color commentary on the NBC Game of the Week but quit during the '73 season and went home to Maine. He knew the game as well as any man alive but couldn't bring himself to talk about his own exploits.

On January 19, 1972, he was elected to the Hall of Fame at age 36, the youngest ever to achieve the honor and only the sixth to make it in his first year of eligibility. He received 344 votes and entered the Hall along with Yogi Berra and Early Wynn.

Sports Illustrated named him "Athlete of the Millennium." He's also the only pitcher named to ESPN's list of the top 50 athletes of the century.

He worked for nine years as a Dodger minor league pitching coach, freely sharing all that was teachable about his genius. He resigned that post in 1990. In 1994 he worked with the Texas Rangers' staff, simply because Kevin Kennedy thought to ask him.

He now travels a lot and plays golf. He took up fly fishing and became a marathon runner. Everything he does he does well. He also shows up at charity banquets, induction ceremonies and funerals. He and Vin Scully were pallbearers for Al Campanis.

He returned to Dodgertown in 1997 to teach at a seminar on sports medicine, where he explained the physics of pitching to a rapt audience of biomechanical experts.

His first marriage ended in divorce, as did his second, in 1997, the same year his sister died.

Sports Illustrated called him "the incomparable and mysterious Sandy Koufax." Incomparable, certainly. But maybe not mysterious so much as incomprehensible—a shy, friendly man who became for six summers the best pitcher in baseball and maybe the best pitcher of all time, a man who put principle before ambition and privacy before celebrity. That really isn't so mysterious, but it surely is rare.

I (Marshall) once sat a few rows behind home plate at Dodger Stadium on a night when Sandy pitched. I don't remember who the Dodgers played or the score or even how Sandy did that night. But I carry an image of him standing on the mound, lean and ramrod straight, eyes on the catcher's target, alone amidst a cheering throng, quiet, dignified, self-contained.

When he threw, the ball seemed to explode in catcher Johnny Roseboro's glove.

I figure watching him was as close to perfection as I'll get on this earth.

CHAPTER 14

Making the World a Better Place
Roberto Clemente

"Anytime you have an opportunity to make things better and you don't, then you are wasting your time on this Earth."
                                                    —Roberto Clemente

"He's the strangest hitter in baseball. Figure him one way, and he'll kill you another."
                                                    —Sandy Koufax

Full name: Roberto Clemente Walker
Nicknames: "Bob," "The Great One"
Position: Outfield
Career: Pittsburgh Pirates, 1955-1972
Career batting average: .317

Career highlights:
- Led the league in batting in 1961 (.351), 1964 (.339), 1965 (.329), and 1967 (.357).
- Paced the league in hits in 1964 and 1967.
- Led the league in triples with 12 in 1969.
- Selected as an All-Star 12 times.
- Won the NL MVP Award in 1966.
- Elected to the Hall of Fame.

The Dodgers let him slip away, and the Pirates nabbed him. Once they did, only Roberto's death could separate them.

Roberto Clemente Walker was born the youngest of four children in Barrio San Anton in Carolina, Puerto Rico, on August 18, 1934. In school he was a track star, specializing in the javelin throw and sprints. But his true love was baseball. He played amateur ball with Juncos Double A Club and then with the Santurce Cangrejeros of the Puerto Rican Winter League.

The Brooklyn Dodgers signed him to a $10,000 bonus and assigned him to their AAA affiliate, the Montreal Royals.

That was their big mistake—a mistake they made sure not to make with their next "bonus baby," Sandy Koufax. At the time, any player receiving more than $4,000 in bonus money had to stay in the majors for a full season. By trying to hide Clemente in Montreal, the Dodgers exposed him to the 1954 player draft. Even though Roberto hit only .257 for the Royals, the Pirates picked him off and signed him for $4,000 on November 22.

When Roberto joined the Pirates the next year, they had just stumbled through three straight 100-loss seasons (in the days of the 154-game season). Clemente's brilliance helped them turn that around.

He spent his entire 18-year major league career—and the rest of his life—there. And what a career and a life it was.

Roberto collected exactly 3,000 hits in compiling a .317 lifetime batting average. But he never looked comfortable before getting any of those hits, constantly rolling his neck and stretching his back as he stood in the batter's box.

He was the National League batting champion four times and collected more than 200 hits in a season four times. He batted over .300 in 13 of his 18 seasons, including a career-best .357 in 1967. He was the N.L. MVP in 1966.

In 1960 he started a streak of eight straight seasons in which he batted no lower than .312. That year he made the first of his 14 All-Star game appearances. (There were two All-Star games that year.)

The next season he won the first of his four batting titles with a .351 average.

Pressure didn't stop him; he got at least one hit in every World Series game in which he played. He hit .310 in the 1960 World Series and topped that with a .414 average, two home runs, two doubles and a triple in the 1971 classic—good enough for series MVP honors.

"The Great One" bridged the gap between North and Latin America, so it was appropriate for Allegheny County to rename the Sixth Street Bridge, which spans the Allegheny River and brings fans to PNC Park, after Clemente.

He was also a superb right fielder, some say the best who ever played. He won 12 straight Gold Gloves and five times led the league in outfield assists. He could track down anything hit near him, often made spectacular catches, and played the tricky caroms off the right field wall at Forbes Field brilliantly.

"Clemente played a kind of baseball that none of us had seen before," Roger Angell wrote after Roberto's 1971 World Series performance, "throwing and running and hitting at something close to the level of absolute perfection."

In 1963 he played in the Hispanic American major league All-Star game, joining stars like Minnie Minosa, Tony Oliva, Orlando Cepeda, Julian Javier, Felipe Alou, Luis Aparacio, Zoilo Versailes, Vic Power, Juan Marichal, Al McBean, Manny Mota and Pedro Ramos. The National League won, 5-2.

On November 14, 1964, he married Vera Cristina Zabala in Carolina, Puerto Rico. Their three sons, Roberto Jr., Luis Roberto, and Roberto Enrique, were all born in Puerto Rico.

He sustained a severe back injury in 1954 and an arm injury in 1959 and came down with malaria in 1964. Still, he played in 140 or more games in eight straight seasons from 1960-67.

His Career Is One Long Highlight Film

His game-winning home run against the Cubs on September 2, 1966, was his 2,000th hit. That season he finally won the MVP Award, edging out Sandy Koufax by 10 votes, despite the Bucs' third-place finish.

In 1969 he dueled Pete Rose for the batting title. In his final at-bat, Rose, leading by .0008, laid down a bunt single to clinch the crown, his second straight.

On July 24, 1970, Pittsburgh gave its star a Roberto Clemente night, and he responded with a couple of hits before leaving the game with a cut knee after making a diving catch on the gravel warning track.

Later that season he collected five hits two games in a row, the first major leaguer in the 20th century to get 10 hits in two consecutive games.

He capped the 1971 season by belting a home run in the seventh game of the World Series, leading the Pirates to a 2-1 win and their first world championship since 1960.

On September 29, 1972, Roberto smashed a double off Met pitcher Jon Matlack in the fourth inning of a game at Three Rivers Stadium. It was his 3,000th hit, and it would be his last.

Flaming Out Like a Shooting Star

His sons were six, five and two when Roberto Clemente died. On New Year's Eve, 1972, Roberto boarded a plane to take medical supplies, food and clothing to earthquake-ravaged Nicaragua. He knew the trip was risky; the weather was bad and the little DC-7 wasn't in the best shape. But previous shipments of supplies had disappeared before getting to the people who needed them desperately, and Roberto wanted to take personal charge of this shipment.

The plane went down almost immediately after takeoff. All five aboard died. Roberto's body was never found.

"I would be lost without baseball," he once said. "I don't think I could stand being away from it as long as I was alive."

He never had to be.

Waiving the rule that a player must be retired for five years before being eligible for the Hall of Fame, the Baseball Writers' Association voted him into Cooperstown the following year, with 393 votes out of a possible 424. He was the first Hispanic to enter the Hall.

The Pirates retired his No. 21 on April 6, 1973, at Three Rivers Stadium, with 51,695 fans cheering their approval.

Baseball commissioner Bowie Kuhn created the Roberto Clemente Award for sportsmanship and community activism.

"He was so very great a man," Kuhn said, "as a leader and humanitarian, so very great an inspiration to the young and to all in baseball, especially to the proud people in his homeland, Puerto Rico."

Curt Shilling and Jim Thome are among the players who have since won the Roberto Clemente Award.

Clemente's memory hasn't faded with the years. On July 11, 1994, the Pirates unveiled a statue of The Great One outside Three Rivers Stadium.

In 1998, on the 25th anniversary of Clemente's induction, the Hall created a special exhibit in its Library Atrium—the first bilingual English/Spanish display in its history. He was the second baseball player ever to appear on a United States postage stamp; Jackie Robinson was the first. Schools all over America and the world bear Roberto Clemente's name.

On April 7, 1999, Allegheny County renamed The Sixth Street Bridge, which spanned the Allegheny River, joining downtown Pittsburgh to the North Side—the Roberto Clemente Bridge, after a man who spanned cultures and united hearts. Fans walk across that bridge now to see the Pirates play in PNC Park.

In 2002, commissioner Bud Selig announced that September 18 would be Roberto Clemente Day. "He will be remembered as a great baseball player and humanitarian," Selig said.

In Carolina, Puerto Rico, a 12-foot-tall statue of Clemente welcomes you to the 304-acre Roberto Clemente Sports City, a part of his legacy that wife Vera and sons Luis Roberto and Roberto Enrique are continuing in his name.

"Clemente is a great hero for all Latin players, especially Puerto Ricans," slugger Juan Gonzalez said.

"Growing up in Puerto Rico, we got to learn a lot about his character," New York Yankee star Bernie Williams said. "[I]t was obvious that not only was he one of the greatest players, but a great human being as well."

"This was a man who could have lived a luxurious life away from the troubles of society and the poverty he faced as a child," writer John Snook noted. "He was not like that. He gave up his life trying to help other people in need."

CHAPTER 15

What Might Have Been
Herb Score

"Calling Herb Score a left-handed Feller is a compliment to me."
— Bob Feller

"Coming on to pitch is Mike Moore, who is six-foot-one and 212 years old."
— Herb Score, Sportscaster

Full name: Herbert Jude Score
Nickname: "Herb"
Position: LHP
Career: Cleveland Indians, 1955-59; Chicago White Sox, 1961-62
Career W-L: 55-46
Career ERA: 3.36

Career highlights:

- Led the league in strikeouts with 245 in 1955 and 263 in 1956.
- Allowed the fewest hits per nine innings in 1956 (5.85) and 1959 (6.89).
- Selected as an All-Star in 1955 and 1956.
- Won the AL Rookie of the Year Award in 1955.

Was Herb Score really worth one-third the value of the entire Cleveland Indians club? The great Ted Williams thought so.

"Score's worth a million as far as I'm concerned," Ted said. "He'll win 280 games before he's through—if he doesn't get hurt."

Ah, but there's always that chance. Players risk injury every time they step on the field. A pitcher is particularly vulnerable, especially a fastball pitcher with a big follow through.

Score's early successes seemed to make a prophet out of Williams. By age 24, Herb Score had already been named Rookie of the Year in 1955 and Sophomore of the Year in 1956. Those first two years as an Indian, Score compiled a 36-19 record, with an ERA of 2.60. In 1955, he broke Grover Cleveland Alexander's rookie record of 235 strikeouts by fanning 245. He went 28 better the next season, whiffing 263. He led the league in both 1955 and 56 with 9.70 and 9.49 strikeouts per nine innings pitched.

He had three pitches—fast, faster and fastest. How fast? Before the radar gun, pitches were clocked using the "foul ball" method.

"About 40 balls are used in a regular game," umpire Larry Napp said. "With Score we need an extra dozen."

"His performance conjured up images of unlimited possibilities," John Benson wrote. "And thinking about those possibilities was part of what made it so much fun to watch him."

Red Sox fans wanted a piece of that joy, and Boston GM Joe Cronin made a pitch for Score. But Tribe general manager Hank Greenberg turned him down. The Indians wanted to revel in the pure beauty of his lightning fastball, which Jack Olsen described as a "classically delivered, full-overhanded fastball, slung in a javelin-like style with the full whip of his six-foot-two frame."

The Indians—and the entire baseball world—would lose the joy of Score's fastball in a split second.

A Million-to-one Shot

Terry Pluto, Cleveland's masterful writer, dates the Indians' self-destruction to Rocky Colavito's trade to the Detroit Tigers on April 17, 1960. But he could well have chosen Tuesday night, May 7, 1957, at 8:05 p.m.

Gil McDougald swung at a Herb Score blazer. Score saw the blur of the ball, and Wally Bock, the Indians' trainer, was running to the mound, towel in hand, to stop the bleeding.

Herb Score credits St. Jude for watching over him before, during, and after his short, brilliant career on the mound.

The "Bear," Mike Garcia, Score's friend and pitching colleague, charged in from the bench to comfort him. Herb asked him what happened to the ball, and Garcia told him McDougald had made it safely to first. He hadn't. The ball caromed off Score's face toward third, where third baseman Al Smith picked it up and threw the runner out. Credit Score with an assist.

Credit St. Jude with one, too.

"St. Jude stay with me," Score prayed as he was carried off the field and taken to Lakeside Hospital.

Romance Replaced By Peril, Peril By Faith

"The moment that pearl leaves Pedro Martinez's hand or Mark McGuire's bat," Tim Kurkjian wrote, "romance is replaced by peril."

When Herb Score let loose with his two-and-two fastball, Gil McDougald's bat became a weapon. Gil connected, sending a scorching liner back through the box at 130 mph.

"For several minutes after the ball hit me in the right eye," Score said, "I was afraid the eye had popped out of my head."

"If he goes blind, I quit baseball," a distraught McDougald said.

Score spent three weeks in Lakeside. He had suffered a broken nose, hemorrhaging, blurred vision, and trauma. His retina was intact, neither detached nor torn. His eye, though, was like "a window covered with rain."

It would be a long recovery.

"A deep religious faith carried him through the dark days and weeks that followed," Gordon Cobbledick wrote. "Herb Score is a genuinely devout young man, and his sublime confidence in his patron saint's watchfulness made him one of the few persons who never felt any doubt that he would come back as good as ever."

Score's devotion to St. Jude was a gift from his mother Anna. She christened him Herbert "Jude" in recognition of Jesus's boyhood friend and faithful companion. Jude was one of the 12 apostles, between James the Less and Simon the Zealot. He's also known as Thaddeus to differentiate him from Judas Iscariot. Jude kept a low profile and is mentioned only occasionally in the Gospel.

During her pregnancy with Herb, Anna prayed to St. Jude for a boy. Three years later, she would invoke his name again. This time it was a parent's worst nightmare. Both of young Herb's legs were crushed right below the pelvis by a bakery pick-up truck.

Doctors feared they'd have to amputate and scheduled an operation the next day. That night a relic of St. Jude was brought to his hospital room. In the morning, X-rays indicated that the bones had worked apart and the operation was cancelled.

"Jude is the workmanlike spiritual mechanic; the one who does his job and moves on," Liz Trotta wrote. "Approaching him takes no energy and is as secret as shouting in a cave for help."

Score's call to Jude on that May night was a gentle whisper.

Little by little, the rain let up, and Herb was ready for a comeback. He refused to give up hope. He was determined that his eye injury be just another bump in the road.

Injury History

He had never gone long without some sort of setback: run over by a truck, bedridden 10 months with rheumatic fever, plus fractured ankles, an emergency appendectomy, two bouts with pneumonia, an acute colon condition, a shoulder separation, and high blood pressure.

Folks compared him to Pete Reiser, the Brooklyn Dodger fireplug whose career ended prematurely due to injuries. Reiser made a habit of running into walls; Score's ailments were more part of his gene pool.

Despite the sicknesses and injuries, Herb Score endured.

He was first noticed as a star pitcher for Lake Worth Florida High School. His lightning-quick fastball placed him at the top of the scouting lists. Fourteen of the then-16 major league teams competed for his premium speed.

Cy Slapnicka, the legendary Indian scout, had the inside track. Cy was a talent-spotter extraordinaire; he signed Bob Feller and Hal Trosky. Both players came from small Iowa towns and had terrific long-term careers for the Tribe. Feller won 266 games in 18 seasons and Trosky, the slugging first baseman, hit .313 in nine solid seasons.

"Cy seemed to talk the farmer's language," Leighton Housh wrote. "And no Iowa town was too small for him to visit."

He nurtured young Herb, becoming good friends of the family. When it was time to sign, friendship trumped dollars. Score signed for a $60,000 bonus.

"All the bids, including Cleveland's, represented so much more than we ever thought was in the world that a few thousand more or less didn't seem to make much difference," Score said. "Besides, 'Slap' was such a nice man that we didn't want to disappoint him."

Turning Wildness into Finesse

Score didn't disappoint, although his progress took time, seasoning, and fine-tuning. Like many young, left-handed flamethrowers, Herb was wild. But the Indians could afford to wait for him to mature, having been blessed with the blue-chip pitching of Feller, Mike Garcia, Early Wynn, and Bob Lemon.

It took about three years.

At age 20, Score was sent to the Indians' Class AAA club at Indianapolis, finishing the season at 2-5, with an ERA of 5.23. The next season he was demoted to Class A Reading, where he continued to struggle. His record improved to 7-3, but he averaged a dozen walks per game.

Slapnicka and the Indians management finally handed Herb over to Ted Wilks, the Indians' Class AAA pitching coach. Slapnicka's instincts had paid off once before when he switched Trosky from a pitcher to an outfielder, and from a right-handed hitter to a lefty.

He was right again. Wilks smoothed out Score's erratic delivery, and Herb went 22-5, striking out 330 in 251 innings in propelling Indianapolis to an American Association pennant in 1954.

"The best pupil I ever had," Wilks said.

In 1955, at age 22, Score debuted in the majors with a victory against the Tigers. It didn't come easily, as he threw 172 pitches, an unheard-of amount with today's strict pitch counts.

Over the next two years, Score just got better and better.

In his rookie year, he fanned 16 Red Sox batters in one game. Afterwards, a reporter asked catcher Hank Foiles why Herb was such a terrific competitor.

"There are a lot of things about him," Foiles said. "He's never too busy for a friend. He has a will to win. And he has an unusual quality. He's open to constructive criticism."

When he took the mound in May 1957 at Cleveland's Municipal Stadium, he was on the verge of pitching greatness. When they carried him off the field, Score's predicted 280 lifetime victories vanished. He would finish 225 wins short.

Short on Victories, Long on Hope

For six long years, he kept climbing to the top of the comeback trail, only to be pushed back down. Each time he battled back.

After his injury, he spent the remaining months of the 1957 season in rehab. The bandages came off, his depth perception returned, and his physical conditioning improved. Only second-guessing and self-analysis remained.

In 1958 he was ready to go, and for one wonderful moment in April, it looked as if he had regained his form. He three-hit the White Sox, 2-0, with 13 whiffs.

In his next start, however, he injured the tendon in his elbow. He spent most of the season in pain, ending up on the disabled list. He managed only five starts and a 2-3 record that year.

The 1959 campaign brought anticipation, as once again, it looked as if Score had fully recovered. At mid-season he owned a 9-4 record, but he nose-dived during the second half, finishing 9-11. Still, he earned the best strikeout-per innings pitched ratio, 8.23. His fastball still befuddled batters.

Still young at 27, Herb believed he could make another comeback. General manager Frankie Lane had different ideas. The day after Lane made his infamous "hamburger for steak" trade (Harvey Kuenn for Colavito), he shipped Score to the Chicago White Sox. In exchange, the Indians obtained righthander Barry Latman. Lane thought a change of scenery would help Herb with his problems.

It didn't.

He spent three frustrating years with the White Sox and even tried a stint with Chicago's Class AAA team in San Diego. But he never connected.

Indianapolis was the knockout punch. In 1963, he hooked up with the Class AAA club for a final try. He failed.

It Wasn't the Line Drive That Knocked Him Out

"You can play baseball for years and years," former pitcher and now ESPN commentator Rob Dibble wrote. "But sometimes mere moments define who we are and who we think we are."

Folks assumed that for Herb Score that defining moment was the shot off the bat of Gil McDougald. But Herb believed he was the same pitcher before and after that tragedy. McDougald's liner didn't do him in, he insisted; arm injuries did.

He was never bitter, never whiny. He continued to believe in himself and move on, despite the setbacks. He continued to have faith, always wearing a St. Jude medallion around his neck.

"[Jude] is, after all, the crucible of hope," Trotta explained. "The one human emotion, the one virtue that keeps mankind afloat—diverting tragedy, healing the sick, comforting the desperate, deciding with some certainty that there is a way out."

Sometimes, the way out isn't what we want or expect.

"We may not be able to choose the moment of our entry into the world, the circumstances that confront us, the choices available, or the consequences that face us for making them," Robert Ellsworth wrote. "But we can always decide how we will respond to the choices and challenges we may have not chosen to confront."

Herb Score responded with courage and a deep faith in God.

While recovering from his eye injury at Lakeside Hospital, Score felt gratitude that so many fans cared about him.

"Here, I saw, were people with their own troubles, most of them, no doubt, far worse than mine," he said. "And yet they were able to put them aside for a while and pray for someone they didn't know. When the realization of what this meant sank into me, it strengthened my decision that I would accept whatever happened—even if I never could pitch again. God had taken care of me for 24 years, and he would help me find something else to do."

Score Climbs into the Booth

One door slams in your face, and another squeaks open, ever so slowly, down the hall.

In 1964, Score traded in his glove for a microphone. The Cleveland Indians remembered their fallen hero and offered him a chance to be a voice to millions of Indian fans. Score jumped at the opportunity.

He had his own style, and for 34 years he treated fans to the ups and downs at the "Big House at the Lake" and later at the Jake.

One devout Indian fan summed up Score's voice this way: "When my dog was a puppy, I would go out in the evening and put Herb Score on the radio to keep him calm."

With the Indians' luck, they needed serenity, and some laughs, like these Herb-isms:

"There's a two-hopper to Duane Kuiper, who fields it on the first bounce."

"I beg your pardon. We are not in Milwaukee. We are in Kansas City… I beg your pardon again. We are not in Kansas City. We just were in Kansas City. We are in Chicago."

His partner, Tom Hamilton, said, "It rekindles your faith in mankind, because you were wondering if these people were going to be stuffy or unapproachable. People like Ernie [Harwell] and the man I broke in with, Herb Score, made you feel like you were one of their peers."

Score left a million broken hearts when he called his final Indians game against the Florida Marlins, Game 7 of the World Series. As he signed off for the final time, he thanked all the fans for their kindness and, as was his way, thought of the other guy.

"[We] hope that whoever sits in this chair next," Score said, "you'll be as kind to them as you have been to me."

CHAPTER 16

A Survivor—On and Off the Field
Joe Torre

"We knew Torre would be back, because he said he would, and his word is good."

—Dave Kindred, *The Sporting News*

Full name: Joseph Paul Torre
Nicknames: "Joe," "The Godfather"
Position: Catcher, First Base, Third Base, Outfield
Career as a player: Milwaukee/Atlanta Braves, 1960-68; St. Louis Cardinals, 1969-74; New York Mets, 1975-77
Career as a manager: New York Mets, 1977-81; Atlanta Braves, 1982-84; St. Louis Cardinals, 1990-95; New York Yankees, 1996-present
Career batting average: .297

Career highlights:

• Led the league in batting average (.363), hits (239), RBI (137), and total bases (352) in 1971.

• Selected NL MVP in 1971.

• Made appearance on the All-Star team nine times.

• Managerial W-L record: 3195-1680 (at end of 2003 season).

Managerial highlights:

• AL Manager of the Year in 1996 and 1998.

J oe Torre has survived serious illness—his own and his brother Frank's—and the rigors of playing and managing in the pressure cooker of New York City, bringing stability to a Yankee team seemingly doomed to be permanent underachievers before he arrived.

He is the calm at the eye of a pinstriped storm.

He's also the only man in history to have been named both Most Valuable Player and Manager of the Year.

Perhaps even more extraordinary, he once got a standing ovation simply for presenting the Yankees lineup card to the plate umpire—in Fenway Park!

Joe Torre is an extraordinary man. He fell in love with baseball early on, and baseball has loved him back ever since.

Joe grew up tough in Brooklyn in the 1950s. He was 18 when the Dodgers moved away. He and the other kids wound rubber bands around paper for a baseball and sawed off a broomstick for a bat.

"If you hit the ball over a first-floor window," he told biographer Tom Verducci, "it was a double. Over a second-story window was a triple. Anything on the roof was a home run."

When he wasn't playing street ball, he played the Ethan Allen All-Star baseball game, learning strategies.

In the summer of his 15th year, he went to visit his big brother Frank, a first baseman with the Milwaukee Braves, and Frank convinced clubhouse man Tommy Ferguson to let his little brother help out and hang out.

Joe wouldn't need a pass from his brother to get into a major league clubhouse for long. He signed with the Braves for a $40,000 bonus and broke in with the Bears of Eau Claire, Wisconsin, in 1960. He took a room at Georgiana "Ma" Farwell's boarding house for $5 a week, and called her on her birthday—December 24—every year for over 20 years thereafter to see how she was doing.

He wound up leading the league with a .344 batting average, copping the title by .001 when he rapped out six hits in a doubleheader on the last day of the season. Combine that with his 16 home runs and 74 RBIs, and you've got the league's Rookie of the Year.

Still just 19, he broke into the big leagues with the Braves at the end of that season. In his first at bat on September 25, 1960, he pinch hit for Warren Spahn at County Stadium and got a base hit off Harvey "the Kitten" Haddux. Next time up he fanned, and that was it for the season—brother Frank's last with the Braves.

He started 1961 at Louisville, but after 27 games, the Braves brought him up to stay. He batted a solid .278 as a semi-regular, with 10 home runs among his 113 hits, good enough to finish second to Billy Williams in the NL Rookie of the Year balloting.

Although never a speedster, young Joe was the trailing runner on a triple steal against the Reds that year, while Henry Aaron made his first steal of home.

After hitting .282 as a part timer the next year, he became a regular in 1963, playing catcher and first base. He hit .293 with 14 home runs and made the All-Star team, as he would for the next four seasons.

He was even better in '64 (.321, 20 home runs, 109 RBI), finishing fifth in the MVP voting. In '65 he blasted 27 home runs and won the Gold Glove for catchers. He also belted a two-run home run in the All-Star game. In '66 he went with the Braves to Atlanta and had his best power year, smacking 36 home runs to go with 101 RBIs and a .315 average.

His numbers fell off a bit the next year, and a broken cheekbone slowed him down in 1968.

In one of baseball's high-profile trades, the Braves swapped their slugging catcher to St. Louis even up for former MVP first baseman Orlando Cepeda. Torre took over for the Baby Bull at first base for the Cards and drove in 101 and 100 runs the next two seasons.

When the Cards shipped Tim McCarver to the Phillies in 1970, Joe moved back behind the plate. But when illness knocked Mike Shannon out of the lineup, Joe moved to third base, and Ted Simmons took over as catcher.

A very handy man to have around, that Joe Torre.

All that moving didn't seem to bother his hitting. In fact, in 1971, at age 30, Joe had the best season of his career and one of the best years of anybody's career. He hit .363 with 24 home runs and 137 RBIs and won the MVP Award. Along with leading the league in average and RBIs, he paced the NL in hits (230) and total bases (352). He even led third basemen in putouts (though he also led in errors).

Joe put in three more solid seasons with the Cardinals, including a memorable game on June 27, 1973, when he hit for the cycle. He stroked a double in the first inning, homered in the third, and tripled in the fourth, giving him all but the "easy" one, a single. Next time up, he hit into a double play. When he walked in the eighth with the Cards rolling to a 15-4 win over the Pirates, Joe wanted manager Red Schoendienst to put in a pinch runner for him, but Red left him in. Joe got a final at-bat in the ninth and came through with the base hit.

"The Godfather", shown here with his top Don (Zimmer), brought stability and championships to a troubled Yankees team. Torre is the only man to win the Most Valuable Player and Manager of the Year awards.

Late in the 1974 season, the Cards traded him to the Mets for pitchers Ray Sadecki and Tommy Moore. The Mets were hoping Joe would solve their problems at third base, but he didn't sparkle in the field or at the plate, where he dropped off to a .247 average with just six home runs in 361 at bats.

His worst day as a hitter had to be July 21, 1975. Four times in a row, Felix Millan singled ahead of him, and four times, Torre hit into double plays, tying the kind of major league record nobody wants.

Joe rebounded in 1976, recording his last .300 plus season at .306, but with only five home runs and 31 RBIs as a part-time player.

One Career Ends as Another Begins

Early the next season, on May 31, 1977, Torre replaced Joe Frazier as the Mets manager. He remained a player for the next 18 games before ending his 18-year playing career, thus becoming the first player-manager in the majors since 1959.

Joe was ready to manage. He'd been studying the game he loved all his life, and as a catcher, he'd been the field general for 903 of his 2,207 major league games.

In his 117 games at the helm that year, the Mets went 49-68, finishing sixth. The best he could get out of the club during his tenure was a .462 percentage and a fourth-place finish in the NL East during the second half of the strike-fractured 1981 season.

He moved on to Atlanta in the NL West the next season, and Torre's Braves won their first 13 games on their way to a division title and an 89-73 finish. But they slipped a notch in each of the next two seasons, finishing a sub-par 80-82.

Perhaps showing their frustration, the Braves were involved in an ugly melee with the Padres in Atlanta in August. After Braves' pitcher Pascual Perez hit Alan Wiggins with the first pitch of the game, San Diego pitchers threw at Perez on four straight trips to the plate. After two bench-clearing brawls and 19 ejections—including both managers—Torre was slapped with a three-game suspension.

On October 1, Braves owner Ted Turner canned Torre, replacing him with Eddie Haas.

Joe had excelled on the field and captured a flag from the dugout. Now he climbed into the broadcast booth for the California (Anaheim) Angels and showed that he could be a fine baseball announcer as well.

He really could do it all.

In August of 1990, he returned to managing, taking over the Cardinals from interim manager Red Schoendienst, who had been filling in after Whitey Herzog's resignation. St. Louis won only 24 of their 58 games under Torre and finished sixth.

Next year, Joe guided the Cards to a second-place finish behind the Pirates in the NL East. They finished a respectable if lackluster third place in each of the next three seasons. When they stumbled to a 20-27 start in 1995, the Cards replaced Torre with Mike Jorgensen.

Torre as manager had posted a pretty good 257-229 record for Atlanta, a so-so 351-354 record with St. Louis, and a downright limp 286-420 record with the Mets. He'd been fired three times and had managed more games than any other skipper without making it to a World Series.

The next season he'd not only get to the Series but win it, in the process restoring the most storied franchise in baseball history to its former glory.

And he'd win the American League Manager of the Year award in the process.

Torre Scales the Baseball Summit

The New York Yankees and their tempestuous owner, George Steinbrenner, had finished second in the East under popular manager Buck Showalter. That wasn't nearly good enough for George, who replaces his managers like some folks change their underwear.

Torre was announcing the Little League World Series when he got the call. He was the new manager of the Bronx Bombers.

Joe was happy to come home to New York and didn't appear to be cowed by his boss's well-earned reputation for reaching down from the owner's box to move the players around on the field. Perhaps the fact that Joe had already been hired and fired by baseball's other most notable owner/eccentric, Ted Turner, prepared Joe for George.

On November 2, 1995, Joe became the 31st manager in Yankee history (depending on how many times you count Billy Martin). He became the fourth ever to manage both the Mets and the Yanks, joining Casey Stengel, Yogi Berra, and Dallas Green.

Seemingly implacable in the dugout or on the phone with his highly opinionated boss, Joe guided a previously troubled team to a 92-70 first-place finish that season. He preached what he practiced: be aggressive on the field and patient at the plate, and don't panic on or off the field.

Faced with the task of winning a world championship for a boss who would accept nothing less, Joe confronted an even bigger challenge in the postseason. While Joe struggled to keep his mind on the playoffs, big brother Frank lay in a New York City hospital waiting for heart surgery.

Frank came through the surgery, and the Yankees whipped Joe's old team, the Atlanta Braves, bringing the championship back to the House that Ruth Built for the first time since 1978.

Joe Torre, MVP, became Joe Torre, Manager of the Year.

The following season, the Yanks won four more games (96) during the regular season, but that was only good for second place in the AL East and a wild-card playoff berth. Then the Bronx Bombers bombed in the first round, dropping a tough five-game series to the Indians.

The season did bring a personal milestone for Torre; on April 30, his Yankees edged Seattle, 3-2, for Joe's 1,000th managerial win.

Did George consider giving his manager the gate after a long (for Steinbrenner) two-year tenure? If he did, he made the best non-decision of his life by hanging onto Torre. As good as his Yankees had been in 1996, they were even better—historically good, in fact—in 1998.

Under Joe's guidance, the Yankees soared to an American League-record 114 wins, taking the East in a walk.

When they hit their only real slump of the season in September, Torre climbed out of character after an especially galling loss to the expansion Tampa Bay Devil Rays, lacing into his team for its less-than-enthusiastic performance. When you don't yell often, it's especially effective when you do; the Yanks heard their leader and won the last seven games of the regular season, roared through the playoffs with a 7-2 record, and then swept the San Diego Padres for the 24th world championship in Yankee history.

Joe earned a second Manager of the Year Award.

Then he got prostate cancer.

Less than three years after brother Frank faced death on the operating table, little brother Joe took a routine physical exam and wound up in surgery. He turned the team over to bench coach Don Zimmer, perhaps the only man in baseball capable of showing less emotion in the dugout, and devoted his energies to recovering his health and getting back to the helm of a Yankee team that was now undeniably his.

Joe came back, just as he said he would. When he emerged from the visiting team dugout in Fenway Park on May 18, 1999, to deliver his lineup card, fans accustomed to booing anything in pinstripes gave him a standing ovation.

And Joe didn't just go back to work. He got back to winning. His Yankees took the Series in 1999 and 2000.

Torre Survives Turner,
Steinbrenner—and Even Wells

If Joe has received praise for surviving tenures with Steinbrenner and Turner, he should probably get a mention for dealing with Boomer as well. Proving that an easygoing guy can also be a disciplinarian when necessary, Joe handled his emotional left-hander, David "Boomer" Wells, with just the right combination of hands-off, let's-make-a-deal, and don't-push-it-buster.

Take Boomer's June 28, 1997 start against Cleveland, in which Wells took the mound wearing his vintage 1934 Babe Ruth autographed cap. It wasn't regulation, and Torre made him take it off after the first inning.

Then there was the May 6, 1988, 15-13 slugfest with the Texas Rangers, during which Wells got lit up for seven runs on seven hits in just two and two-thirds innings. Joe lashed him afterwards, not for getting roughed up, but for not seeming to care.

Then Joe sought out his troubled pitcher in a quieter moment and let Boomer unload.

"I feel like you don't show confidence in me," Wells reportedly told his manager. In particular, he said Joe was getting relievers up too quickly behind him.

Torre listened, considered, and acted, giving Wells more time to work his way out of trouble. Two starts later, Wells didn't have any trouble at all. He pitched a perfect game.

"Baseball, it's a game of life," Torre says. "You play it every day. And when you have a problem, unless you talk about it or deal with it, it's going to get worse."

Torre even survived the tempest surrounding the 2003 publication of Boomer's book, *Perfect I'm Not: Boomer on Beer, Brawls, Backaches, and Baseball*, written with Chris Kreski. (Apparently, it was an "unauthorized autobiography," as Boomer denied some of the stuff he had supposedly written.)

Joe also met the challenge when Steinbrenner went out and bought him troubled slugger Jose Canseco from the Devil Rays for the stretch drive in 2000. Joe had no place to put Canseco except on the bench, but he got Jose and the team through the potential crisis just fine.

And when Joe wanted a player, he hasn't been shy about making a phone call. When the Yankees signed Oriole free agent Mike "Moose" Mussina before the 2001 season, Mike said a deciding factor in his decision to sign was the call he got from Joe Torre.

Joe Torre: CEO?

Appreciation for his managerial style goes well beyond the base-ball world. In an April 16, 2001, article in *Fortune* magazine, Jerry Useem asserted that Joe just might be "the model for today's corporate managers."

Here's Useem's reasoning. "Consider: For five seasons he has taken a collection of rookies and retreads, recovering drug addicts and born-again Christians, Cuban defectors and defective throwers, and created a workplace that, were it not for the particular job requirements, would surely qualify for *Fortune*'s list of the 100 best places to work."

"I try to understand what motivates other people," Joe told Useem, who calls him "a master organizational psychologist" with exceptional "emotional intelligence."

Joe doesn't have a lot of rules: show up on time, no excessive facial hair, no loud music in the clubhouse. He shuns clubhouse meetings and rah-rah speeches in favor of one-on-ones with his players. He stays with a player in a slump. The tenser the situation, the calmer Joe becomes. He's intense but not tense.

He also takes the heat from the front office, serving as effective buffer between Steinbrenner and the players. Whereas Steinbrenner demands perfection, Torre stresses preparation, effort and resiliency.

There's "no guarantee you're going to win," he says, "but you're going to come out here ready to play. You judge how good a team is by how they respond to the negative stuff."

His teams respond very well indeed. On May 12, 2002, the Yankees whipped Minnesota, 10-4, giving Skipper Joe his 1,500th career win.

Joe the player, manager, and "organizational psychologist" is also Joe the author. In 1997 he teamed with Tom Verducci to pen his autobiography, *Chasing the Dream: My Lifelong Journey to the World Series*, and in 1999, with Henry Dreher, he wrote *Joe Torre's Ground Rules for Winners: 12 Keys to Managing Team Players, Tough Bosses, Setbacks and Success*.

Nobody manages them better than Joe.

The Joe and Billy Show

Of all Joe's famous teammates over the years, none is more famous—or a bigger Yankee fan—than comedian Billy Crystal. Longtime friends, Torre and Crystal partnered up to promote "Finding Our Families, Finding Ourselves," a multimedia exhibit at the Museum of Tolerance in Los Angeles. The show displays the personal histories of notable Americans, including Crystal and Torre, athletes Kareem Abdul-Jabbar, Michelle Kwan and Steve Young, author Maya Angelou, and musician Carlos Santana.

Torre's favorite aspect of the show is the chance it affords visitors to begin a hands-on computer search for their own ancestors.

"You realize there are things you want to find out about yourself," he told *Sports Illustrated*. "I know for years we were ashamed, or were supposed to be ashamed, that we had divorce and abuse in our family. I think this exhibit helps so many other people to be open with it."

Crystal calls Joe before every Yankee playoff game. The message is always the same: "We eat together, we win together." It's a tradition they started in 1999.

Crystal says Gary Cooper would have been a good choice to play Torre in the movie version of his life, "with a little Mel Gibson and a little Samuel Jackson."

So far that movie wouldn't include an induction scene at Cooperstown. Joe received 29 votes, or 35.8 percent, on the 2003 balloting of the Veterans Committee, about the same percentage he received as a former player and manager on the baseball writers' ballot.

Joe felt let down, he admitted to *New York Daily News* reporter Bill Madden—but not for himself.

"I am disappointed Gil [Hodges], [Ron] Santo and Roger Maris…weren't elected," he said. But for himself? "I never had any hopes of being elected," he says. "[I]t should be hard. It's a special place."

We think Joe's a perfect candidate, and we hope the Hall doesn't wait until Joe's managerial career is over to vote him in. He has excelled on the playing field and in the dugout, and he's one of baseball's very best good guys, in and out of the ballpark.

If they do film the story of his life, Joe should play himself. He's proved he can do everything else.

CHAPTER 17

Second Chances
Tommy John

"I have four basic pitches—fastball, curve, slider and change-up—plus eight illegal ones."

—Tommy John

"Every pitching arm is doomed."

—Jane Leavy

Full name: Thomas Edward John, Jr.
Nicknames: "Tommy," "TJ," "the bionic arm"
Position: Left-handed pitcher
Career: Cleveland Indians, 1963-64; Chicago White Sox, 1965-71; Los Angeles Dodgers, 1972-78; New York Yankees, 1979-82 and 1986-89; California Angels, 1982-85; Oakland A's, 1985
Career W-L: 288-231
Career ERA: 3.34

Career highlights:
- Led the league in shutouts in 1966 (five), 1967 (six), and 1980 (six).
- Topped the league in W-L percentage in 1974 at .813 (13-3).
- Led the league in fewest walks per nine innings with a 1.58 mark in 1982.
- Finished in the top five in ERA five times.
- Finished second in Cy Young voting twice.
- All-Star in 1968, 1978, 1979, and 1980.

By midseason in 1974, Dodger lefty Tommy John was enjoying his pitching prime, winning at a .813 clip (13-3). He should have been picked for the All-Star game at Three Rivers Stadium but remarkably was overlooked on the National League roster.

Since arriving in Los Angeles in 1971 from the Chicago White Sox, he had gone on a 40-15 streak, posting a fine 2.83 ERA. At 31, in 12 major league seasons, he'd logged 2,165 innings on his fine left arm.

Then on July 17, the arm went numb.

The Dodgers were leading Montreal, 4-0. T.J. was breezing along, heading for his 14th victory, until the Expos' Willie Davis led off the fourth inning with a drag bunt single. Tommy walked Bob Bailey on a tough 3-2 call, and up came first baseman Hal Bredeen.

John threw him a sinker that didn't sink. It just floated.

"A 'nothing' sensation," Tommy said.

He tried another sinker, with the same non-result. Tommy walked off the field and onto the examining table. The medical team, public relations staff, and front office folks huddled. At first, they reported that John had a muscle spasm.

He didn't. X-rays don't lie. John had suffered a "torn ulnar collateral ligament." No matter what you call it, Tommy John was damaged goods.

Occupational Hazards

Firemen inhale smoke, doctors lose sleep, construction workers wrench their backs, and pitchers blow out their arms.

But Tommy got a second chance. Orthopedic surgeon and team doctor Frank Jobe brought Tommy's arm back to life.

"The elbow is almost a hinge, which is a simple joint," Jobe said. "The shoulder has four joints involved and 21 muscles. They need to all be in good shape and functioning in a synchronous pattern."

John's elbow had unhinged, and odds were against Jobe's bionics making it work again—and surely not at the major league level.

But Tommy had nothing to lose. He could either take the knife or slam the door on his pitching career.

"Doctor Jobe had been level with me from the start," Tommy said, "and I felt sure he felt that he would never see me pitch again. But I felt I had a secret weapon, that nothing was impossible with God. And I also knew that whatever I had to do to get my arm back to shape again—no matter how tedious, how long, or how strewn with booby traps the path might be—I would stick to it until I reached the goal, or until the last faint flicker of possibility was extinguished."

On September 25, more than two months after his "nothing sensation," Tommy John had the surgery that's now named after him. Two years earlier, Doctor Jobe had removed bone chips from the same elbow. Before that operation Tommy had asked him to "put in a Koufax fastball."

This time Doctor Jobe rolled John's odometer back to zero by transplanting the tendon in Tommy's right wrist to his left elbow. Six weeks later, his arm looked like a claw. It took a second operation to work out the kinks. During round two, they untwisted the ulnar nerve. Since the doctors also found scarring, they re-channeled the nerve into a new position, then prayed for regeneration. Regenerate it did, but very slowly.

Just a Game of Pitch and Catch

Up until then, Tommy had always been a fast worker. He notched his first major league victory for the Cleveland Indians in 94 minutes. He shut out the Orioles and their starter Robin Roberts on three hits with only 73 pitches.

This time he would have to take a lot of time, and he would need great patience. It's best to rehab without your eye on the clock. Ask the Braves' John Smoltz or the Reds' Jose Rijo. Both prolonged their recovery by returning too soon.

Doctor Jobe succeeded in his delicate mission. Now it was up to Tommy. After removing the splint, he began shoulder and arm strengthening exercise, then proceeded to wrist and forearm. His wife, Sally, helped.

"For a while, Sally was my catcher," Tommy says. "We'd turn on the porch lights late at night and play catch."

Sally was more than his catcher. Along with Dodgers' head scout Ben Wade, she provided inspiration and support. St. Paul gave him a big assist, too.

"One piece of scripture sustained me and became like a mantra to me," John said.

"'For with God, nothing shall be impossible.'"

He graduated from the backyard to the bullpen and finally to pitching batting practice. For six days a week, he would work his arm back to shape. On the seventh day, the arm rested.

On average, it now takes 12-18 months to fully recover from Tommy John surgery. But Tommy was the first to succeed, and his journey took 19 long months.

Tommy John defied Father Time, in part due to the elbow surgery that now bears his name, by sticking around baseball for 26 seasons.

When teammate Jimmy Wynn said, "Damn T.J., you've got it back, man," Tommy knew that his grueling regime was paying dividends.

Doctor Jobe's surgery had put more treads on his arm. Now Tommy felt ready to take it for a test ride.

God Doesn't Pitch

It's one thing to pitch in practice, quite another to pitch with your future at stake.

In his first start of 1976, on April 16, T.J. pitched five innings against Atlanta, picking up the tab for a 3-1 loss.

After the game, Dodger manager Walter Alston upped the ante. "We're giving you one more shot," he said. "Then we've got to decide what we're going to do with you."

After a shaky first inning in his next outing, he threw seven shutout innings against the Astros. Unfortunately, he was dueling J.R. Richards, who did the same.

That earned him another start, and that's all he needed. Tommy beat the Pirates, 7-1. He was back, and 40,000 Dodger fans knew it, rising to their feet in the eighth inning to cheer him.

He ended that season at 10-10 with a 3.09 ERA. He started 31 games, pitched 207 innings, and captured the 1976 *Sporting News* National League Comeback of the Year Award and the 12th annual Fred Hutchinson Award for honor, dedication, and courage.

As is his style, Tommy took little credit for his achievements.

"His ego has always been so small," Thomas Boswell wrote, "he could hide it in his glove."

Tommy gave the credit to a higher power.

"God (as near as I can tell) has never taken the mound in a big league game," he said. "But He gave me the strength to attempt what virtually no one else thought I could do. Without Him, I would have been lost."

Paradise Regained

From 1977-1980, Tommy split his time between Los Angeles and New York and was dominant in both leagues. He went 79-35 with a 3.21 ERA and tossed a dozen shutouts. In 975 innings, he gave up a scant 45 homeruns. He conquered the 20-win plateau three times and made the All-Star team in '78, '79, and '80. How he missed the 1977 game is a mystery, as he was the runner-up in the National League

Cy Young balloting. He achieved runner-up Cy Young status again as a Yankee in 1980.

In a 1979 *Sport Magazine* article, American League hitters got a rare opportunity to rate opposing pitchers. They lavished praise on Tommy John, who ranked 11th overall.

"That sinking fastball starts at the knees and seems so slow," Ted Simmons remarked. "You feel you can golf the ball 450 yards to the green. But by the time you finish swinging, the damn thing's at your ankles."

Tommy tested the free agent waters in 1979. It was Milwaukee, Kansas City, or George Steinbrenner. T.J. selected George, $2.8 million, and three years.

The Yankees finished a disappointing 13.5 games back of the Baltimore Orioles that year but took the American League East flag the next, winning 103 games.

On June 7, 1980, T.J. won his 200th game when he two-hit the Seattle Mariners. Tommy was all the way back.

At 12:30 a.m. on June 12, 1981, baseball players threw down their bats and balls and went home. As a result of the 49-day strike, John started only 20 games. He ended the season with a mediocre 10-9 record but managed his best ERA (2.63) since 1968.

He also created a piece of trivia history. Due to the strike-induced split season, T.J. became the first and only pitcher to start and win two opening games in one season, and both against the same team. He bested the Texas Rangers 10-3 in the traditional April opener, pitching eight innings, giving up seven hits and three runs, en route to his 44th win in Yankee pinstripes. In Act II, he pulled the curtain up again, beating the Rangers 2-0. This time he went seven innings, giving up only two hits at Yankee Stadium before 40,373 fans.

But soon after this gala homecoming, Tommy and his wife were hit by a staggering personal tragedy. Their young son, Travis, fell from a third-story window.

Tommy was in Detroit for a game against the Tigers when Sally's frantic call reached Briggs Stadium. Travis had suffered a "serious cranial injury" and lay comatose in intensive care at Point Pleasant Hospital.

Coincidence or Miracle?

"As a wise man once put it," Tommy John said, "coincidence is God's way of remaining anonymous."

The "coincidental" location of Sally's car saved Travis' life. When Sally first arrived at her friend's house, she parked in the middle of the driveway. She had second thoughts and rolled the car closer to the house so her sister and her kids could have more room. When Travis tumbled three stories, he landed on the car's hood, breaking his fall. If the car had stayed where it had been, he would have hit the concrete head first.

Travis swallowed his tongue and was turning blue when Sally reached him on the ground. She darted down the stairs so fast that she was still holding her bottle of nail polish. She pried his mouth open so he could breathe.

A policeman happened to be in the area. He rushed over and assisted with the quick transport to the emergency room of Point Pleasant Hospital. On the way, the police car dodged traffic, saving precious time. Doctors performed 90 minutes of surgery.

Meanwhile, Tommy wondered how he could make it from Detroit to New Jersey. There were no direct flights to New Jersey. Bob Zancl's name popped into Tommy's head. His golfing partner of that morning had a private plane. It was not available, but Bob knew a friend whose plane was.

Tommy arrived at the hospital by 2 a.m.

In Los Angeles, Tommy's friend Doctor Stu Seigel heard the news on the radio. He did a computer search for the best in the business and came up with Fred Epstein. Doctor Epstein took the case—and became part of the family.

A 2001 *ABC News Nightline* show referred to Epstein as "The Messenger."

"He's been in the trenches of the operating room." Laura Palmer said, "fighting to give children back their childhood which are held hostage by brain and spinal cord tumors."

Doctor Epstein worked his magic with Travis.

He put Travis into a deep coma to reduce swelling, then drilled into his skull to insert a life-saving device that measured brain pressure.

Good Night Moon

During many long nights that followed, Sally John read Travis his favorite story, *Good Night Moon*, reciting this funny, rhyming tale about a bunny who wishes "Good Night" to everything in his "great green" room. He even says "Goodnight, nobody."

In Travis's hospital room, Tommy and Sally never said goodnight to their hopes and prayers.

"All the prayers that are being said out there are going to enter Travis through you," New York cardinal Cooke told them. "Just keep telling

Travis day after day how much you love him and how God loves him. I'm sure he can hear you. Travis will get better through these prayers."

He did. After a month in the hospital, Travis came home.

Outfoxing Father Time

"Playing baseball was the farthest thing from my mind," Tommy says. "I was going to go out, though, and do what I do best—throw a baseball." He kept throwing it for the Yankees until he was dumped the next season.

First it was arbitration, then contract woes, and finally a mediocre performance. T.J. was dealt to California for a player to be named later. His career seemed to be over when the Angels released him in 1985. But Tommy wasn't ready to quit. During the next seven years, he pitched for minor league clubs in Modesto, Madison, Oakland, Fort Lauderdale, and, finally, made it back to George's place in the Bronx in 1987. At age 44, he went 13-6 with the Yankees.

Along the road to this comeback, folks took advantage of the chance to see a pitching great. For his start with the Madison Muskies, 3,500 fans jammed stands made to accommodate 3,000. One of those fans, Leon Varjian, self-appointed team mascot and creator of many inventive "Fish" cheers, passed out "Tommy John Fan Club" membership cards.

Tommy faltered in the first, yielding a couple of runs. But then he found the rhythm, thrilling the fans and befuddling the A-league batters by hitting the catcher's glove with an assortment of curves and sinkers. Folks knew they were watching a major league pitcher.

Don't Close the Book on Tommy John

His last triumphant journey began on April 4, 1989, when he was the opening-day pitcher for the Yankees. At age 45, T.J. beat the Twins, 4-2. He did it in his usual style, twice freeing himself from bases-loaded jams.

Wasn't it Satchel Paige who said he would pitch forever? Old Satch didn't quite make it, and neither did Tommy John. But almost.

He's now in his 30th season in baseball. In 2003, he became the pitching coach for the Edmonton Trappers, the Montreal Expos' Class AAA affiliate.

"There's a sense of relief when I look back on my career, knowing that it's over," Tommy said. "The only thing I'd do differently is learn the change-up much earlier, because it's such a devastating pitch. Other than that, I wouldn't change a thing. I feel things happened the way God intended."

We'd change one thing. T.J. belongs in the Hall of Fame.

He's been on the ballot since 1995. In nine attempts, he's averaged 116 votes, close to 25 percent of the total votes. That leaves him well short of the 75 percent magic number. His 288 major league wins give him the most of any pitcher eligible but not in the Hall.

"While almost every other pitcher in baseball gives up gophers, John kills 'em," Tom Boswell wrote. "Can't hit what you can't excavate. A long blast off John only bounces twice before it gets through the infield."

"Tommy John is a con artist, a finesser, a tempter," Reggie Jackson said. "He's the kind of guy who will throw you a pitch flat, a foot out. You say 'He's got nothing.' You don't know he's done it on purpose. Next pitch is inside. You miss. He's a teaser. He tries to entice you with something that looks good but isn't quite."

John doesn't reside on the lofty plateau with Sandy Koufax, but there's plenty of room at Cooperstown to hang his plaque. He belongs there on guts alone.

His inscription might read something like this:

THOMAS "TOMMY" EDWARD JOHN JR.
ONE OF BASEBALL'S GOOD GUYS

CHAPTER 18

Don't Call Him Catfish
Jim Hunter

"Thank you, God, for giving me strength and makin' me a ballplayer."
—Jim Hunter

"You don't get anything by doing nothing."
—Albert Hunter, Jim's daddy

Full name: James Augustus Hunter
Nicknames: "Jim," "Catfish"
Position: Right-handed pitcher
Career: Kansas City/Oakland Athletics, 1965-74; New York Yankees,
    1975-79
Career W-L: 224-166
Career ERA: 3.26

Career highlights:
- Led the league in wins with 25 in 1974 and 23 in 1975.
- Posted the top ERA in the AL in 1974 with a 2.49 mark.
- Topped the league in innings pitched at 328 in 1975.
- Selected as an All-Star in 1966, 1967, 1970, 1972, 1973, 1974, 1975, and 1976.
- Threw a no-hitter and perfect game.
- Elected to Hall of Fame.

On Catfish Hunter Day, September 16, 1979, the Yankees presented Jim with a pickup truck, a television set, a set of luggage, a couple of shotguns, and a Hawaiian vacation. Twenty years later, Yankee fans rose slowly to their feet, silently remembered Jim, and then gave him a rousing ovation.

Jimmy would have loved the scene—not for himself, but for the cheering crowd, the full house, Yankee camaraderie, the clips of his past pitching mastery, veteran public address announcer Bob Sheppard's kind words, and of course, a Red Sox-Yankee match up.

But Jim was gone, a victim of Lou Gehrig's disease.

"A human shield had risen around the Hall of Fame pitcher," Michael Paterniti wrote, "that just kept sucking his body of its vibrancy and motion."

He lost his year-long struggle to amyotrophic lateral sclerosis at age 53. Yet his spirit was very much alive on that warm September afternoon at Yankee Stadium.

"You always like to go out a winner," Hunter said in 1979. "Nobody likes to go out a loser." 55,000 Yankee fans made sure he didn't.

The Guy Next Door

"Take away his exquisite right arm and his uncanny ability to make an opposing hitter feel good about going 0-for-4 against him," Murray Chass wrote, "and Jimmy Hunter could have been the next-door neighbor who came over occasionally to say 'hi' and maybe see if there was something he could do, like repair the item the man of the house couldn't make work."

Ask a fourth grader from Ms. Larson's Union Grove Elementary School in North Wilkesboro, N.C., who his hero is, and he'll say Jim "Catfish" Hunter. Kids around those parts understand the simple life of hunting, fishing, and playing baseball. Catfish Hunter did, too.

James Augustus Hunter was born in Hertford, North Carolina, a town of fewer than 2,200 people and "home to the world's largest s-shaped bridge."

He caught the pitching bug early, hurling for Hertford grammar school. Along with his three brothers, the Nixon clan (one of the Nixons, Billy, is the father of Red Sox right fielder Trot Nixon), and the neighborhood kids, he played ball all summer long. Hunter led Perquiman High School to the AA State Title as a junior and runner-up his senior year. He also was an All-Star football player and ran the 440 in track.

But he loved playing baseball best.

George Steinbrenner landed a huge free agent when he snagged Jim "Catfish" Hunter from the Oakland A's in 1974.

"If you don't want to play—go home," Jim said. "That's the way I always thought about playing baseball." Jim wanted to play.

He played for 15 major league seasons, compiling a won-loss record of 224-166, with an ERA of 3.24. During one five-year span from 1971-1975, he won over 20 games each season. He pitched in six World Series, with a record of 5-3 and an ERA of 3.29. He was voted to the All-Star team in eight seasons and won the Cy Young award in 1974, besting Ferguson Jenkins.

On December 31, 1974, Hunter signed with the New York Yankees, where he spent the next five years, as George Steinbrenner said, "Teaching a new generation of Yankees how to win."

Then at age 33, Jim called it quits and went back home to Hertford.

The Bigger the Game, the Better He Pitched

Kansas City Athletic scout and fellow North Carolinian Clyde Kluttz first noticed Jim's pitching abilities. Clyde, a journeyman major league catcher for nine years, understood pitchers. He also had a knack for discovering talent and thought Jim had those special intangibles needed for success.

"He rarely relied on just what he saw on the field," Jim later said. "No, with Clyde, a visit to the family preacher or a school principal told him as much or more than what he saw on the diamond."

Kluttz's intuition paid off. He made a phone call to his boss, and soon Charles O. Finley was making tracks to North Carolina. Hunter came out of the back roads of Hertford to meet him in 1964.

Finley liked what he saw and immediately signed him to a $75,000 bonus. He also hung the name "Catfish" on him—a name Hunter never liked.

"Leadfoot" might have been more appropriate. On a hunting excursion, Hunter's brother accidentally fired buckshot into Jim's right foot. Finley sent him to Mayo Clinic to remove several bone chips and 16 pellets. The injury caused him to sit out the 1964 season.

In 1965, at age 19, he began his career with an 8-8 slate, not bad for a pitcher who never wore a minor league uniform.

Three years later, the Athletics had moved to the Oakland Coliseum. On May 8, 1968, 22-year-old Jim Hunter pitched the first perfect game in the American League since 1922, when Charlie Robertson of the Chicago White Sox bested Detroit 2-0.

For six innings, it was a scoreless duel between Hunter and the Twins' Dave Boswell. In the seventh inning, Hunter delivered the first run himself with a bunt. The next inning he came through again, singling in two insurance runs.

He entered the ninth leading 4-0. He retired the first two batters easily—pinch hitter Johnny Roseboro on a ground out and catcher Bruce Look on a strikeout. Hunter had thrown 96 pitches and was within one out of perfection.

The Twins called on Rich Reese to pinch hit for relief pitcher Ron Perranoski. Reese ran the count to 3-2, and then it was foul ball after foul ball, after foul ball, after foul ball. On his 11th pitch, Reese finally struck out.

Hunter relied on an assortment of fastballs and sliders, throwing only one curve ball, three change-ups, and a whole bunch of foul balls. He had pinpoint control on all his pitches.

That night also marked the return of Joe Rudi from Vancouver. He made a tough catch on a sinking, slicing line drive. Sal Bando made another terrific play at third, stabbing Harmon Killebrew's hard grounder and throwing him out. Only five balls were hit out of the infield.

Too bad only 6,298 Oakland fans witnessed Hunter's masterpiece, but one of them was his boss. A jubilant Charlie Finley promised Catfish a $5,000 bonus. Hunter's father had doubts.

"Tell me all about that $5,000 when you get it," he said.

Emerging as a Star

Hunter didn't break the .500 barrier until 1970, and then he exploded. From 1971-74, he won 88 and lost only 35 games. His ERA was consistently below 3.00, as he became the ace of a great Oakland staff. The A's took three World Series, with Jimmy winning a third of the A's World Series victories during 1972-74 with a perfect 4-0 record.

"Cat could actually move the ball inch by inch. Control was his greatest asset," A's catcher Dave Duncan said. "You'd see a guy swinging at a ball one inch out of the strike zone. The next ball was two inches out. Then three. Boom. Boom. Boom... [V]ery few people have excellent control over all the strike zone—in, out, up, and down. Cat did."

In 3,449 career innings, he yielded only 954 walks. In 1974 he walked only 46 in 318 innings.

In October, 1974, the A's won their third consecutive World Series, and Jim won the Cy Young Award. Then he went to Finley, asking for the $50,000 tax-deferred annuity payment he had negotiated in lieu of half his salary. But Charlie O. faced a basic tax conundrum: if Hunter could defer it, then Finley couldn't deduct it. The payment was due August 1, 1974. It never came, and Jim called for binding arbitration.

Finley and Hunter went to arbitration on November 26, 1974. The panel consisted of one part baseball player association (Marvin Miller), one part owner lackey (John Gaherin), and the swing man, an honest broker named Peter Seitz.

Bowie Kuhn and Charlie Finley hoped for a slap on the wrist. Instead, Seitz used a hammer.

"You have to consider the magnitude of the breach," Seitz said. "Finley, for whatever reasons, withheld one-half of Hunter's compensation for a full year."

Kuhn and Finley were sunk. Jim became a free agent, and a bidding war broke out.

The Yankees Go Fishing

Twenty-two teams wanted a piece of the Cat. (Only Detroit and Baltimore demurred.) The bidding occurred in the law offices of Cherry, Cherry, Flythe, and Evans in Ahoskie, North Carolina. Senior partner J. Carlton Cherry was the one-time bus driver for Hunter's Ahoskie American Legion Post 102 team. Besides being an excellent navigator, he was a formidable deal maker.

For two weeks, teams haggled, hassled, wrangled, bargained, and negotiated over terms, money, and perks. The cash war finally boiled down to the New York Yankees vs. the San Diego Padres, a duel between George "Top Gun" Steinbrenner and Ray "Hold the Mayo" Kroc.

The Yankees held the ace in the hole—Clyde Kluttz. Hunter's trusted friend had jumped ship from the Kansas City scouting department to become field director of player development for the Yankees. Hunter gave his price to Kluttz, who brought the news to Steinbrenner.

"Well," Kluttz told Hunter, a smile on his face, "I don't know if they'll give it to you, but let's go find out."

Jim was looking for $3,484,626 and guarantees. The Yankees wanted titles. Jim got his money and five years. The Yankees landed an ALCS championship and two World Series rings.

Hunter Does New York

"New York," Jim said in 1971, "still scares me." Four years later, he was scaring New York Yankee opponents. In 1975, his first season with New York, Hunter went 23-14 with an ERA of 2.58. He led the league in innings pitched (328) and complete games (30) and was runner-up to Jim Palmer for the Cy Young Award.

The Athletics were left perplexed. "It's just like a trade," former teammate and friend Sal Bando lamented, "except we didn't get anything in return."

The next year Hunter helped the Yankees win their first American League pennant since 1966. He went 17-15 with a 3.53 ERA, pitching a workhorse load of 298 innings.

On September 16, 1976, Hunter notched his 200th win at the tender age of 31. (Only Cy Young, Christy Mathewson and Pete Alexander have hit the 200 mark before age 31.)

In the first game of the ALCS, he bested Kansas City Royals pitcher Larry Gura, 4-1, hurling a neat five-hitter. The Yanks went on to beat Kansas City in five games but lost the World Series to Cincinnati in four straight.

But 1976 was just a warmup. The Yanks won back-to-back World Series against the Dodgers in 1977 and 1978.

Due to arm problems, Jim tailed off in 1977 to a 9-9 mark. Thanks to a pair of doctors, Hunter managed a sensational comeback despite diabetes and arm problems in 1978.

During spring training, doctor Sheldon Nassberg diagnosed Jimmy with Type I diabetes. He treated Jim and told him how to control the disease through diet, exercise and insulin injections.

Hunter became an "A" student and, true to his character, became a spokesman for the American Diabetes Association.

In June, a second doctor, doctor Maurice Cowen, successfully "manipulated" Hunter's right arm.

"While he was under general anesthesia, I manipulated his arm back into the cocking position—something I could never have done while he was awake," Cowen said. "It made this resounding noise—a big pop! Someone in the room said, 'Ah shit, we broke his arm.'

"We immediately took an X-ray, but I honestly didn't think I had broken it, because I hadn't used that much force. So I continued to stretch his arm back and forth."

Luckily, the good doctor was right. What they heard was a piece of ligament breaking off. Jim could now cock his arm. He ended the season with a 12-6 record. Trailing the Yankees by one game, the Red Sox needed a Yankee loss to force a playoff. On the final day, Hunter lost to the Indians 9-2, setting up that "cheap" Bucky Dent fly ball home run to left as the Yankees beat the Red Sox in a one-game playoff.

Hunter bounced back from that Red Sox loss and helped propel the Yankees to a World Series victory against the Los Angeles Dodgers. Catfish received credit (with a little help from Goose Gossage) for the final Game 6 win when they defeated the Dodgers 7-2.

Hunter Spits Out His Last Chaw

The Yankees had a disastrous 1979 season, falling from first place to fourth. It was also a tough year for Hunter. Besides going 2-9, within a three-month period he lost his good friend Clyde Kluttz, his father Abbott, and close teammate Thurman Munson. These deaths stung Jim.

"From that time on," Hunter said, "I've gotten down on my knees every night and thanked God for my life; not for what I've accomplished or who I am, but simply for being alive, for making it through another day happy and healthy."

At the end of his five-year contract, Hunter retired.

"I'll miss the guys, the feeling of belonging with a team," Hunter said. "But 15 years is enough. I want my kids to know me and I want to know them."

For close to 20 years, Jim worked his farm, hunted, fished, coached, and hosted an annual old timers baseball game in Hertford. Each spring, you could find him working with young pitchers at the Yankees complex in Tampa.

"An opportunity to teach and forget farming and fertilizer for six weeks," was Hunter's description of spring training.

He passed on pitching tidbits like this, from his "Pitch Like a Pro" pamphlet, co-written with Yankee pitching coach Sammy Ellis:

"Don't get discouraged. Play under competitive conditions whenever possible and never get too high or too low mentally before or after a game. Pitch every game as if it is your last. It could be.

"Life is filled with suffering, but it also contains many wonders."

In September of 1998, Hunter, like another great Yankee, Lou Gehrig, was diagnosed with ALS.

"ALS is not a rare disease, but it is uncommonly brutal," Mark Reiman said. "In the United States alone, someone dies from ALS and another is newly diagnosed every 90 minutes—more than 15 people per day. While our minds remain sharp and active, we become buried alive inside a useless shell of a body."

Mark ought to know. He's the co-founder, publisher, and editor-in-chief of *Incredible People Magazine*. He was diagnosed with ALS in 1991. To create awareness of ALS and to share a message of hope and determination, he became the first person to sing a national anthem in every major league park in one season (1998). Reiman was selected to the Board of Directors of the Catfish Hunter ALS Foundation.

Like Mark, Catfish learned to cope with the disease

"I think it was his never-give-up competitive spirit that helped Catfish endure," Reiman said. "As long as he was breathing he would do whatever he could to win, which in this case meant helping find a cure for ALS and helping those who have ALS."

That's why the Hunter Foundation is in business today.

"Since the beginning of time, history has never been about what happens to us, because bad stuff happens to everyone." Reiman said. "Instead, it's about how we respond to those circumstances. Each morning I wake up thankful to have one more day to make a difference in the world through what I can do, even if that is just love my friends and family. I believe with all my heart and soul that our greatest value on this earth has very little to do with arms and legs and has everything to do with a positive attitude and a loving spirit."

Jim Hunter would agree.

His legacy as a pitcher was built in Kansas City, Oakland, New York, Hertford, North Carolina and Cooperstown, N.Y. His legacy as a person was formed from the lessons learned on the farm and from his family.

"The last time we saw him was in Florida during spring training," Yankee coach and former teammate Chris Chambliss said. "It was comforting to see his sense of humor was still there. That's what made him special. Catfish was upbeat about everything."

Indeed, Catfish was a wonder. A wonderful husband. A wonderful father. A wonderful friend. A wonderful teammate.

And, oh yeah, a wonderful pitcher.

People wishing to remember Jim Hunter can send donations to: P.O. Box 47, Hertford, NC, 27944. Make checks out to Jim "Catfish" Hunter ALS Foundation.

CHAPTER 19

Baseball's New Iron Man Restores the Game's Glory

Cal Ripken Jr.

"He is the man. He is the man."

—Sammy Sosa

"I'm honored to be on the same field as him."

—Alex Rodriquez

Full name: Calvin Edwin Ripken Jr.
Nicknames: "Cal," "Junior"
Position: Third base, Shortstop
Career: Baltimore Orioles, 1981-2001
Career batting average: .276

Career highlights:

• Led the league in extra base hits in 1983 (76) and 1991 (85).

• Led the league in runs (121), hits (211), doubles (47), and at bats (663) in 1983.

• Led the league in total bases in 1991 with 368.

• Selected as an All-Star 19 consecutive years beginning in 1983.

• Named Rookie of the Year in 1982.

• Earned AL MVP in 1983 and 1991.

- Selected as All-Star MVP in 1991 and 2001.
- Won the AL Golden Glove Award in 1991 and 1992.
- Eligible for the Hall of Fame in 2006.

Major League career records:

- Most consecutive games played: 2,632.

"He played in 2,130 consecutive games, not counting World Series contests," Jack Sher wrote of Lou Gehrig in the October, 1948 issue of *Sport Magazine*, "and there isn't a ballplayer alive who won't tell you that this record will stand forever."

Don't blame Sher for being a rotten prophet. Everybody thought Lou's record for endurance would stand forever.

Of course, when Sher wrote those words, Cal Ripken Jr. hadn't been born yet. When he was, he was born to be a baseball player.

Once he started playing, he just didn't want to quit. Cal never took a "mental health" day. He never took a day off because he had a cold or the flu. He didn't sit out for a twisted ankle or a badly sprained knee, didn't even give in to back spasms or a broken nose.

Cal showed up for work every day, no matter what. And when he did, he had to hit 95 mph fastballs and field shots deep in the hole at shortstop and gun runners out at first. He did it day after day, game after game, with uncommon excellence.

When he finally took a breather, he hadn't just broken Gehrig's unbreakable record. He'd shattered it, playing 2,632 games in a row, 502 more than the legendary Iron Horse.

Then he gracefully took himself out of the lineup, so his manager wouldn't have to make the decision to end the most amazing expression of durability and dedication in baseball history.

In the process, he lifted the game out of its morass of labor disputes and allegations of drug use and reaffirmed that a ballplayer could be a model of good citizenship on and off the field.

All those seasons when he never called in sick, he wasn't doing it to set a record.

"[Y]ou are challenged by the game of baseball to do your very best day in and day out," he said. "And that's all that I've ever tried to do."

Cal didn't just show up and put in his innings. He performed at a consistent level of excellence, in the field and at bat, for two decades, all of it spent with the team he always wanted to play for, the Baltimore Orioles.

His numbers are staggering: 3,001 games, 3,184 hits, 1,647 runs, 432 home runs, 1,695 RBIs.

He hit 353 of his homers as a shortstop. When he hit one on July 15, 1993, off Scott Erickson, he passed Ernie Banks as the game's greatest slugging shortstop. Alex Rodriguez ended the 2003 season only a few home runs short of Ripken's record.

He set the standard in the field, too. He led the league in assists in 1983 and set an American League record for assists by a shortstop with 583 in 1984. He led the league again in '86 and '87, led in putouts in 1985, and in double plays in 1983 and 1985 (while also leading all major league shortstops in home runs, RBIs and slugging percentage each year from '83-'86). In 1990 he posted the highest single-season fielding percentage ever for a shortstop, .996.

During the streak that will forever be associated with his name, he played with three dozen different second basemen. While he was the O's one and only shortstop, the other teams in the bigs fielded 337 of them.

His streak was longer than the next 15 active players' streaks combined.

"Stubbornness is usually considered a negative," he said, "but I think that trait has been a positive for me."

The Beginning of the Streak

On May 30, 1982, Cal Ripken Jr. broke into the Baltimore Orioles' starting lineup. He played third base that day and batted eighth against the Toronto Blue Jays.

Sixteen and a half years later, on September 20, 1998, he pulled himself out of the starting lineup in the Orioles' final home game of the season, against the Yankees.

In between, he didn't miss a game—not one—for 2,632 games.

A few days after Cal started playing regularly, he started another, less noted streak. He played the full nine innings on June 5 against the Twins and didn't miss a play for 8,243 consecutive innings spanning 904 games between the years 1982-1987. Not one inning! And that doesn't even count the 82 postseason innings he played in 1983.

Now that it's over, the number seems as unattainable as a mountain peak on Mars. Cal played hurt. He played sick. He played when he wasn't hitting. He played when the game "didn't mean anything"—as if there could ever be a meaningless baseball game to Cal Ripken. And he played brilliantly at the game he was born to play.

Born in Havre de Grace, Maryland, on August 24, 1960, Cal grew up in nearby Aberdeen. The Orioles were always his team.

Through sickness, injury, and slumps, Cal showed up for work 2,632 days in a row, playing with brilliance and grace all the while.

His father was a ballplayer, and so were his uncles, Oliver and Bill. One day Cal Sr. brought an old pitching machine home from the ballpark, and Jr. began working on his swing. He hung out with Dad at the ballpark, and by age 16, they were letting him shag fly balls during Orioles pregame workouts. Once in a while, they even let him suit up and catch batting practice, which his dad threw.

He earned All-State honors at Aberdeen High School, graduating in 1978. The Orioles drafted him as a pitcher in the second round (48th pick overall) of the June free agent draft, and he broke in with Charlotte, North Carolina of the AA Southern League. He made the big club as a third baseman in 1982, at the age of 21.

After 27 games at third base, his manager, Earl Weaver, moved him over to shortstop in a game against Cleveland and left him there, despite the disapproval of the grandstand managers, who said that, at six foot four and 220 pounds, Cal was too big to be a shortstop.

He finished his rookie season with a solid .264 average, 28 homers and 93 RBIs, good enough for Rookie of the Year honors. Nobody was keeping track yet, of course, but the streak stood at 118 games.

The sophomore jinx stood no chance against him. In 1983, Cal hit .318 with 27 homers and 102 RBIs, and led the league in hits (211), doubles (47), and runs (121). He became the first player ever to be Rookie of the Year and Most Valuable Player in consecutive seasons.

He capped the season by making the final putout in the '83 World Series, helping the O's defeat the Phils in five games for their first world championship since 1970.

Some Near Misses
on the Way to Immortality

In game 444 of the streak, on April 10, 1985, Cal sprained his left ankle during a pickoff play in the third inning against the Texas Rangers. He didn't even leave the game, and X-rays later detected no break.

The Orioles had an exhibition game at the United States Naval Academy in nearby Annapolis the next day, and Cal sat the game out. But he was back in the lineup the next day against Toronto, keeping the streak alive. He ended another fine season (.282 average, 26 home runs, 110 RBI) with the streak at 603.

He played straight through in 1986, keeping both his game and inning streaks going, and for the fourth straight year led AL shortstops in home runs (25), RBIs (81) and runs (98) while batting .282.

On September 14, 1987, at Toronto's Exhibition Stadium, the Blue Jays bombed the Orioles with 10 home runs in an 18-3 rout. With the game far out of reach, the O's manager sent Ron Washington out to play shortstop in the bottom of the eighth inning, giving Cal his first inning off after 8,243 straight.

The manager who made the move was Cal's dad, Cal Ripken Sr.

"What the hell," Sr. explained after the game. "He couldn't have hit a 20-run homer."

From his new perspective in the dugout, Cal later admitted, "I didn't know what to do with myself...[I]t was the strangest feeling...I was lost. No doubt about it."

The senior Ripken excused his son early in several other games that season when the outcome was no longer in doubt.

Cal's brother Bill was playing second base for the O's, marking the first time in major league history that a father had managed two of his sons.

The next season Jr. endured a streak of another kind, an 0-29 batting drought in April, the longest of his career. But he kept playing and started hitting again. On June 25, 1988, at Boston's Fenway Park, the streak reached 1,000 games.

By playing in his 1,208th straight game the next year, Cal passed Steve Garvey for the third longest streak in history. The year after that he climbed past Everett Scott, who played for the Yankees and Red Sox from 1918-1925, with 1,308 games to claim second place behind Gehrig.

He hit only .250 that season, his lowest mark for a full season in his career, but he still led the team in home runs with 21, RBIs with 84, and runs with 78. He also went 95 games and 431 chances without an error, both records for a shortstop. He finished the 161 game season with only three errors in 681 chances.

Cal had a brilliant season in 1991, capturing his second MVP award. He hit .323 and drove in 114 runs; his 34 home runs were the most by a shortstop in 22 years. He also sparkled in the home run derby before the All-Star game that season, swatting 12 home runs in 22 swings. The next day, against the considerably tougher pitching of former teammate Dennis Martinez, Cal belted a three-run homer, earning game MVP honors.

He finished that stellar season having played in 1,573 straight games.

The following September 11, during game 1,713 of the streak, Cal twisted his right ankle legging out a double against Milwaukee. Typically, he stayed in the game and was back in the starting lineup the next day.

He had a down year at the plate, hitting just .251 with 14 homers, but was nearly flawless in the field as he posted that record .996 fielding percentage, a 95-game errorless streak, and just three errors all season.

June 6, 1993, Cal played in consecutive game 1,790 against Seattle in Baltimore, but a 20-minute fight almost cost him the streak. Cal's spikes caught in the infield grass during the melee, and he twisted his right knee badly. By game time the following day the knee was badly swollen and very painful. Cal went out to take infield as usual and assured his manager and teammates that he was good to go.

"It was the closest I've come to not playing," he admitted later.

A month later he hit his 278th home run as a shortstop, surpassing Hall of Famer Ernie Banks as the greatest slugging shortstop ever.

He sailed into the 1994 season, hitting his 300th career home run on May 24 against Milwaukee. The streak hit 2,000 on August 1 in Minneapolis, bringing Cal to within less than a season of Gehrig's mark.

And then, on August 12, 1994, the players walked out, contract negotiations with the owners having caved in two days before. After 34 days of on-again, off-again meetings, the owners voted 26-2 to cancel the rest of the season. Marge Schott of the Reds and Peter Angelos of the Orioles cast the only dissenting votes.

For the first time since 1903, there was no World Series.

Like everyone else, Cal packed up and went home, his streak on hold at 2,009 games, 21 shy of Gehrig.

Nothing was settled during the off season, and the owners talked about fielding teams of replacement players. If it came to that, would Cal honor the strike and scuttle the streak or keep his record alive by playing with the replacements?

There was never a question in his mind; he would join his teammates on the sidelines. The game would come ahead of individual honors. It always had for Cal.

Orioles owner Angelos stepped up, saying he wouldn't employ replacement players. "We have a special problem in Baltimore with the Cal Ripken streak," he explained, "an extraordinary accomplishment by Cal and one that we certainly will do everything to avoid harming."

Fortunately, the question was never called. The players settled, and on a belated opening day in Kansas City on April 26, the game and Cal's streak resumed.

Adulation for the Hometown Hero

On September 5 the fans jamming Baltimore's Camden Yards roared as Cal took the field. When the game became official in the bottom of the fifth inning, they stood and gave their hero a five-minute ovation. He had played in 2,130 consecutive games, tying Gehrig.

The next inning, Cal parked one into the leftfield seats, and the place went up for grabs. If anyone had needed a reminder, Cal had given it to them. He didn't just show up and put in his innings. He played!

The next day, before another packed house and a huge national television audience, Cal powered a home run in the fourth inning. But the big moment again came after the top half of the fifth. As the Angels took the field, the huge banners hanging from the warehouse wall beyond the rightfield fence rolled over like a giant odometer, the "2," the "1" and the "3" staying in place as the "0" was replaced by a "1."

Cal had done it.

He had reached the unreachable, broken the unbreakable, done the impossible.

For 22 minutes, the fans cheered, shouted, clapped, hugged, grinned and cried as Cal took a long victory lap around the park, reaching out to touch as many hands as he could reach.

"Tonight I want to make sure you know how I feel," Cal told the hushed fans as he stood at home plate. He told them he had always dreamed of being a big leaguer and playing for the Orioles. "For all of your support over the years," he said, "I want to thank you, the fans of Baltimore, from the bottom of my heart. This is the greatest place to play."

He thanked his father, who inspired him "with his commitment to the Oriole tradition and…taught me to play the right way…From the very beginning, my dad let me know how important it was to be there for your team and be counted on by your teammates."

He thanked his mom, "a unbelievable person…my inspiration."

He praised his teammate, Eddie Murray, "who showed me how to play this game, day in and day out," and thanked him for his example and his friendship.

He thanked his wife, Kelly, who enriched his life, he said, "with her friendship and with her love…for the advice, support, and joy you have brought to me, and for always being there. You, Rachel, and Ryan are my life."

Finally, he invoked the spirit of the great player whose record he had just surpassed.

"Tonight I stand here," he said, "overwhelmed, as my name is linked with the great and courageous Lou Gehrig. I'm truly humbled to have our names spoken in the same breath."

Their true link, he told his fans, wasn't the streak but "a common motivation—a love of the game of baseball, a passion for our team, and a desire to compete at the very highest level.

"I know that if Lou Gehrig is looking down on tonight's activities, he isn't concerned about someone playing one more consecutive game than he did. Instead, he's viewing tonight as just another example of what is good and right about the great American game."

"Whoever picks up a bat or puts on a glove," Cal continued, "from major league superstar to sandlot player, is challenged by the game of baseball to do their very best day in and day out.

"And that's all that I've ever tried to do," Cal concluded.

With his incredible accomplishment and his inspired words that night, Cal helped restore faith in the game he loves so much and to heal the wounds inflicted by the rancorous strike of the past season.

What Do You Do for an Encore?

Then Cal did what Cal had always done; he kept right on playing baseball—every day.

He finished the season by playing in his 2,153rd straight game. He put up fair numbers at the plate, hitting .262 and driving in 88 runs, and led all A.L. shortstops with a .989 fielding percentage and 100 double plays.

Sports Illustrated and *The Sporting News* both named him Sportsman of the Year. Loads of other honors followed.

Even so, Oriole manager Davy Johnson moved Cal to third base the next season, ending his streak of consecutive starts at shortstop at 2,216 games. But The Streak went on.

Cal sustained a bizarre injury at the All-Star game that year, his 13th straight as a starter. During the pregame photo shoot, White Sox pitcher Roberto Hernandez lost his balance and, swinging his arms out, belted Cal, breaking his nose.

Cal had the nose reset, started the game, and played into the seventh inning.

That season Cal enjoyed his first career three-homer game, which included a grand slam. Brother Bill hit a homer in the same inning as one of Cal's shots. The next day, Cal hit number 334 to move past Eddie Murray into first place on the Orioles' all-time list. He finished the season at .278 with 26 home runs and 102 RBIs and broke another Gehrig endurance record, playing in all of his team's games for the 14th straight year, his 16th season with the O's.

In 1997 back spasms almost forced Cal out of the lineup in Anaheim, but he played through the pain, as he had always done. He moved over to third base for good that season and helped lead the Orioles to the American League East flag. He hit .348 in a losing play-off series with Cleveland and hit his first postseason home run.

He finished that season with 2,478 consecutive games. Since breaking Gehrig's record, he had played in 346 straight games, which by itself was the second longest streak among active players, behind Jeff Bagwell's 351.

Cal's autobiography, *The Only Way I Know*, came out that year. On June 3, he signed 2,200 copies for fans, who kept him at the park until 3:00 a.m.

The next night he hit a home run against the Yankees.

The End of the Streak and the Beginning of the Rest of His Life

Before the final home game of the 1998 season, Cal approached Orioles manager Ray Miller shortly before game time and quietly told him he would sit out that night.

There was no announcement. Cal didn't want any fuss. Ryan Minor simply trotted out to third base to start the game. After the first out, the visiting Yankees figured out what was going on. The players stood at the top of the dugout steps and gave Cal a standing ovation, and the Camden Yards fans quickly followed suit.

Fifty-three outs later, The Streak was over at 2,632 games. For the first time since May 30, 1982, Cal Ripken Jr. had missed a game.

One of Cal's managers, Earl Weaver, had earlier put The Streak in perspective.

"It's inconceivable that anyone could play shortstop, third base, or even center [field] in so many games," Weaver said. "It's just something that can't happen. You can't play 2,000 big-league games in a row the way he has."

Cal had done the seemingly impossible.

"To me," he wrote in *Count Me In*, his baseball book for children, "the game wasn't about breaking a record, because I never set out to top Gehrig's mark. It just happened. It was really about playing the game I love the only way I know how—trying my best every day."

Less than two weeks before the opening of the 1999 season, Cal Ripken Sr. died of lung cancer, and Cal Jr. mourned. On the field, back problems left him unable to swing a bat or bend to field a grounder without severe pain. In April he went on the disabled list for the first time in his life.

It appeared that the Iron Man might at last be finished. But you just never want to count this guy out. When he reentered the lineup, he went on a tear, finishing with a career-high .340 batting average and hitting a home run every 18.4 at bats, his best ever. On June 13 in Atlanta, he had the first six-hit game in Oriole history, including two home runs and 13 total bases. In early September he hit his 400th career home run, becoming only the 20th player in history to reach that plateau.

On April 15, 2000, Cal went three for five against the Twins, becoming the 24th player in history to reach 3,000 hits (and only the seventh to combine them with 400 home runs).

He had done it all.

On June 19, 2001, two months shy of his 41st birthday, Cal made a simple, inevitable, shocking announcement: "I'm retiring, and I'm not going to play baseball anymore."

He said he wanted to be with his family and to work with youth in baseball. The current season would be his last.

The announcement came on the 98th anniversary of Lou Gehrig's birth.

"I don't see this as an ending so much," he said. "I'm not stopping something. I'm just moving on. The reality is that players can't play forever."

He had us fooled.

"I have a big interest in teaching baseball, youth initiatives, creating a fun environment, promoting baseball at the…grassroots level," he said. "Baseball has afforded me the experience and the opportunity. Now maybe I have a platform to make a significant difference."

As if he hadn't already.

"I accomplished what my skills, ability and determination allowed me to," he said.

He got three hits on Cal Ripken Jr. Day, hit a home run and won the MVP in the All-Star game, and became the seventh player to play in 3,000 big-league games.

"So many good things have happened to me in the game of baseball," he said. "When I do allow myself a chance to think about it, it's almost like a storybook career. You feel so blessed to have been able to compete this long."

He could remember specific hits all the way back to high school, he told an interviewer, "but my wife says I can't remember what day the garbage goes out."

Cal Produces Off the Field, Too

While the rest of the world focused on The Streak, Cal had been preparing all along for the day he would hang up his spikes. He and wife, Kelly, had long supported adult literacy through the Baltimore Reads program, and in 1992 they established a foundation to expand their charitable and personal giving. His "Because We Care" program supplied Orioles tickets to kids and adults who would otherwise never get to see a game. He also donated millions of dollars to youth baseball programs.

He received the Bart Giamatti Caring Award and the Roberto Clemente Award in recognition of these and other contributions. For his work with youth baseball, the Babe Ruth League changed the name of its largest division from "Bambino" to "Cal Ripken Baseball."

In "retirement," Cal threw himself into facilitating more ways to enhance the game he loves and has devoted his life to. He bought the Utica Blue Sox of the New York-Penn League for $3 million, moved the club to his hometown of Aberdeen, and renamed it the Ironbirds.

With brother Bill, he created and manages Ripken Baseball, which oversees the Ironbirds and other projects. He put up $6 million of seed money to build a 110-acre baseball complex, the Aberdeen Project, with a 6,100-seat stadium for the Ironbirds and six youth stadiums modeled after famous major league parks. His baseball youth academy provides camps, clinics and tournaments for young players. The first academy drew 850 campers and coaches for four weeks of baseball.

Ripken Baseball has created a two-hour instructional baseball CD-ROM, with Cal and Bill, along with former major leaguers Joe Orsulak and John Habyan, to teach baseball skills and The Ripken Way of playing the game.

Ripken Baseball created a consulting subsidiary, Ripken Management and Design, to help municipalities interested in obtaining a minor league franchise with all phases of planning and stadium development. They'll even help you design and build a "Ripken Signature Baseball Stadium" for your new team and then manage the maintenance for you.

Cal was the complete ballplayer on the field; he's the complete businessman off it.

Aberdeen's City Hall now houses a Ripken Museum, devoted to the lives of Cal Sr., Cal Jr., and Bill. Along with all the photos, bats, balls and jerseys, the museum hopes to embody the spirit of loyalty, dedication, and perseverance that defines "The Ripken Way."

A Baseball Star—and Much More

"Cal is a bridge, maybe the last bridge, back to the way the game was played," Joe Torre said. "Being a star is not enough. He showed us how to be more."

"Cal's meant a lot to baseball," pitcher Randy Johnson said. "He's been almost like the ambassador for the game."

"We are thrilled to play beside him," former teammate Brady Anderson said.

"Cal Ripken embodies all that the Orioles stand for, all that Baltimore stands for, and really, all that this country stands for in terms of his dedication and his work ethic," said Oriole owner Peter Angelos.

Slugger Mark McGwire summed it up in six words: "There will never be another Cal."

Even if some superman comes along one day to break Cal's mark, there will truly never be another Cal Ripken Jr., just as there's never been another Lou Gehrig. Like the Iron Horse before him, Cal contributed so much to the game. Beyond baseball, he provides an example of what is best in humanity: courage, dedication, and loyalty.

CHAPTER 20

Praising God All the Way
Dave Dravecky

"Today we're going to witness a miracle."
—Roger Craig, manager of the Giants, August 10, 1989

Full name: David Francis Dravecky
Position: Left-handed pitcher
Career: San Diego Padres, 1982-87; San Francisco Giants, 1987-89
Career W-L: 64-57
Career ERA: 3.13

Career highlights:

• Posted a 2.93 ERA in back-to-back seasons in 1984-85.

• Won a career-best 14 games in 1983.

• Selected as an All-Star in 1983.

In September, every game counts, pennant races heat up, and daily standings become front-page news.

For Bay Area fans, September 1987 was pure delight. Their Giants were on fire, going 17-8 in the final month and clinching the west title for the first time in 16 years. Since July 4, San Francisco had torn up the league, winning at a .614 clip (51-32).

Newly acquired Giants Dave Dravecky and Kevin Mitchell led the second-half charge. In 18 starts for the Giants, Dravecky went 7-5 with a 3.20 ERA. Mitchell chipped in with 15 homers, a .306 batting average and a slugging percentage of .530, and the Giants finished the year at 90-72, earning a dance with the Cardinals for the pennant.

September was also when Dravecky first felt the lump.

"Running my hand along my left arm, I found a firm, round shape under the size of a quarter," Dravecky says. "It didn't hurt. It didn't show. And I paid it little attention."

He was too busy living his dream.

Chasing the Dream

As a kid, Dave's heroes were Sandy Koufax and Vida Blue.

"They were incredible athletes—I watched them pitch, and I loved them," Dave said. "I dreamt of being a left-handed flame-thrower just like them."

Dravecky was a southpaw like Sandy, but he didn't throw heat.

"I am what is called a finesse pitcher," he said. "I do not have over-powering stuff. My fastball rarely reaches 90 miles per hour, and my slider doesn't break a foot. I get outs by surprising batters, by keeping them off balance, and by putting the ball within an inch or two of where I intend it."

By age 26, Dave was not only fooling batters but also grabbing the attention of San Diego management. The Padres called him up from Hawaii of Pacific Coast League in June of 1982, and he responded by going 5-3, with an ERA of 2.57.

The next season, he was named to the 50th All-Star game, held at Comiskey Park in Chicago. There, Dravecky's star shone brightly for the senior circuit. Although the American Leaguers shellacked the National, 13-3, Dave pitched two innings of shutout baseball, retiring Gary Ward, Rod Carew, Robin Yount, Fred Lynn, George Brett and Lance Parrish. Jim Rice was the only batter to reach first when he singled.

His comeback from cancer was miraculous, and Dave was quick to credit his faith in God. When cancer finally ended his career and took his left arm, Dave figured that God had something else he wanted him to do: the Dave Dravecky Foundation of Hope.

Dave finished the season at 9-8 with eight saves and an ERA of 2.93.

Sports Illustrated named him to its 1985 "Team of your Dream" line-up.

"He pitched in 50 games last year, starting 14," Steve Wulf wrote. "He was indispensable to the Padres, who might have given the Tigers a better series had Dravecky gotten one of the starts."

Indeed, his postseason record was sparkling.

In 1985, after losing the first two games to the Cubs, San Diego rallied to beat Chicago in five games. Dravecky relieved in three games, giving up only two hits in six innings. He continued his mastery against the Tigers with four and two-thirds innings of scoreless pitching.

His postseason ERA against Chicago and Detroit was 0.00.

Two years later, Dave put up nine more zeroes, bringing his scoreless postseason record to 19 and two-thirds innings when he two-hit the St. Louis Cardinals in Game 2 of the 1987 NLCS.

By this time though, he was wearing the Giants' orange and black. On July 4, 1987, the Padres and Giants lit up a firecracker deal. Seven players traded uniforms. San Diego sent pitchers Dravecky and Craig Lefferts, along with outfielder Kevin Mitchell, to San Francisco for third baseman Chris Brown and a trio of pitchers—Keith Comstock, Mark Davis, and Mark Grant.

After his two-hit gem against the Cards' John Tudor in Game 2, Dravecky and Tudor faced off again in Game 6.

"My pitching that night was better than in my first playoff game," Dravecky said. "I didn't walk a man, and I struck out eight in six innings. The damage was all done by one of those little things."

Little, but towering. The lights at St. Louis's Busch Stadium did him in.

"[Candy] Maldonado saw the glare of an extra-terrestrial spaceship or the lights above third base in the second inning," George Vecsey wrote. "He spotted Tony Pena's fly to right field but then lost it. He went into a defensive slide on the wet turf, and the ball ticked off him for a triple."

Jose Oquendo hit a sacrifice fly to right field, with Pena scoring the only run of the game, as Dave lost a heartbreaker, 1-0.

Golden Gaters' hearts broke too, when suddenly, Giants bats went dead. The next night, the Cards' Danny Cox shut down Roger Craig's squad, 6-0. The Giants, who had been averaging 4.6 runs in the first five games, couldn't produce a single run.

Shattering the Dream

That lump in Dave Dravecky's left arm just wouldn't go away. In January 1988, a Magnetic Resonance Imaging test revealed torn muscle fiber and scarring. Doctors described the lump as an "organized hemorrhage hematoma." The prognosis was inconclusive—no abnormalities, keep an eye on it, and make sure it doesn't misbehave.

His fellow pitcher and good friend Atlee Hammaker suggested a second opinion. Dave said no. He was full of optimism.

"You know something, baby?" Dave told his wife, Janice. "I think 1988 is going to be my year."

It wasn't.

Dave began the season where he left off in the playoffs, besting Fernando Valenzuela and the Dodgers, 5-1, with an Opening Day three-hitter. But by June he was on the disabled list with a sore shoulder. He underwent arthroscopic surgery to repair a frayed tendon and remove scar tissue.

The pain persisted. He failed his rehab assignment with the Giant's Class AAA Phoenix affiliate and was done for the season.

And the lump wouldn't go away.

"It stood out on the side of my arm like half a golf ball, Dravecky says. "And nearly as hard as one, too."

Second Opinion

One year from the day Dave noticed the lump, Doctors reexamined his arm. This time the MRI showed a "soft tissue mass on the end of the deltoid muscle."

A biopsy was next. The nightmare followed. Dave's lump was a tumor, of the angry "desmoid" variety—not life threatening, but to anyone who pitches for a living, career ending.

Dr. Muschler, Dave's orthopedic surgeon, told him that after surgery he would never pitch again.

"If I never play again, Doc, I'll know that God has someplace else he wants me,"

Dravecky said. "But I'll tell you something else. I believe in a God who can do miracles."

The seven-hour surgery was painfully invasive. Removing the cancer "was a little like prying a thick layer of paraffin off a tin can," Dravecky said.

He lost most of the function of his deltoid muscle but none of his faith. He faced months of grueling rehabilitation, but with amazing tenacity and determination, he defied the doctor's predictions.

"I was enough of a realist to know that the odds were against my coming back," Dave said. "I knew I might not make it. My part, I believed, was to do everything possible, to try with all my might. Then, if I couldn't pitch, God would have other, better things for me to do."

Reclaiming the Dream

Almost three months after surgery, Dave was given a green light to throw—not a baseball—but a football. But Dr. Muschler was still apprehensive about Dave's humerus bone. To destroy the cancer cells, Muschler had frozen the bone during what is known as cryosurgery, making the bone more fragile.

"If we went too quickly, the area of dead bone might crack before the rest of the bone had grown strong enough to take over," Dravecky said. "The whole bone might crack."

He was willing to take the risk, and by early July, he was ready to pitch his first simulated game. By the end of the month, he had pitched two complete games for the Class A San Jose Giants. On August 4 he was elevated to the Class AAA Phoenix Firebirds.

With a sellout crowd looking on, he seven-hit Tucson, eking out a 3-2 win. He was now ready for his second major league debut.

A Dozen Standing O's

His first start had came on August 8, 1982, with the San Diego Padres. He'd gone six innings, giving up only four hits and allowing only a single run to the Cincinnati Reds.

Now, seven years later, God was giving him another shot at the Reds.

When Dave defeated the Reds in 1982, Pete Rose had already left Cincinnati for Philadelphia. On August 10, 1989, Charlie Hustle was back in uniform, this time managing the Reds.

"He's back, and it's great for him," Rose said. "I hope he loses."

But a million others were pulling for Dave. When he took the mound at Candlestick, his mere presence made a huge impact, as big as Dave's heart and soul.

"We want to believe in miracles," Ira Berkow wrote. "That is why the comeback of Dave Dravecky of the San Francisco Giants was so dramatic, so inspiring, and why it received so much attention across the nation."

Dave didn't disappoint the 34,810 fans. After seven innings, he had given up only a double by left fielder Joel Youngblood.

"Roger Craig said later that in all the decades he'd played and coached," Dave recalled, "he'd never seen so much emotion at a game. It was half revival, half baseball game."

Dave began to lose steam in the eight inning. He gave up three runs to make it a tight 4-3 ball game, but he got through the inning, with ace closer Steve Bedrosian warming up behind him. "Bedrock" came on in the ninth, but not before fans had given Dave his 12th standing ovation of the day. Bedrosian retired the side in order and handed Dave the victory. Dave handed it to Jesus.

"I want to give praise and glory to Jesus Christ for allowing me the opportunity to come back and play again," he said.

A Taste of Honey

Dave's next start was on the road in Montreal.

"I was looking for a chance to win my second game of the season," Dravecky said. "I was back to normal, and this was a normal game. That's the way I wanted it."

Unlike his outing in San Francisco, the atmosphere in Montreal was much more subdued. Once again, Dave was putting up zeroes and Matt Williams was driving in the runs. Entering the bottom of the sixth, the Giants were ahead 3-0.

The Expos' Damasco Garcia opened the inning with a homer. Dravecky's next pitch hit Andres Galarraga. Tim Raines came strolling to the plate. Dave checked Galarraga at first, then delivered a fastball.

"I heard a loud popping noise," he said. "The sound was audible all over the field. It sounded as though someone has snapped a heavy tree branch."

The ball sailed wildly. Fans watched in horror as Dravecky lay on the mound, face up, writhing in pain.

He was sent to Queen Elizabeth Hospital, where X-rays showed that the "snap" was a fracture adjacent to where his cancer had been removed.

Dr. Muschler doubted the break would end Dave's career. "He's already proven his shoulder, without the deltoid muscle, is capable of performing at that level," he said. "This fracture isn't going to change his ability."

Muschler was wrong. Dave would never pitch again.

His comeback had lasted only five days, but Dave climbed the mountain. He never won a Cy Young Award, reached the 3,000 strikeouts plateau, or threw a no-hitter, yet he managed to inspire thousands of people with his hard work, determination, and faith in God.

"I still marvel at how he accepted the frustration, the pain, the disappointment," Vin Scully said, "and put it all in the right perspective."

Dave officially retired from baseball in November, 1989. From the mountain, he was about to sink into the valley.

Hitting the Skids

The lump just wouldn't go away, not until doctors finally had to amputate the arm in June of 1991.

Struggling with cancer and disability put a tremendous strain on Dave and Jan's relationship. Despair and grief welled up. Depression bore down on their marriage and their faith.

"For the first time in [Jan's] life, God didn't make sense," Cynthia Norman wrote. "'After all,' Jan questioned, 'How could a loving God allow so much suffering?' Pain and confusion left her angry with God. Accusations of hidden sin and inadequate faith only intensified her feelings of helplessness and guilt."

In her book, *Let's Roll*, Lisa Beamer wrote about the tragic death of her husband on September 11, 2001: "In those days following the crash, this truth became even more real to me. God knows exactly what we need, when we need it."

It took time, but the answers came for the Draveckys, in the form of a doctor, a psychologist, a friend, and a teammate. Doctor McGowen, Doctor Townsend, Sealy Yates (Jan's friend), and Atlee Hammaker showed up bringing their gifts.

Slowly, the Draveckys emerged from the darkness. Dave said:

"I used to see everything in black and white; now I see the shades of gray in between. I used to be dogmatic and think there was an answer to everything; now I realize a lot of things don't have answers. I used to think I could keep God in a box; now I believe his ways are too deep for any box to contain. I used to depend on myself; now I depend more on God; I used to be preoccupied with my own needs; now I am learning compassion for the needs of others; I used to view Christ's death on the cross intellectually; now I view it more emotionally. Through my own suffering, I have become more aware of this. And I love him more as a result."

Their awareness and love turned into the Dave Dravecky Foundation of Hope.

During the past 12 years, they have helped thousands whose lives have been devastated by cancer.

By serving others, the couple found peace.

Dave's pitching career came to a premature end when cancer struck. With God's help, he was able to muster the courage to fight back. We believe his comeback was a miracle.

CHAPTER 21

You Can't Keep a Good Man Down
Jim Eisenreich

"I had to stop being ashamed of myself. After awhile, you get tired of that."

—Jim Eisenreich

Full name: James Michael Eisenreich
Position: Outfield, first base, designated hitter
Career: Minnesota Twins, 1982-84; Kansas City Royals, 1987-92; Philadelphia Phillies, 1993-96; Florida Marlins, 1997-98; Los Angeles Dodgers, 1998
Career batting average: .290

Career highlights:

• Finished 10th in the league in triples (seven) and ninth in the league in stolen bases (27) in 1989.

• Hit a career-best .361 in 1996.

He was an emerging star with a bad case of rookie stage fright. That's what folks figured.

But the uncontrollable verbal and physical tics that plagued him soon drove Jim Eisenreich off the baseball diamond. Jim has Tourette's Syndrome, a neurological disorder he has been able to control through medication, determination and courage.

After numerous comebacks and nearly three years out of professional baseball, Jim fought his way back to the majors, playing well enough to be named the Kansas City Royals' Player of the Year in 1989. Six years later, when he got his first chance to play every day, at age 36, he batted .316 for the Philadelphia Phillies. He was hitting .361 the next season when a foul tip broke his left foot.

A career .290 hitter with over 1,000 hits, Jim won't get into the Hall of Fame, but his guts on the field and his work off of it with kids who share his disease earn him a spot among baseball's greatest good guys.

A Promising Beginning

As a kid, Jim endured twitches and verbal outbursts, but doctors just figured he was hyperactive. Despite his mysterious behavior, he was able to pursue his passion for baseball.

The Minnesota Twins drafted Jim in the 16th round in 1980. After a short apprenticeship in the Midwest League, Jim vaulted all the way from A ball into the big leagues with the Twins in 1982. On April 30, while patrolling the outfield in the Metrodome, he collapsed with convulsions and had to leave the game. On the team's next road trip, the bleacher bums in Boston's Fenway Park taunted him. When his twitching became uncontrollable, Jim had to take himself out of the game. He was hospitalized five days later, on May 9.

Folks figured the pressures of being in the major leagues had gotten to him, but Jim knew there was something seriously wrong with him. Doctors eventually confirmed his instincts.

Jim had Tourette's.

After just 34 games, with Jim hitting .303 with 13 stolen bases, his rookie season was finished.

Twitching Sickness

There is a name for Jim's disease now, and we're certainly more enlightened about it than back when folks called for the exorcist or burned the sufferer as a witch. A documentary called *Twitch and Shout* helped bring Tourette's out in the open. We now know that Tourette's runs in families and that the symptoms usually begin in childhood. We know that boys are much more likely to get it than are girls and that Tourette's is often linked with obsessive-compulsive disorder. It's estimated that about three percent of children have it, although many with mild symptoms go undiagnosed.

But children with Tourette's are still teased and stigmatized, and the rare sufferers whose Tourette's includes coprolalia (spontaneous, uncontrollable swearing) are often ostracized.

A few brave and determined individuals have been able to succeed in the most unlikely of professions. The Tourette's honor roll includes an NBA basketball star and a disk jockey somehow able to control his verbal outbursts whenever the mike is open.

It also includes Jim Eisenreich.

Jim tried to come back for a second season with the Twins, but after only two games, he went to manager Billy Gardner and told him the Tourette's was giving him more than he could handle.

The following year was little better. But after just 12 games, humiliated by his condition and ridiculed by fans, he put himself on the voluntary retired list and went home to St. Cloud, Minnesota. His once-promising career was apparently over. He worked in an archery shop and played a lot of softball.

"I did dream about coming back," he said. "All I needed was to have enough confidence in myself."

One of Baseball's Great Comebacks

With medication and courage on his side, Jim was determined to make another run at the majors. On October 2, 1986, the Kansas City Royals gave him his chance, claiming him on wavers. In 1987 he hit a blistering .382 for KC's AA team in Memphis. The big club called him up for 44 games at the end of the season, using him primarily as a pinch hitter and DH. On July 2, he hit his first major league homer in five years to lead the Royals to a 10-3 victory over the club that had first signed him, the Twins.

WE WANT YOU!
TO BE A CHAMPION

Jim Eisenreich overcame Tourette's Syndrome and salvaged his major league career, becoming a star and winning a World Series championship with the '97 Marlins. Today, he helps kids who share his disease in fulfilling their dreams.

Jim Eisenreich, major league dropout, was now the Royals Player of the Year.

He platooned in the Royals' outfield for three more seasons, peaking in 1991 with a .301 average.

But Jim wanted to play every day. So he left the Royals as a free agent after the 1992 season and signed with the Phillies on January 19, 1993. The Phils figured to use him as a left-handed bat off the bench, but Jim also began coming in as a late-inning defensive replacement for Wes Chamberlain in right during the Phils' drive to the pennant in 1993. He hit .318, started all six games in the World Series, and drove in seven runs. Philadelphia sportswriters honored him as the year's "Most Courageous Athlete."

"Yeah, it is kind of surprising," Jim admitted to *USA TODAY*. "I pretty much expected to be a pinch-hitter who got an occasional start when somebody needed a rest or got injured. Then I started hitting, and guys did get hurt, and they found out I could still catch the ball."

He hit over .300 in each of his next three seasons for the Phils and got his chance to be their everyday rightfielder in 1995, at age 36. He responded by hitting .316. The next season he was hitting .361 through 113 games when an injury ended his best-ever season.

From the start of the 1993 season through 1995, he actually received more starts than any other Philly player.

Again a free agent, Jim signed a two-year contract with the Florida Marlins. He contributed to the Marlins' 1997 world championship season by hitting .280 and played outfield and first base. He capped the season by hitting a home run in the third game of the World Series against Cleveland.

After just a few games the following year, Jim was part of the Marlins' roster purge, going to Los Angeles with Bobby Bonilla, Gary Sheffield, Charles Johnson, and Manuel Barrios for Todd Zeile and Mike Piazza. He hit just .197 in limited service with the Dodgers and ended his 15-year career at the end of the season.

"My calling in life was not to be a superstar ballplayer," he told *Baseball Weekly* in 1995. "I have another job to do—to be a quality player, help my team win, and show kids who have Tourette's what they can accomplish."

Throughout his playing career, Jim invited kids with Tourette's to visit him in the dugout before and after games. He traveled all over the country, talking about the disease, taped a public service announcement, and played in charity golf and bowling tournaments. He also had a role in a video for kids called *Handling It Like a Winner*.

His success on the playing field serves as testimony and inspiration to those with Tourette's and teaches us all never to write off someone because of illness or handicap.

CHAPTER 22

Reluctant Role Model
Jim Abbott

"[T]hey told me Abbott was the All-American boy—almost too good to be true. But he's surprised me. He's better than that."
—Mark Marquess, Stanford University baseball coach
and Jim's coach for the 1988 Olympic team

"I've learned that it's not the disability that defines you...[I]t's how you deal with what the disability presents you with...I have never felt slighted."
—Jim Abbott

Full name: James Anthony Abbott
Nickname: "Jim"
Position: Left-handed pitcher
Career: California Angels, 1989-92 and 1995-96; New York Yankees, 1993-94; Chicago White Sox, 1995, 1998; Milwaukee Brewers, 1999
Career W-L: 87-108
Career ERA: 4.25

Career highlights:

• Threw a no-hitter.

• Placed third in Cy Young voting in 1991 after finishing fourth in the league in wins (18) and ERA (2.89) in 1991.

Jim Abbott once won 18 games in a season for the California Angels. Six years later, he lost 18 in a season for the same team. That averages out to a pretty ordinary 10-year career: 87 wins, 108 losses, and a 4.25 ERA.

But Jim threw a no-hitter, won an Olympic gold medal, and was the first baseball player ever awarded the Sullivan Award as the nation's outstanding amateur athlete. He leapt right from college into the big leagues, and he later accepted a demotion to the minors and worked his way back to the show. There's nothing average or ordinary about any of that.

And when you consider that he did it all with only one hand, he becomes extraordinary.

He'd rather you didn't consider that, though. He'd rather you just thought of him as a left-handed pitcher, not a one-handed one.

Jim was born on September 19, 1967, in Flint, Michigan, a strapping baby boy who grew to be big, strong, and athletic. Jim was perfect in every way except for the stump where his right hand should have been.

From an early age, this one-handed boy wanted to be a pitcher.

"I loved throwing a baseball," he said. "It is so important to find something in life you love."

When he was five, doctors fitted him with a hook to replace his right hand. He wore it for about a day and a half before ditching it.

Other kids taunted him, calling him "crab" and worse, but he didn't let that stop him from competing.

"I didn't grow up thinking about not having a right hand," he told *Time* magazine. "I just strove to be normal."

Nobody taught him how to catch and throw one-handed. "My dad and I did what was necessary to play catch," he said. "We didn't form the basis for a major league career. We just played catch."

His parents were very supportive, he said, simply by allowing him to try whatever he wanted to do. "I don't ever remember a concession to the fact that I had one hand," he added.

He spent hours bouncing a ball against a wall, whipping his glove off his stump and onto his left hand to field the rebound, then clamping the glove under his right arm, plucking the ball with his left hand, and firing the ball to the imaginary first baseman.

"Growing up, sports were my way of gaining acceptance," he said. "I guess somewhere I started thinking if I was good enough on the field, then maybe kids wouldn't think of me as different. Honestly, I hid behind sports."

He got so good at throwing and catching, so swift and so smooth transferring his glove, folks didn't notice he was doing it unless somebody pointed it out. That's the way he liked it.

He was the starting quarterback on his high school football team, leading them into the finals of the Michigan state championships.

The Toronto Blue Jays drafted him in the 36th round, but he chose to go to the University of Michigan on a baseball scholarship. There he compiled a fine 26-8 career record with a 3.03 ERA. He was named to Team USA in 1987 and carried the American flag in the opening ceremonies of the Pan-American Games at the Indianapolis Speedway, an experience he describes as "spine-tingling." Then he helped his team to a silver medal. The U.S. Baseball Federation gave him its Golden Spikes award as the best amateur player in the country.

The Sporting News named him the left-handed starting pitcher on its 1988 college All-America team, and he represented his country in the 1988 Olympics, pitching the U.S. to a gold medal with a complete-game 5-3 victory over Japan. First baseman Tino Martinez supplied all the muscle Jim needed with two home runs and four RBIs.

The California Angels drafted Jim in the first round of the amateur draft that year and brought him right up to the majors, a move some considered a publicity stunt. But he could throw serious heat, punctuated by a sharp-breaking curve and a nasty slider, the kind of stunts any team can use.

Before he could become a pro, Jim faced one more hurdle. He obviously couldn't hide the ball in his glove, as every other pitcher did, so a sharp-eyed hitter could have determined from his grip what pitch was coming.

"I do something where I kind of twirl the ball," Jim explained. "It's nothing more than guys do inside their glove."

But did Jim's twirl violate the rule against a pitcher "moving the ball to deceive a runner at first base"? The commissioner of the American League watched Jim pitch in spring training and cleared the move. After that, Jim said, "Nobody ever said a word about it."

He made his major league debut on April 8, 1989, lasting only four and two-thirds innings in a 7-0 loss to Seattle. But after a rocky start, Jim settled into the starting rotation, posting a 12-12 record and a 3.92 ERA.

He spent the next season in the starting rotation, too, going 10-14 with a 4.51 ERA.

Jim Abbott readily admits that wanting to be a pitcher is an illogical choice for a kid born without a right hand. But his major league no-hitter proves that folks with disabilities can not only survive, but flourish—even in professional sports.

Going Beyond "Normal"

Then in 1991, at age 23, Jim Abbott emerged as one of the best pitchers in baseball. In 34 starts that year, he went 18-11 with a fine 2.89 ERA.

He actually had a better ERA (2.77) and more complete games (seven) the following season, but the Angels scored only two and a half runs a game for him. His 7-15 record didn't fool the Yankees, though. They sent first baseman J.T. Snow and pitchers Russ Springer and Jerry Nielsen to Anaheim and brought Jim to the Big Apple to pitch on baseball's center stage.

He made 32 starts in 1993, going 11-14 with a 4.37 ERA. One of those starts, on September 4 against the Cleveland Indians, was especially memorable.

After the Tribe knocked him out in the third inning in Cleveland, the Yankees gave Jim an extra day's rest, throwing him against the Indians again when they got home to Yankee Stadium. Jim must have had that last game on his mind as he walked leadoff man Kenny Lofton. But Felix Fermin banged into a double play, and Jim retired the side without trouble.

"I remember it was a cloudy day," he recalled. "A day game, the kind of game I like to throw."

He surely must have liked what he was throwing this cloudy day. Things got quiet in the Yankee dugout as Jim mowed through the Indian order inning after inning. Earlier in the season, Jim had carried a no-hitter into the eighth inning against the White Sox, but Bo Jackson broke it up with a single. Nobody wanted to say anything that might jinx him this time.

Apparently nobody did. Jim walked four more batters but didn't let any of them get past first base, allowing only six balls to be hit out of the infield in cruising to the first no-hitter at Yankee Stadium since Dave Righetti did it 10 years prior.

Jim enjoyed one more season in pinstripes, posting a 9-8 record with a 4.55 mark, and then the Yankees traded him to the White Sox. He won six games for Chicago in 1995 before they sent him back to Anaheim. He notched an overall 11-8 record for the season, with a 3.70 ERA.

From the Top to the Bottom

In 1996 his fastball deserted him, followed quickly by his confidence. He absorbed beating after beating for Anaheim, losing 11 in a row. The Angels tried bringing him in from the bullpen, a first for him in his career, and when that didn't help, they sent him down to the minors to try to work out his mechanics.

"What it turned into was a...real odyssey," he says of his only experience with the long bus rides and cheap motels of the bush leagues. "I came across great people, saw a lot of different things, and it wasn't all bad." But, he admitted, "I don't know why to this day that I did it."

Whatever the reason, it didn't help. Jim finished the season 2-18 with an astronomical 7.48 ERA.

"It was tough," he admitted. "Really, there's no other way to put it. On the grand scale—obviously, we're playing Major League Baseball, making a lot of money—it certainly doesn't compare with some of the other things that people go through in life. But for me—I took it too hard. Maybe that was my personality. Maybe I didn't like being so vulnerable. You come out of it hopefully stronger."

He spent the summer wondering if his career was over. "Somewhere deep inside, I wasn't sure," he said.

He gamely went to spring training with the Angels in 1997, but they released him before opening day.

Jim spent a year out of baseball, he and wife Dana enjoying their new baby girl. He could have simply retired, having gone so far. But when the White Sox offered him a tryout in 1998, he grabbed the chance to pitch again.

The good news, he recalled, was getting the call in September to join the big club. The bad news? He would be facing his old team, the Yankees, the hottest team in baseball.

Jim beat the Yanks that day and went on to win four more starts without a loss.

He gave baseball one more go in 1999, signing with the Milwaukee Brewers as a free agent. This presented him with one more challenge. As a career American Leaguer, Jim had never had to face major league pitching. But the Brewers had recently switched to the National League. Without the DH, Jim Abbott would have to bat.

No problem. On June 15, in a 7-4 Brewer loss to the Cubs, Jim stroked his first major league hit. He had, after all, belted a triple off Rick Reuschel in Scottsdale during spring training in 1991.

He could pitch. He could hit. And he could field. Jim went through four of his 10 major league seasons without making an error and had a career .976 fielding percentage, with just nine errors.

It's Not What's Gone—but What's Given

"I really feel that, to have an effect, to be someone that can be pointed to as an example," Jim told a writer for his alumni news service, "is to be good" at what you do. He wanted to show, he said, "not only that you can survive—make it—but that you can flourish."

His playing days over, Jim has shared his life lessons with groups all over the country. He tells kids to find what they love to do in life and do it. "Baseball wasn't the most logical choice for someone with one hand," he admits, "but I loved it.

"When you fail," he counsels, "get back up and try again. Leave no room for excuse…Listen to that voice deep within you. It knows."

CHAPTER 23

A Long Way from Shining Shoes
Sammy Sosa

"Sometimes I want to cry a little bit, because only I know where I came from. Only I know what I've been through."

—Sammy Sosa

"Sosa is to Chicago what the queen's guards are to Buckingham Palace or Old Faithful is to Yellowstone."

—Tom Verducci

Full name: Samuel Peralta Sosa
Nicknames: "Sammy," "Slammin' Sammy"
Position: Outfield
Career: Texas Rangers, 1989; Chicago White Sox, 1989-91; Chicago
    Cubs, 1992-present
Career batting average (through 2003): .278

Career highlights:
- Led league in home runs in 2000 (50) and 2002 (49).
- Earned the RBI crown in 1998 with 158, and in 2001 with 160.
- Finished first in runs scored three times.
- Topped the league in extra base hits with 89 in 1999.
- Led the league in total bases three times, including a career-best 425 in 2001.
- Selected as an All-Star six times.
- Named NL MVP in 1998.

Who has hit the most home runs over a five-year period in the history of major league baseball?

Babe Ruth would certainly be a good guess. Over a five-year stretch starting in 1927 and ending in 1931, the Babe stroked 255 of them (while his running mate, Lou Gehrig, was ripping 196 batting right behind him).

But trivia buffs know the Babe's a poor second to Sammy Sosa.

Starting in 1998, when he raced Mark McGwire to break the single-season home run record, Sosa hit 293 home runs in five years. In that period, he hit 51 more than Barry Bonds. He also drove in more runs than anyone else in that stretch, his 710 RBIs putting him 39 ahead of runner-up Manny Ramirez.

That dizzying run left him with 499 home runs at the end of the 2002 season. He no doubt would have blasted through the 500 barrier that year, but an injury robbed him of nine games at the end of the season.

He had to wait all winter, but he didn't have to wait long once the 2003 season began. On April 4, during the seventh inning against the Cincinnati Reds, Sammy took a 1-2 fastball from Scott Sullivan into the right field bleachers at Great American Ball Park in Cincinnati.

With that swing, Sammy Sosa became the 18th major leaguer in history to reach the 500 home-run plateau and the first Latin American player to scale that height.

Along the way, he also might have set the record for coming the longest way to achieve stardom. His dad died when Sammy was only seven. At age 14, he quit school and took to the streets of San Pedro De Macoris to sell orange juice and offer "the best shoe shines in the Dominican Republic," earning pennies to help support his mother and six brothers and sisters.

"Dirt poor" would have been a step up.

He couldn't afford baseball equipment, so he did what the other kids in the neighborhood did, fashioning a glove out of a milk carton, a bat out of a tree branch, and a ball out of a taped-up sock.

When you want to play baseball, you find a way. His boyhood hero was Roberto Clemente, the first Latino to make it into the Hall of Fame.

Sammy didn't pick up a real baseball bat until he was 14 and began playing in various small leagues in Santo Domingo. Swinging that tree branch must have been good training; when Texas Ranger scouts Omar Minaya and Amado Dinzey saw him two years later, they signed him to a $3,500 bonus, despite noting in their report that he looked "malnourished."

Sammy went from shining shoes on the street of San Pedro de Macoris to slammin' baseballs over major league fences at a staggering pace. Baseball has been very, very good to him—and he's been great for baseball.

Sammy gave all but $200 of the bonus money to his family and treated himself to something he'd never had before—a used bicycle.

After a brief apprenticeship in the minors, Sammy skipped right over AAA ball and made his major league debut on June 17, 1989, at Yankee Stadium. He started the day in Tulsa, Oklahoma, raced to make a flight, and arrived at New York's LaGuardia Airport only two and a half hours before the first game of a scheduled doubleheader between his Texas Rangers and the legendary Yankees.

He took a taxi to the House that Ruth Built, pulled on jersey number 17, and went out to take batting practice against coach Tom House, the former Reds reliever who had caught Hank Aaron's 715th home run ball.

He hit House's first pitch out of the yard. So much for intimidation.

Sammy batted leadoff for the visiting Rangers that night and lined the first strike of the game from Yankee pitcher Andy Hawkins into left field for a clean base hit. In the sixth inning, he pulled a double down the third base line for his second major league hit.

In his sixth game in the bigs, he powered his first major league home run off Roger Clemens at Fenway Park. Three days later, he pounded out four hits in a game against Cleveland. After 60 at bats, the skinny kid from the Dominican Republic was batting .317 and had a home run off a future Hall of Famer.

He was confident. He was aggressive. But he wasn't ready. He slipped into a one-for-24 slump starting July 4, and by July 20 he was hitting just .238 in 84 at bats, and he still had just the one home run. Ranger general manager Tom Grieve sent him down to AAA Oklahoma City, and three days later, traded him to the White Sox, along with pitcher Wilson Alvarez and infielder Scott Fletcher, for Harold Baines and Fred Manrique.

Former Ranger owner George W. Bush drew a big laugh during the 2000 presidential campaign when he called the trade his biggest mistake as an adult. Lots of folks complained about the trade at the time, to be sure. They thought the White Sox had gotten robbed! White Sox catcher Carlton Fisk was especially vocal in his disgust.

"Harold and Freddy for one major league player," he said. "Harold Baines. Harold Baines. You know what I mean? Harold Baines."

The one major leaguer he was referring to wasn't Sosa. He was talking about Fletcher.

In 13 games at AAA Vancouver, Sammy hit a blazing .367 and, Fisk's poor opinion of him aside, the Sox called him up to the big club. Sammy caught up with his new team at the Metrodome in Minneapolis, put on uniform number 25, and rejoined the big leagues. He drew walks in his first two at-bats, something he rarely did in those days, singled his next two times up, and then, in the ninth inning, clobbered the ball six rows up in the left-field seats off reliever David West for his second big league home run.

Despite this strong beginning, Sammy still wasn't ready. He struggled in his three years with the Sox, averaging just .240 and nine home runs a season, along with a ton of strikeouts. He showed promise during the 1990 season, becoming the only American Leaguer that year to reach double digits in doubles, triples, home runs, and stolen bases, but he hit just .233 and struck out 150 times. He also made 13 errors.

The Sox sent Sammy back to the minors for a short stay and then traded him across town to the Cubs for George Bell in March of 1992. They even had to throw in pitcher Ken Patterson to sweeten the deal.

You can't really blame the Sox. The slender six-footer had never hit more than 15 home runs in a season at any level, and he had a disturbing habit of chasing low, outside breaking pitches out of the strike zone. Who could have known that he would become one of the greatest sluggers in the history of the game?

From Trade Bait to Star

Sammy was feeling the pressure when he got to Wrigley Field. He needed to support his family back home, and baseball was all he knew. He had to stick this time.

He made his debut with the Cubs on March 31, 1992, in a soggy spring training game against the Seattle Mariners at HoHoKam Park in Mesa, Arizona. Sammy was standing in centerfield when Harold Reynolds took off from first base, trying to steal second, and Cubs catcher Rick Wilkins errantly fired the ball into center. Sammy charged, scooped up the ball, and fired it somewhere in the vicinity of Camelback Mountain. Reynolds scored easily, and Sosa had an error the first time he touched the ball as a Cub.

That first year was pretty much a washout. He hit just .211 with one RBI over his first month, then fractured his right hand and left ankle in separate injuries, losing 95 games while recuperating from the injuries.

But the season wasn't a total loss. In his first game back after a Dennis Martinez pitch had broken a bone in his hand, Sammy batted lead-off and took Doug Drabek's first pitch out of the park. He got two more hits that night, but the fans were paying more attention to pitcher Greg Maddux, who was making his first start since announcing that he would be leaving the Cubs at the end of the year.

Sammy battled back to .260 by the end of the year, with eight home runs. The numbers weren't much, but something to try to build on.

Next season, playing full time, he had his first solid season, slamming 33 home runs and knocking in 93 runs. He also swiped 36 bases, becoming the first Cub ever to join the elite 30/30 club.

The *Chicago Tribune's* legendary baseball columnist, Jerome Holtzman, liked what he saw when Sammy reported for the 1994 season.

"At 25, he is developing into a superstar," Holtzman wrote. "Sosa seems to have matured, as if he suddenly realizes his potential."

He averaged over 35 home runs and 100 RBIs the next four seasons and delighted the crowd with his hustle, charging full speed out to right field at the beginning of each game, a huge grin on his face. Fans also loved the "Sosa hop." When he knew he'd hit one out, he jumped straight up before starting his charge around the bases. Some said he was showing up the pitcher, but the hop was just more evidence of Sammy's exuberance and the joy he takes in playing the game.

And then there was that gesture of his—touching his heart with the index and middle fingers of his right hand, then bringing the fingers to his lips and blowing kisses. As he does, he murmurs, "Para ti, Mami" ("For you, Mommy").

He hit .300 in 1994, renewed his membership in the 30/30 club in 1995, hit 40 home runs in 1996, and drove in 119 runs in 1995 and 1997. On May 16, 1996, he became the first Cub ever to hit two home runs in one inning. When a Mark Hutton pitch broke Sammy's wrist and forced him out of the lineup on August 20 that year, it snapped a string of 304 straight games played.

Sammy was a star, and in 1997 he signed a star's contract, four years, $42 million. This time he didn't buy a used bicycle; he bought a 60-foot yacht. And the kid who had grown up with six siblings in a two-room apartment bought his mother four houses.

Still, the Cubs were never contenders in any of those years, and after the 1997 season, Cub manager Jim Riggleman ripped Sosa for not being more of a team player.

From Star to Superstar

Sammy got off to a slow start in 1998, with just nine home runs through May 24. Meanwhile, St. Louis Cardinal slugger Mark McGwire was tearing up the league with 24 homers by the same date. Even so, an improved Cub team showed signs of being a contender, especially when young fireballer Kerry Wood took the mound.

One of Sosa's early-season home runs netted him another career record—a most strange one. When he belted career home run number 210 on April 15, he broke Bob Horner's major league record for most home runs without a grand slam from the start of a career. Slugging Sammy had still never cleared the bases with a blast.

Sammy had been tinkering with his swing, and this perhaps accounted for his slow start. New Cub coach Jeff Pentland had sent him videotapes to study over the winter, and Pentland and Cub Hall of Famer Billy Williams worked with Sammy all spring to get him to lower his hands, shorten his swing, and be more selective.

The work started to pay off on May 25, when Sammy cracked two home runs against Atlanta. Then he caught fire. Starting with those two home runs, he launched the greatest power barrage in the history of baseball, clubbing 21 long balls in the 30 days from May 25 through June 23. He hit 20 home runs in June alone, the most ever hit in a single month.

And one of those blasts erased the one small stigma on his home run record. Career homer 248, which came July 27 against the Diamondbacks, was Sammy's first grand salami, after 4,428 at-bats.

The next day he hit another one, his second grand slam in four at bats. He was the first Cub ever to hit grand slams in consecutive games and only the 18th big leaguer to accomplish the feat.

Sammy eventually caught up to McGwire in the home run race during 1998, and the two of them closed in on Roger Maris's single-season home run record of 61, set in 1961. On August 19, with McGwire watching from first base, Sammy hit number 48 off Kent Bottenfield, to pull ahead of McGwire for the first time all season. But Big Mac hit consecutive blasts later in the game to retake the lead.

As the duel drew international attention and reporters flocked to interview the two sluggers, the world discovered Sammy's exuberance and joy. He maintained that McGwire was "the man" and would be the one to set the record. When Big Mac drew criticism for using a controversial testosterone-boosting drug, Sammy drew laughs when he revealed that he, too, relied on a drug supplement—Flintstone vitamins. During a Labor Day weekend press conference, he made his oft-quoted assertion that "Baseball been berry, berry good to me."

Home run number 57 came on September 4 against Pittsburgh. With it, Sammy surpassed Hack Wilson's Cub single-season mark, set 68 years before.

On September 12 he became just the fourth player in big-league history to reach the 60 home run plateau when he went deep off Brewer Valerio de los Santos in a 15-12 Cub win.

Sammy was standing in right field on September 8 when Big Mac hit record-breaker number 62 off Steve Trachsel at Busch Stadium. Sammy ran in from the outfield to hug his friendly rival, who lifted him off his feet.

On September 13, with the Cubs battling the Mets and the Giants for the National League wildcard playoff spot, Sammy launched two mammoth Wrigley Field shots to tie McGwire at 62 as the Cubs edged the Milwaukee Brewers, 11-10. The crowd of 40,846 gave him a six-minute standing ovation and three curtain calls after the game winner. Sammy tapped his chest and blew kisses as tears streamed down his face.

"I've never been more emotional," he said later. "When I got 62, I have to say it was unbelievable...I couldn't believe what I was doing."

He wasn't done yet. When he came up with the bases loaded in the eighth inning of a tie game in San Diego on September 16, Padre fans stood and cheered him as if he were one of their own. Sammy promptly belted his third grand slam of the season and his career, and the fans called him back out of the dugout with a standing ovation.

A week later, against his "cousin" Brewers in Milwaukee, he hit numbers 64 and 65, tying Hank Greenberg's 1938 record of 11 multiple home-run games in a season. Two days later he hit number 66 in Houston. For the second time he was ahead of McGwire. For about 47 minutes, Sammy Sosa had hit more home runs in a season than any player in history. Then Big Mac struck again in St. Louis, and the race was again knotted.

McGwire hit four more homers over the last two games of the season to set the new major league standard of 70 home runs in a season, since eclipsed by Barry Bonds's 73.

But the Cubbies beat the Giants in a one-game playoff at Wrigley to claim the wildcard playoff spot, and Sammy was the NL MVP, capturing 30 of 32 possible first-place votes. He hit .308 and led the majors with 158 RBIs, 134 runs scored, and 414 total bases.

"It's a beautiful year," Sammy said.

From Superstar to Legend

He was no longer "just" a star. He was a superstar now, one of the game's elite. His 66 home runs were the most ever in a season by a Latin American player, and in his native Dominican Republic he was an idol—a living legend.

"Sosa has no idea what he is doing for our country," said countryman, pitcher Jose Rijo. "He has come a long way from a big struggle in his life."

Sammy was in Japan for a postseason goodwill tournament when Hurricane George struck the Dominican Republic, razing the island and leaving more than 100,000 without food or shelter.

Sammy stepped up, sending 30,000 pounds of rice, 30,000 pounds of beans, and barrels of pure water to his countrymen through the Red Cross. He helped fund the rebuilding of houses and launched the Sammy Sosa Charitable Foundation to further the education and health care of children in the United States and the Dominican Republic. The Foundation raised $700,000 for his country and helped several other Latin American countries with food and money in time of crisis.

So, what would Super Sosa do for an encore when the 1999 season began? After an uncharacteristically fast start in spring training, he started slamming home runs again, and this time McGwire was chasing him for the title.

On September 19, 1999, Slammin' Sammy took a 2-2 pitch over the centerfield wall, becoming the only player ever to hit 60 home runs in two different major league seasons. When Babe Ruth hit 60 in 1927, he broke his own record of 59, set in 1921, but he never reached 60 again. Nor did Roger Maris.

Sammy's wife, mother, and son, Michael, were in the stands to see him do it.

"I have to say that what I've done today is actually more special that what happened last year," Sammy said. "It's something no one else has ever done. I'm extremely proud of that."

Big Mac again edged him out for the home run crown, 65-63, the third and fourth highest single-season home run marks ever. Sosa had now hit more than 60 home runs two years in a row—and failed to win the home run title both times.

He didn't climb the 60-home run mountain in 2000, and the Cubs floundered under new manager Don Baylor. But Sammy had another great season, hitting .320 and driving in 138 RBIs. And his 50 home runs were enough to net him his first home run crown.

The Cubs rewarded their superstar slugger with a four-year, $72 million contract.

He went out and had another spectacular season in 2001. Highlights included the Cubs' first win at Busch Stadium in 13 tries over two seasons. Sammy led the way with a two-run shot and a grand slam and made a diving catch to save a run.

On August 22 he hit three home runs in a game for the second time in two weeks. With the Cubs far ahead of the Brewers, manager Baylor took Sammy out after the sixth inning, removing any chance of his tying the major league mark of four home runs in a game.

Four days later, he slammed two more against the Cardinals, numbers 50 and 51 for the season, thus joining Babe Ruth and Mark McGwire as the only players ever with four 50 homerun seasons.

The records continued to fall. His 52nd homer of the year, hit on August 28, tied Ruth for most home runs hit over seven consecutive seasons with 343. But Sammy was far from finished. September 23 he became the first man in history to hit three home runs in a game three times in one season.

His 60th came on October 2, but despite it, the Cubs were eliminated from wildcard contention. Now Sammy stood alone—the only player in history with three 60 home run seasons.

In his last at-bat of the season, he hit number 64 to set Cub records with 98 extra base hits and 425 total bases in a season. His 160 RBIs were the most in the National League since Chuck Klein's 170 in 1930.

The first time Sammy made his charge out to right field after the tragedy of September 11, 2001, he carried an American flag with him. He showed the colors again as he circled the bases after a home run, his way of showing his love for his adopted homeland.

2002 was another disappointing year for the "wait'll next year" Cubs, and Sammy had what was for him a "poor" year. Imagine hitting .289, belting 49 home runs, and driving in 103 RBIs and having it be a drop-off from previous years' production. That's the kind of superstar Sammy Sosa had become.

Those 49 dingers left him one short of 500 for his career as he entered the 2003 season. On April 4, he took care of that.

The Cubs' home opener was scheduled for April 7, but snow delayed it a day. With the temperature hovering at 32 degrees and snow flurries in the air, Sammy and Hall of Famer Ernie Banks, "Mr. Cub," the only other Cubbie to hit 500 home runs, threw out simultaneous first pitches.

But once the cheers died down, Sammy hit the worst three months of his career. On April 20, a Salomon Torres fastball struck him flush in the side of the head, shattering the batting helmet that saved his life. He sat out a few games, and then an infected toe forced him onto the disabled list on May 10. In all he missed as many games as the previous six years combined. When he returned on May 30, he struggled to find his stroke.

And then, on an otherwise routine ground out against the Tampa Bay Devil Rays, Sammy's shattered bat was found to have cork in it, and he was suspended for seven games. He said it was a mistake, that he used the bat in batting practice and for hitting exhibitions. Officials X-rayed all 74 of his other bats and four of his bats featured in the Hall of Fame and found nothing amiss. Still, cynics doubted his explanation, and many of the Chicago sportswriters turned on him.

When he returned to action June 8, to mixed cheers and jeers, he hit a homer in his first game and went on a hitting tear that carried him past immortals Ted Williams and Willie McCovey on the all-time homer list.

"It's a situation I've never been in before, with the way people said things about me," he told *Sports Illustrated*'s Tom Verducci. "What I learned from it is it makes you stronger. I've put it all behind me."

Then Sammy went out and helped the "wait'll next year" Cubbies make the playoffs. Despite missing 25 games, he finished the regular season with 40 home runs—number 40 coming in the division-clinching win against Pittsburgh—and 103 RBIs, marking the unprecedented ninth straight season the he'd knocked in 100 or more.

Sammy is the game's reigning slugger, one of the game's most exciting and loved players, and one of its finest humanitarians. He is happily married to wife, Sonia, and adores his four kids—Keysha, Kenia, Sammy Jr. and Michael.

Like his childhood hero, Roberto Clemente, he is a great right fielder and a great hitter. Like Clemente, Sosa wears number 21. And like his idol, he gives back to the country that raised him and the people he has never forgotten.

Also like Clemente, Sosa will one day be in the Hall of Fame—along with other Latin stars like Orlando Cepeda, Juan Marichal, and Tony Perez—alongside Babe Ruth, Roger Maris, Mark McGwire, Barry Bonds, and the game's other great sluggers.

To his devoted Cubs fans, and especially to the bleacher bums out in right field, whom he salutes each time he takes the field, he will stand as the greatest of them all.

CHAPTER 24

Hitting for Extra Bases
On and Off the Field
Carlos Delgado

"If you had a son, you'd like him to be like Carlos."
—Cito Gaston

Full name: Carlos Juan Delgado Hernandez
Position: First base, designated hitter
Career: Toronto Blue Jays, 1996-present
Career batting average (through 2003): .284

Career highlights:

- Led the league in doubles (57), extra base hits (99), and total bases (378) in 2000.
- Led the league in RBI in 2003 with 145.
- Finished in the top ten in home runs each season from 1998-2003.
- Finished second in AL MVP voting in 2003.
- Selected as an All-Star in 2000 and 2003.

Carlos is already the Blue Jays' all-time home run leader, and judging by his performance in 2003, he's a long way from done.

But it's his off-field heroics that earn him his spot in our good guys lineup.

He'll do just about anything to make a kid smile, and he isn't afraid to put it all on the line for the people of his native Puerto Rico.

"Carlos has a great way with kids," said Kim Sokoloski, manager of communications and development for the Make-A-Wish Foundation of Toronto. "He knows how to make them feel comfortable, how to make them laugh."

Ask four-year-old Dequan, whose wish was to get to throw out the first pitch at SkyDome, Toronto's baseball field, on the Blue Jays' Make-A-Wish Day. He turned shy as his big moment drew near, but Carlos took his hand and led him onto the field. Dequan ran to the mound, eager to show his friend how well he could pitch.

Anything for the kids.

He has refurbished two ballparks in poor areas of Toronto. He provides game tickets for underprivileged kids. He visits the schools, encouraging kids to work hard on their studies.

He helped organize a big fundraiser for Special Olympics, the Sports Celebrities Festival, and served as honorary chairperson for the festival in 2000.

"Carlos is a guy that will do the little extra," according to Glenn MacDonell, executive director of the Ontario Special Olympics. "[I]t makes him that much more a gentleman."

He started his own organization, the Extrabases Foundation, to help fund charitable groups dedicated to improving the lives of kids in Canada, the U.S. and Puerto Rico. One of those organizations, Casa Juan Bosco, helps kids in Carlos's hometown of Aguadilla, Puerto Rico. Carlos visits whenever they invite him.

"He does whatever he can to show the kids he is there for them," said Elba Perez, who works with the program.

Many athletes avoid taking stands on political issues because they don't want to alienate fans or lose potential commercial endorsements. Not Carlos. In April, 2001, he joined singer Ricky Martin and boxer Felix Trinidad to take out full-page ads in the *New York Times* and the *Washington Post* to ask the navy to stop using the island of Vieques, off the eastern coast of Puerto Rico, as a bomb-testing site.

"Puerto Ricans are like my family," Carlos said. "If people are being hurt in your family, you are going to take a different perspective on things. It's something I believe in."

The Making of a Slugger

As a kid growing up in Puerto Rico, he played baseball because "everybody there plays baseball," he said.

He credits his parents with giving him confidence in himself and solid values to live by. He stays close to his family, hopping a plane as soon as the season's over to head home.

Carlos was just 16 when he signed with the Jays in October 1988. He broke into professional baseball with St. Catharine's in 1989, moving up to Myrtle Beach, Dunedin, Knoxville, and finally the Jays' AAA team in Syracuse before making the big club in 1994.

Garth Iorg knew what the Jays had when he managed Carlos at the AA level, calling him a "consummate power hitter," the kind who can "carry a team on his back offensively for weeks at a time." At six foot three and 235 pounds, Carlos has the broad shoulders made for such heavy lifting.

He started hitting homers as soon as he hit the bigs in 1994, swatting nine of them, with 24 RBIs and 25 walks in 43 games. But then the player strike ended the season, and he went back down to Syracuse.

He made the Jays out of spring training next season, but in 91 at bats, he hit just .165 with three home runs, and the Jays sent him down again.

"[A] lot of kids get discouraged when they get sent down," former Jays' manager Cito Gaston said. "[But] he went down there and just got better."

Carlos rejoined the Jays in 1996, mostly as a DH. In his first full season, he hit a hard .270, with 25 homers and 92 RBIs. He had arrived to stay.

He'd always worn number 21, but when the Jays signed Roger Clemens, Carlos gave the Rocket the 21 in exchange for number 25.

When John Olerud left in the off season, Carlos became the Jays' everyday first baseman, despite having off-season surgeries on his wrist and knee. He also injured his shoulder diving for a ball in a game in Puerto Rico in January and couldn't play again until mid-April.

"My wrist was the one thing I was scared of," he said, "because that's the bread and butter for me."

He had another solid year in 1997, batting .262 with 30 home runs and 91 RBIs. He liked being part of the action on the field, too. "If you

Carlos Delgado will do just about anything to make a child smile—including funding numerous charities throughout Canada, the United States, and his native Puerto Rico. He makes plenty of Blue Jay fans smile as well with his remarkable hitting.

have a bad day at the plate," he noted, "you can contribute on the field. When you're DH-ing, you sit around two or three innings, and then you got to crank it up to hit."

Carlos cranked it up often, averaging 39 homers a season over the next five years. He not only hit home runs; he hit long home runs. One of his blasts hit the Windows Restaurant at the SkyDome, and another cleared the roof of old Tiger Stadium.

In 1999 he cracked 44 long balls, and his 134 RBIs tied George Bell's Blue Jay record for RBIs in a season. And he did all that by September 22, when an injury again ended his year early. In the eighth inning of a Jays' 14-9 win over the Red Sox, Carlos fouled a pitch off his right leg, fracturing the bone.

Once again he came back strong from injury. The next season he belted 41 home runs and drove in 141 runs, hitting a gaudy .344.

Carlos had become a star, and he got a star's reward. On October 20, 2000, the Jays signed their star to a four-year, $68 million contract, making him the highest-paid player in the game at the time.

On the same day, he won the Hank Aaron Award as the best overall hitter in the American League. Three days later, *The Sporting News* named him its Player of the Year.

He went out the next year and showed that he was worthy of the accolades. In an April 4 game against the D-Rays, he slammed three home runs. Two weeks later, he hit three more in one game, this time in a 12-4 win over the Royals.

But all that was just a prelude to his performance near the end of the 2003 season. On September 24, 2003, he arrived at the SkyDome feeling sluggish and sick. He took cold medicine and caught a quick nap in the clubhouse and, typically, said he was ready to play.

Was he ever!

Carlos went out and became just the 19th man in big league history to slam four home runs in a single game. The last one came in the eighth inning when, with more than 13,000 fans up and screaming, Carlos launched a mighty drive off the restaurant in the center field stands.

For his encore, he belted a grand slam on the last day of the season, setting a new Blue Jay record for RBIs in a season with 145.

He should continue to be a big hit for years, with the bat, with his teammates, and with the fans—and with the many kids who receive his generosity and his love.

CHAPTER 25

Turning Two Is a Family Matter
Derek Jeter

"Until you hit 1.000 and have no errors, you'll always have something to work on."

—Derek Jeter

"If you have a little, you give a little back. If you have a lot, you give a lot back."

—Dorothy Connor, Derek Jeter's mother

Full name: Derek Sanderson Jeter
Nickname: "D.J."
Position: Shortstop
Career: New York Yankees, 1995-present
Career batting average (through 2003): .317

Career highlights:
- Led the league in runs with 127 in 1998.
- Topped the league in hits (219) and times on base (322) in 1999.
- Finished third in AL MVP voting in 1998.
- Selected as Rookie of the Year in 1996.
- Selected as All-Star game MVP and World Series MVP in 2000.
- Five-time All-Star.

What would you call someone who makes $10 million dollars a year, has matinee idol good looks, dates singer Mariah Carey, hangs out with Tiger Woods, and laughingly calls George Steinbrenner "Boss Man" to his face?

How about "wholesome," "refreshing," "unaffected," "shy" and "kind"? All those words fit when you're talking about Derek Jeter.

But before we get to any of that, we really have to talk about The Play.

Many call it the most heads-up play they've ever witnessed on a baseball diamond.

In Game 4 of the 2001 American League division playoff series against the Oakland Athletics, with the Yankees struggling to avoid elimination, an errant peg from the outfield missed the cutoff man, and Jeremy Giambi—then a member of the Athletics—seemed certain to score. Suddenly Derek Jeter flashed across the diamond, scooped the ball and shoveled it to catcher Jorge Posada, who tagged Giambi out.

If you somehow missed seeing one of the thousands of replays of The Play, don't worry. It will make the highlight films for the ages.

But Derek is no one-play wonder. Just as the debate raged in the '50s (and continues to this day) over who was the greatest centerfielder—Brooklyn's Duke Snider, the Giants' Willie Mays, or the Yanks' Mickey Mantle—folks today argue among Jeter, Boston's Nomar Garciaparra, and the Rangers' Alex Rodriguez for greatest shortstop honors.

But Derek may be best remembered, not for The Play, not even for the career, but for his efforts off the field, where his Turn 2 Foundation helps turn at risk kids around and get them headed toward productive and satisfying lives.

Give Credit to Grandmother

Derek Sanderson Jeter was born on June 26, 1974, to Charles Jeter and Dorothy Conner in Pequannock, New Jersey. When Derek was four, he and sister Sharlee moved with their parents to Kalamazoo, Michigan. By the time he was six, Derek's maternal grandmother had already introduced him to pitch-and-catch and made a Yankee fan out of him.

Right about then, young Jeter was determined to play for the Yankees, and he adopted Hall of Famer Dave Winfield as his idol. He read Winfield's autobiography and decided to be like him both on and off the field. Winfield was the first major athlete to start his own charitable foundation, and even as a kid, Derek wanted to do the same.

D.J. brings new meaning to the baseball term "turning two." His family-run Turn 2 Foundation turns at-risk kids into high achievers.

His dad was his first coach, pitching to him for as long as he wanted and coaching his Westwood Little League team.

Derek's training in leadership began early, too. His parents asked him to mentor little sister Sharlee on the difficulties she would face being biracial. (Their father is African American, their mother Caucasian.) Big brother modeled patience and forgiveness.

Derek starred for the Kalamazoo High School baseball "Maroons," hitting .557 with seven home runs as a junior and .508 his senior year, with four home runs and 23 RBIs in 23 games. His slugging percentage was a staggering .831 and his on-base percentage .637. He also swiped 12 bases in 12 attempts. The American Baseball Coaches Association noticed, naming him the 1992 High School Player of the Year.

He played basketball with the same competitive fire, hitting the game-winning three-point shot against Portage High.

The Yankees made him the first high school player chosen in the 1992 free agent draft (he was the sixth selection overall) and offered him an $800,000 signing bonus.

Derek had starred in the classroom as well, earning admittance into the National Honor Society, and several colleges were after him. But he followed his dream and signed with the Yankees.

They started him out at Class A Tampa, where he had a miserable time adjusting to life away from home. He missed his parents, his sister, his high school sweetheart, Marisa Novara, and his best friend since fourth grade, Doug Brio.

Tampa "might as well have been another planet," he wrote in his autobiography.

He hit a puny .202 that first season, but the Yankees stuck with him, moving him to Class A Greensboro, where he hit a solid .293. Then in 1994 D.J. tore up AA ball, hitting .377 for Albany, and vaulted right to AAA, where he hit .349 for Columbus. *The Sporting News* tabbed him its Minor League Player of the Year for 1994.

He started the next season at Columbus, but on May 29, 1995, he made his big-league debut with the Yankees. He played in 15 games and hit .250 that year. Although the Yanks sent him back down to Columbus to finish the season, manager Joe Torre announced at the end of the season that the starting shortstop job was his to lose in 1996.

Derek didn't lose it.

Rookie of the Year and Emerging Star

Once Derek got his hands on his dream job, he wasn't about to let go. He hit .314 in his first full season and scored 104 runs, plenty good enough for Rookie of the Year honors. Then, he hit .360 in the three postseason series, helping the Yankees to a world championship over the Atlanta Braves. He was already building a reputation for coming through in the big games.

He fell off slightly in 1997, batting .291 but still scoring 116 runs and again helping New York into the playoffs, where Baltimore knocked them out.

These two solid seasons were but a prelude to stardom, however. In 1998 Derek emerged as one of the game's top performers, batting .324, swiping 30 bases, and scoring 127 runs. He also popped 19 home runs and drove in 84 runs, earning his first appearance in the All-Star game and finishing third in the MVP voting.

He again topped himself in the postseason, batting a torrid .353 in the Yankees' four-game sweep of the San Diego Padres.

In 1999 he was even better, hitting a career-best (so far) .349, clubbing 24 home runs and topping 100 RBIs (102) for the first time. He also scored 134 runs and posted an on-base percentage of .438 and a slugging percentage of .552.

And he again sparkled in the postseason spotlight, batting .375 in the playoffs as the Yankees beat Atlanta again in the World Series.

In 2000, he hit .339 and compiled his third straight 200-plus hit season, only the third Yankee (after Lou Gehrig and Don Mattingly) to do so. He was the MVP in the All-Star game in Atlanta, amazingly the first Yankee to win the honor. And he was again Mr. Clutch in the "Subway" World Series against the Mets. He hit .408 with two doubles, a triple, and two home runs in the five games, leading the team to victory and earning series MVP honors.

Making the Plays—and The Play

Despite their dominating performance in 2000, the Yankees weren't favored to repeat as champs the next season, and they appeared headed for elimination in the first round of the playoffs when they dropped the first two games of their best-of-five series against the Athletics. With the series moving to Oakland for games three and four, most folks were ready to award the series to the A's.

But then Derek made The Play, cutting down Giambi at the plate and turning the series around. The Yankees beat the A's and then the Seattle Mariners before falling to the Arizona Diamondbacks in the World Series.

Jeter slipped below .300 in 2002 but had another solid season, batting .297, stealing 32 bases, and scoring 124 runs (third best in the league). He matched his 2001 hit total with 191.

Now an established star playing on baseball's center ring in Yankee Stadium, Derek ran into adversity on Opening Day in 2003. Scrambling to reach third base before Toronto Blue Jay catcher Ken Huckaby could apply a tag, Derek suffered a shoulder separation when he collided with the catcher's shin. He missed 36 games, with rookie Erick Almonte and veteran backup Enrique Wilson filling in at shortstop.

When D.J. came back, owner George Steinbrenner named him the 11th team captain in New York Yankee history, following players like Gehrig, Mattingly, Thurman Munson, and Ron Guidry. The honorary title had been vacant since Donnie Ballgame retired in 1995.

"When he first came here, the other players seemed to gravitate toward him," his manager, Joe Torre, commented. "So I thought this day would come eventually."

Derek displayed his leadership on the field when a pop fly dropped between Jeter and two outfielders, a play one of them should have made. Pitcher David Wells showed his teammates up with his gesture of disgust at the missed opportunity. D.J. trotted to the mound and had words with "Boomer."

"You don't do that," he remembered saying, "and you know it."

The next day, Wells apologized.

Foundation Gives Kids the Boost They Need

There's a lot more to Derek Jeter than what we see on the field and in the credit card ads on television.

His parents instilled in him a desire to serve others, so it was natural that Derek enlisted his family to create the Turn 2 Foundation in 1996 to support and develop programs to help at-risk children. He first discussed the idea with his father in a hotel room of the Ritz-Carlton in Dearborn, Michigan, in September 1996.

The original design was to prevent and treat teenage substance abuse, but the programs Turn 2 creates or supports have gone way beyond that, addressing nutrition and fitness, providing tutoring and mental health counseling, and stressing parent and teacher involvement in the kids' lives.

According to Paul Attner, writing in *The Sporting News*, it is "the most unique athlete-initiated foundation in sports—family-based, family-directed, successful beyond anything the family had envisioned."

Turn 2 programs flourish in places like the Jackie Robinson Center in Harlem and the Lincoln International Studies School in Kalamazoo.

At the Kips Bay Boys & Girls Club in the Bronx and the Kalamazoo Boys & Girls Club, Turn 2 backs a drug, alcohol and lifestyle program for kids six to 18.

Turn 2 partners with the New York City Parks and Recreation Department to offer free baseball clinics and after-school programs for kids in Harlem and the Bronx.

Turn 2 also awards scholarships; the first Jackie Robinson/Derek Jeter Scholar recently graduated from MIT with a triple major.

"What has happened to the foundation is above and beyond what I ever envisioned," Derek wrote. "We are reaching a lot of kids, and I am very proud of it."

Turn 2 is a family affair for the Jeters. Derek's parents run the foundation, while sister Sharlee directs the programs.

"I wanted it to be something the family could do together," Derek explained. "And it had to be hands-on. I just didn't want to give money; I wanted to be involved…And I have the best parents in the world. I could trust them."

Although Turn 2 isn't just about money, in its first five years of existence, the foundation poured more than $1.5 million into its programs and partnerships. To make sure the work will continue long after Derek retires from baseball, Turn 2 has created an endowment fund, already well over $1 million.

The Jeters and Turn 2 have won numerous awards for their work, including the 1997 Joan Payson Award for community service, the New York Press Photographers' annual "Good Guy" Award in 1998, and the Baseball Writers Association of America Joe DiMaggio "Toast of the Town" award in 1999.

Finding Role Models Everywhere

D.J. credits his parents for his values and work ethic, but he says he has found role models everywhere.

Two of them, Alex Rodriquez and Nomar Garciaparra, are often compared to Jeter, and in fact, folks mistake Rodriquez for Jeter and vice versa. Alex calls D.J. "my best friend," and Derek says the Ranger superstar is "like my brother."

He credits Don Mattingly with teaching him about the game and about life.

Derek also tries to emulate Michael Jordan, who is "classy and dignified," he said, on and off the court, and Tiger Woods, with whom his manager, Joe Torre, compares him for his presence and his passion for winning.

Jeter calls his manager "Mr. Torre" out of respect and seeks his advice almost daily.

But you don't have to be a superstar to be a role model for Derek Jeter. He said he's learned a great deal from teammate Luis Sojo, for example, and his parents and his grandmother remain the biggest influences in his life.

He is fiercely loyal to family, friends and teammates. Boyhood buddy Doug Brio is still his friend, as is high school sweetheart Marisa Novara. When teammate Darryl Strawberry was suspended for the third time for drug abuse, Derek went to him and told him that he loved him and supported him in his efforts to turn his life around.

Derek is keenly aware of his responsibility to the folks who only know him at a distance, too, and he accepts the challenge of being a role model gratefully and gracefully. His behavior must be exemplary at all times, he believes, on and off the field.

"You never know who's watching," he said simply.

He understands that he lives in an unreal world and that he has been allowed to live out his dream. He takes nothing for granted.

"I'm just an ordinary guy," he insisted, "with extraordinary dreams."

Derek Jeter made his dreams come true. Now he's helping others do the same.

CHAPTER 26

You Can't Keep a Good Woman Down
Ila Borders

"I'm a baseball player. That's all I do."

—Ila Borders

"I believe God gave me my talent…If I don't use that talent, I'm doing something wrong."

—Ila Borders

Full name: Ila Borders
Position: Left-handed pitcher
Career: Saint Paul Saints, 1997; Duluth-Superior Dukes 1997-99;
    Madison Black Wolf, 1999-2000; Zion Pioneerzz, 2000

From the day her daddy took her to her first baseball game at Dodger Stadium when she was 10, Ila Borders knew she wanted-ed to be a baseball player.

"I really learned to appreciate the game from my dad," she said. "When I was younger, we were always watching a game on TV, going to the ballpark, or playing catch…My dad taught me everything I know. He's like a coach to me. But he's never made me feel uncomfortable or pushed me to get into it. He's just really excited for me and always real-ly supportive."

She would need that support. Ila didn't want to play softball with the girls; she wanted to pitch in the major leagues.

Many players climb the ladder from Little League up through high school to college, but relatively few make the jump to professional baseball, let alone The Show. The odds are just too long, the competition too tough. So, what are the odds of a woman even getting a toehold in the first rung of that ladder?

Ila Borders faced down those odds and the barriers, enduring abuse, profanity and shunning—sometimes from teammates as well as opponents. Once, at age 14, she struck out a boy in a key situation, and his girlfriend came down out of the stands to attack her. In the early days, her father sometimes had to escort her off the field. Later, she made the walk alone—except that she always carried her strong faith in Jesus Christ with her.

Faith, ability and hard work made her the first woman to get a college baseball scholarship and the first to pitch a complete game for a college team. And when in 1997 she played in a game for the Northern League St. Paul Saints, she became the first woman to pitch in men's professional baseball.

She missed being the first woman to play in any capacity in men's pro ball by a few years. Lee Ann Ketcham and Julie Croteau played for the Maui Stingrays in the Hawaiian Winter Development League in 1994. Even so, Ila's achievement was so singular and so significant that her glove and jersey from that game now hang in Cooperstown.

Then she went on to become the first woman to start a men's pro game and the first to win one.

In doing so, she has surely made a statement for equal rights and equal opportunity for women. But that was never her aim. She just wanted to play baseball—at the highest level and against the best competition her God-given talents would allow for.

She's five foot 10 and whip thin. Her long brown ponytail streams behind her when she fires one of her assortment of pitches—curve, screwball, changeup, and a fastball that may or may not have topped out at 82 mph, depending on whose radar gun you believe.

"You definitely sometimes run into an attitude in the league about a woman playing," she said of her time with the Saints, "but it's only in the minors that I've heard 6,329 people [a sellout crowd in St. Paul] chanting my name and cheering for me when I take the mound. I hate to say it, but after being hassled for so long, it gives me chicken skin to hear the PA in every city play Roy Orbison's 'Pretty Woman' or the Doors' 'Love Her Madly' every time I run out of the bullpen to pitch."

Faith, ability, and hard work enabled Ila to become the first woman ever to win a game for a men's professional baseball team.

With Friends Like These...

It was a long run from the southern California suburb of La Mirada, where she grew up, to the mound in St. Paul.

Ila played baseball with the boys starting in Little League. At age 12, she faced 18 batters in a game and struck out every one. She started playing semi-pro ball two years later. She was her team's Most Valuable Player at Whittier Christian High School, and her performance induced Southern California College (SCC) in Costa Mesa to offer her a scholarship.

"No one ever knows until the opportunity is presented," SCC Vanguard coach Tim Fortugno noted. He praised her work ethic and her "outstanding" changeup.

Although she was the first woman to get a baseball scholarship, she wasn't the first to pitch in a college game, as has been widely reported. Jodi Haller beat her by four years, pitching for St. Vincent's College.

But Ila wouldn't be content with just pitching. She wanted to win.

She had long ago learned to screen out the taunts of opponents, but she was shocked when her SCC teammates turned on her.

"In college I went through what no person should ever go through," she says. "I'd turn around during practice, and I'd have baseballs thrown at my head. I'd go out to my car and find my tires had been slashed. I found I always had to be alert and watch my back."

She was especially hurt because SCC was a Christian college. Her faith in Christians was deeply shaken for a long time, she admits, but the abuse couldn't touch her belief in God.

"I drew strength from Psalm 37:3-4," she said. "'Trust in the Lord and do good...Delight yourself in the Lord and He will give you the desires of your heart.'"

She had to prove herself day by day, she said. "I'm just trying to keep focused on my goal to go on to something higher than this."

In her first start for SCC, she held NCAA Division III Claremont-Mudd to five hits and one run, becoming the first woman to pitch a complete-game victory in a men's collegiate game. In 19 and one-third innings (seven starts and two relief appearances) that season, she posted a 2-4 record with a fine 2.92 ERA.

"By the middle of the season, I was just a pitcher on the team, not the girl pitcher," she said. "That's the way I want it."

She patterned herself after Angels' pitcher Chuck Finley. "I'm a finesse pitcher," she said, "and I'm trying to establish the outside corner."

But she slumped her sophomore year, going 1-7 with a 7.20 ERA for a team that finished 21 games under .500. Her junior year she worked only 24 innings out of the bullpen.

She transferred to nearby Whittier College for her senior year, pitching 81 innings and going 4-5 with a 5.22 ERA. Her teammates there were much more accepting, she said.

The opposition wasn't. Ila batted 11 times that season; she was hit by a pitched ball 11 times.

When her college career ended in the spring of 1997, Ila, then 22, sorted through her options. She had a degree in kinesiology and worked as a substitute teacher in the off-season, but that was for later. She wanted to be a professional baseball player, to see how far ability and hard work would take her. Several Japanese teams were interested in her, as were the Colorado Silver Bullets, an all-women's team that toured the country for several seasons starting in 1994 playing amateur and semi-pro men's teams.

"Even though I could have made more money in some of those situations," Ila said, "I wanted to play in the best league I could find that would give me a chance. The Northern League is independent, with a reputation as being good, quality baseball—equal to the Double A level minor leagues."

Ila got her chance when the St. Paul Saints gave her a tryout.

A Foot in the Door with the Maverick Saints

Lots of folks think it was a publicity stunt. They have their reasons. The team's owner, Mike Veeck, is the son of Bill Veeck, the legendary owner/promoter who once sent three-foot-seven Eddie Gaedel up to pinch hit for the St. Louis Browns. Son Mike was in fact doing promotions for his old man in 1979 when his ill-fated "Disco Night" blew up in his face, forcing the Chicago White Sox to forfeit the second game of a doubleheader.

Bill Veeck lived by the credo that baseball should be fun, and son Mike makes it plenty of fun in St. Paul. At a Saints' home game, you can get a haircut in a real barber chair behind home plate or a relaxing massage from a genuine nun, sister Roselind Gefre. When the plate umpire needs a new supply of baseballs, the team mascot, a pig, brings them.

So you'd have some justification for accusing Mike Veeck of putting a uniform on a woman and sticking her out on the mound as a sideshow to boost attendance.

You could, that is, until you realized that every St. Paul Saints game is already a sellout, weeks, even months in advance. Veeck didn't need Ila to fill the stands.

Saints manager Marty Scott made the decision to keep her on the roster. She made the club, Scott said, "by the skin of her teeth, based on her work ethic, based on other rookies in camp who didn't perform up to our expectations. But now it's up to her to pitch well to stay."

Scott liked the movement on Ila's pitches, liked her command and location, and thought she could help the team.

He must have had his doubts after her historic first appearance. It came on a Saturday night against the Sioux Falls Canaries on May 31, 1997. The crowd of 3,335 at Sioux Falls stadium gave her a standing ovation as she trotted to the mound. But she hit the first batter she faced, Paul Cruz. She appeared to have retired the next batter, Michael Dumas, on a groundout to shortstop, but the umpire called a balk on the pitch. Dumas then lined a full-count pitch back at Borders. She knocked it down but threw wildly for an error, allowing Cruz to score. When John Tsoukalas followed with an RBI double to right center, Scott gave Ila the hook. The Canaries won, 11-1.

"I think we were both a little nervous," Tsoukalas told reporters. "I know she had to be really nervous...Nobody wants to get out by her, so I think that's going to make it even tougher for her."

"I did awful," Ila said. "It's as plain as that...That was the most nervous thing I've gone through in my entire life, and I failed."

Former major league pitcher Steve Howe, on his seventh suspension for drug violations, pitched one and two-thirds innings in that game. Afterwards, he had consoling words for Ila.

"I remember how I felt as a rookie in the Houston Astrodome. I couldn't even spit, so you have to show her some respect. I just told her, 'Hey, been there, done that,'" said Howe.

"She'll be given another chance," manager Scott said. "I think we owe her that."

Good to his word, he ran her back out the next day—to another standing ovation—and this time Ila retired the side.

"My first year was nothing but survival," she said.

Not everyone hoped she'd make it. Sioux City Explorers coach Ed Nottle was heard to utter, "Every time she pitches, it hurts the integrity of the league."

After Ila pitched in a few more games for St. Paul, the Saints traded her to Northern League rival Duluth-Superior.

"I was shocked at first, and a bit disappointed," she said. "The guys on the Saints had been really great to me, and the fans in St. Paul were friendly as well."

So Ila was truly a professional now. She had endured her first trade—for a .181 hitter named Keith English. If she thought the trade bothered her, she should have heard English, who lamented, "I was traded for a girl!"

The trade had lots of upsides for Ila. She stood to get more chance to pitch with the perennial doormat Dukes than with the league champ Saints. Her new teammates greeted her warmly and treated her fairly. And if the crowds were smaller than in St. Paul, they were every bit as enthusiastic and supportive. And Ila could make a big difference at the gate for the Dukes; when she pitched, attendance doubled or even tripled at Wade Stadium, a 1930 Works Progress Administration relic in the shadow of a train trestle near Lake Superior.

Ila Comes Through for the Dukes

The Dukes surprised everyone by making a run for the second-half pennant. As contenders, they used Ila sparingly, a mop-up inning here and there, and her ERA soared to over seven. Even so, in the first round of the playoffs for the Northern League championship, Dukes manager George Mitterwald got Ila up in the bullpen. And then, with the game on the line and the opponent's best hitters coming up, he called for Ila.

As she trotted in, the crowd chanted, "I-la! I-la! I-la!"

They continued to roar as Ila got the first two batters on pop-ups but quieted when she walked the third. After getting two quick strikes on the next batter, Ila heaved a sigh and reached back for that something extra pitchers always seek in such moments. She found it, firing a called third strike to end the threat. The cheering then wasn't for a woman pitcher; it was for a clutch performance by the home team pitcher.

That was enough for the Dukes to offer her a contract to come back in 1998, giving her the chance to achieve two more milestones.

The Dukes fell out of contention early, and Ila started getting more work in relief, six appearances totaling 10 innings. Then, on Thursday, July 7, she got her first start, the first start ever by a woman against the men. With 2,266 cheering her on at the Wade, she faced the Sioux Falls Canaries—and took a 2-1 lead into the fifth inning. But she tired and yielded solo home runs to Benny Castillo and Eddie Gerard.

The Dukes lost the game, 8-3, but Ila won a major victory. Her line—five innings, three hits, three earned runs, two walks and two strikeouts—was credible and earned her another start a week later.

"I wish I could have gotten that win," she said after the game. "But I wanted to keep my team in the game, and I wanted to pitch the best I can. I think I did those things, and I'm proud of that."

Next time out, against the Thunder Bay Whiskey Jacks, she again hit the wall at about 75 pitches but this time escaped with no decision. So Mitterwald handed her the ball again, on Friday, July 24, 1998, against Sioux Falls at the Wade. Mark that date well. Ila Borders made baseball history that night.

Somber pregame ceremonies marked the 50th anniversary of a terrible tragedy. On July 24, 1948, the bus carrying the Dukes from Eau Claire, Wisconsin to St. Cloud, Minnesota, crashed head on with a truck in St. Paul, killing four players and seriously injuring many others. One of the survivors was a kid named "Red" Schoendienst, who went on to a sparkling 19-year career in the majors.

Then Ila took the hill and breezed through the first four innings, carrying a 1-0 lead into the fifth. That's where she had hit the wall in previous starts, and she got in trouble again quickly. C.J. Martin worked her for her first walk of the night, and Jason Klam roped a line drive toward the gap. But centerfielder Brian Ralph caught up to the ball, whirled, and fired a bullet to first to double off Martin. When Rich Rodriques grounded out routinely to end the inning, Ila had escaped.

If she and the Dukes could hold on, it would be the first ever victory for a woman in men's professional baseball.

The Dukes pushed across another run in the home half, and Ila entered the sixth inning and uncharted territory. The number nine hitter flied out to Ozzie Canseco, Jose's twin brother, in left, but the leadoff man, Craig Dour, drew the second pass of the night from Ila and promptly stole second.

Ila got the second out but now faced Eddie Gerald, a .338 hitter who was already 2-2 against her that night, representing the tying run. With the crowd roaring on every pitch, Gerald took her deep into the count, slamming one long foul down the left field line. And then Ila struck him out swinging on a nasty curveball to end the threat and bring the crowd to its feet.

"Big Poppa" Lewis polled a long home run over the 380-foot marker in dead center off Canaries' starter Brian Grant in the bottom of the sixth to make the cushion 3-0. The bullpen then took over for Ila—and made it much too interesting.

It all came down to Edgar Tovar batting against the Dukes' closer, Emiliano Giron, with two outs, the Dukes up, 3-1, and the tying runs on first and second.

Giron fired a fastball, and Tovar swung hard, sending a high fly ball to center. Ralph faded on the ball, settled under it, and made the catch at exactly 10:08 p.m.

The crowd of 3,048 bathed Ila and her teammates with cheers and chanted for Ila, who hung around for an hour to exchange congratulations for autographs.

"It was kind of like having a dream your entire life and then getting it," she said. "It was awesome. I've been told 'no' my whole life...It was like a fairy tale."

In Ila's next start, against the Fargo-Morehead Redhawks on the road, Hawks manager Doug Simunic threatened to forfeit the game rather than exposing his team to the indignity of facing (and possibly losing to) a woman. He had reason to worry. Although she didn't get the win, Ila spun another six innings of shutout ball.

That 12-inning scoreless streak attracted the attention of Mike Wallace and his CBS *60 Minutes* crew, who were at the Wade for Ila's next start. Unfortunately, Ila didn't have it that night. In an inning and a third, she gave up seven runs, including three home runs, two by Marty Neff, as the Sioux City Explorers beat her, 9-3.

Undaunted, she opened the 1999 season with Duluth-Superior, but the Dukes traded her to the Madison Black Wolf on June 10. Again Ila swallowed her disappointment and made the most of her new opportunity. Madison manager "Dirty Al" Gallagher developed an unusual strategy for using her. Of her 15 appearances, 12 were starts. Gallagher let her pitch the first three innings and then, regardless of the score or her performance, pulled her, to prevent her from tiring, he said, and to keep opposing hitters from timing her off-speed pitches the second time through the lineup.

Ila responded with a staff-best 1.67 ERA, giving her a combined 3.64 ERA with the Dukes and Black Wolf for the season. But the plan had a downside; Ila couldn't qualify for a win, since starters must pitch at least five innings. She did pick up her second professional victory, however, on June 17, in relief at Fargo, her only decision of the season.

She opened the 2000 season with the Black Wolf but pitched little and asked for her release on June 9. She caught on with the Zion Pioneerzz in St. George, Utah, where, in five appearances totaling eight and two-thirds innings, she gave up nine earned runs. After the Feather River Mudcats reached her for three runs off what she thought was her best stuff, she announced her retirement from baseball on June 29, 2000, at age 26.

She had gone as far as she could go.

She Never Did It for 'Women'

If anyone needed proof of Ila's pioneer status, it came late in 1999, when she took her place beside Hillary Clinton, Supreme Court justice Ruth Bader Ginsburg and other notables in a special exhibition of photographs by Annie Leibowitz called simply "Women."

But Ila downplays her status. "This was never meant to be a statement for women," she says. "I just love to play baseball.

"My responsibility is to work hard and do my best for Christ…No matter what happens, God will still love me, so He's really the only One I have to please."

Ila was now ready to pursue new goals, perhaps teaching high school science or P.E. and coaching baseball. She went back home to La Mirada, California, and began working at a daycare center.

But whether she admits to it or not, Ila Borders is a symbol and an inspiration for every little girl who wants to play hardball with the boys. With enough ability, enough courage and faith, and a strong work ethic, they just might make it. No one dare tell them they can't.

Ila Borders did it.

CHAPTER 27

The Voice of the Dodgers
Vin Scully

"He paints the picture more beautifully than anyone who's ever called a baseball game."

—Dick Enberg

Name: Vincent Scully
Nicknames: "Vinnie," "Vin"
Career: Announcer, Brooklyn/Los Angeles Dodgers, 1950-present

He learned from the master.

Vin Scully apprenticed with the great Red Barber in Brooklyn, reading commercials and filling in for an inning or two. He was also responsible for going down to the field to get the starting lineups from the managers before each game. One day Red glanced at the cards Vinnie gave him and asked why the number three hitter in the Brooklyn order had been dropped to fifth.

"I didn't know," Vin recalled. "That's the last time I said those words to the Old Redhead. Be prepared, he taught me."

Vin learned his lesson well. He's been prepared for everything the Dodgers and baseball could toss at him ever since.

This is a case of the student surpassing the teacher. In his day, Red Barber was the best. But as great as Red Barber was, Vin Scully is better. Vin Scully is the best.

Imagine that you have a good friend who also happens to be one of the most knowledgeable baseball fans ever born. Imagine that this friend is happy to sit down with you and describe each day's game for you. He weaves in great stories but never gets in the way of the action. As a bonus, he has a great voice and a marvelous command of the language.

That's Vinnie. When he describes a game, you see it better than if you were there.

For over half a century, Vin has been inviting fans to "pull up a chair" and spend some time enjoying Dodger baseball.

His commentaries often become a kind of improvisational prose poem. His call of the ninth inning of Sandy Koufax's perfect game in 1965 has been anthologized with the greatest baseball literature.

He also knows when to keep quiet. His eloquent silence after Kirk Gibson's game-winning home run against the Oakland A's in the first game of the 1988 World Series intensified one of baseball's great moments.

Vin transcends the game, his commentary often touching on the human condition. He is more than baseball's greatest announcer; he is one of America's great storytellers.

Along with being the voice of the Dodgers for all these years, Vin has worked for the networks since the late '50s, calling baseball, football and golf. He teamed with Joe Garagiola on NBC's *Game of the Week*. In a case of perfect typecasting, he also played the announcer in the Kevin Costner movie *For Love of the Game*.

But he's at his best on the radio—just you, Vinnie and the game.

He introduced Los Angeles to the Dodgers in 1958, at the same time introducing millions of southern Californians to the intricacies of the game.

"When a game is on the air," Robert Creamer wrote after Vin had been in Los Angeles for a few years, "the physical presence of his voice is overwhelming. His pleasantly nasal baritone comes out of radios on the back counters of orange juice stands, from transistors held by people sitting under trees, in barber shops and bars, and from cars everything—parked cars, cars waiting for red lights to turn green, cars passing you at 65 on the freeway, cars edging along next to you in rush-hour traffic jams."

Thirty five years later, the description still fits—except that we'd have to change the "65" to "75 or 80."

"Vin Scully's voice is better known to most Los Angelinos than their next-door neighbor's," Creamer concluded.

Fans bring their transistors to Dodger Stadium so that Vin can enrich the game they're watching. "It keeps you on your toes," Vin

When you hear Vin Scully—the voice of the Dodgers for over half a century—describe a game on the radio, you see the game better than if you were actually there. He is one of America's great storytellers.

noted. "When you know that just about everybody in the ballpark is listening to you describe a play that they're watching, you'd better call it right."

Thumbing through the record books during a slow game in 1960, Vin noticed that it was umpire Frank Secory's birthday. "Let's have some fun," he told the fans. "As soon as the inning is over, I'll count to three, and on three everybody yell, 'Happy birthday, Frank!'"

Then he had second thoughts. What if, when he said "three," he was greeted by stony silence?

He shouldn't have worried. The crowd roared out its birthday greeting, and Secory looked up, startled and pleased.

When Vinnie calls a game, he sets it in time and place and defines its importance. As the game unfolds, he creates its mood and theme, blending anecdotes and descriptive details with his game coverage. He discusses strategy so the listener can anticipate the plays.

Concepts that usually apply only to literature—tempo, tone, texture—enhance his broadcasts. Add a musical voice, rich diction, and perfect-pitch inflection, and you have a symphony for one human voice.

His vivid commentary matched the level of Sandy Koufax's perfect game in 1965.

"And you can almost taste the pressure now. Koufax lifted his cap, ran his fingers through his black hair, then pulled the cap back down, fussing at the bill. Krug must feel it, too, as he backs out, heaves a sigh, took off his helmet, put it back on and steps up to the plate."

Vin called Sandy's three other no-hitters and many more, including Bill Singer's.

"They call him 'Billy No-No,'" Vin reported that night. "The no-no is because of the way he runs. When Bill Singer runs, his head shakes from side to side, and Don Drysdale once said, "Here comes 'Billy No-No.' And the message board in left field just underneath the scoreboard where it says 12,455 [the attendance], it says 'no-no.'"

After that game, Vin drew on his experience to further enrich the fans' appreciation of the event. "When he was interviewed on the postgame show in Atlanta after pitching seven and two-thirds innings of no-hit ball," Vin recalled, "Bill said, 'I'll get one one of these days,' and one of these days is July the 20th."

Vin also called every pitch as Don Drysdale broke the major league consecutive scoreless inning record.

"Drysdale takes a little walk back of the rubber. Picks up the resin bag and drops it again. McCovey moving the bat back and forth…Every member of the Giants on their feet at the base of the dugout steps, everyone!"

He described the first eight innings of Big D's fifth consecutive shutout as "eight blanks" and his 44 consecutive shutout innings as "forty-four pearls on a string. He needs one more."

It came down to one of the most controversial moments in baseball.

"The bases are loaded," Vinnie reported, "nobody out. The batter is Dick Dietz. But down through the years it just wouldn't be the Giants and Dodgers if it didn't wind up this way."

The next pitch hit Dietz, seeming to force in a run and break the streak. But the plate umpire directed Dietz to remain at the plate, and chaos erupted. Vin calmly told his audience that the ump "could have conceivably said that Dietz did not make an effort to get out of the way." That's exactly what happened; Vin had remembered and correctly applied rule 6.08. The man knows baseball.

"Oh, can you picture it?" he concluded. "If you had presented this script three days ago, the only word would have been 'balderdash,' and maybe one or two others."

Vin creates his verbal art without a script, without editing. His is a living commentary on baseball's work in progress.

When Dodger pitcher Orel Hershiser broke Drysdale's record two decades later, Vin was there to call each inning—with Double D in the booth with him.

"Eugene O'Neil wrote a great line," Vin told his audience. "He said there's no present and no future. There's only the past over and over now. And that's what we're looking at. The past, 20 years ago. We're looking at it again. Remarkable!"

When a crippled Kirk Gibson hobbled to the plate in the bottom of the ninth inning of the first game of the 1988 World Series to pinch hit against the Oakland A's, Vin was there.

"And look who's coming up? [He lets the crowd have its say here.] All year long they looked to him to light the fire, and all year long he answered the demands until he was physically unable to start tonight with two bad legs."

When Gibson fouled off a pitch, Vin said he was "shaking his left leg...like a horse trying to get rid of a troublesome fly."

The tension built. "So the Dodgers, trying to catch lightning right now. 4-3 A's. Two outs. Ninth inning. Not a bad opening act. High fly ball into right field! She is gone!"

And then Vin's eloquent silence let the roaring fans underscore the moment.

Vin, Sandy Reach Perfection Together

Of all his broadcasts, Vin will be best remembered for his call of Sandy Koufax's perfect game. Vinnie's commentary was as perfect—and as improvisational—as the game itself.

Vin, who had been at Ebbets Field the day Sandy tried out for the Dodgers, told the radio technicians to turn on the tape recorder for the ninth inning, as he always did when a Dodger was working on a no-hitter. Vin always emphasized the date at such times, so his words would create a record for the pitcher to keep. For Sandy on the night of September 9, 1965, he added the exact time to further place the event in history. Here's Vinnie in the ninth:

"There are 29,000 people in the ballpark and a million butterflies…And Koufax with a new ball, takes a hitch at his belt and walks behind the mound. I would think that the mound at Dodger Stadium right now is the loneliest place in the world…

"The time on the scoreboard is 9:44, the date, September 9, 1965. And Koufax working on veteran Harvey Kuenn…

"Sandy ready, and the strike one pitch. Very high, and he lost his hat. He really forced that one. That was only the second time tonight where I have had the feeling that Sandy threw instead of pitched. You can't blame a man for pushing just a little bit now. Sandy backs off, mops his forehead, runs his left index finger along his forehead, dries it off on his pants leg, all the while Kuenn just waiting…

"It is 9:46 p.m. Two and two to Harvey Kuenn. One strike away… Sandy into his windup. Here's the pitch! Swung on and missed! A perfect game!"

Vin then kept his mouth shut and the field mike open for 38 seconds to let the crowd roar. When he spoke again, it was to say:

"On the scoreboard in right field, it is 9:46 p.m. in the City of the Angels, Los Angeles, California, and a crowd of 29,139 just sitting in to see the only pitcher in baseball history to hurl four no-hit, no-run games. He has done it four straight years. And now he capped it. On his fourth no-hitter, he made it a perfect game."

And Vinnie called it perfectly.

Learning from the Master

Vin Scully was born in New York City and grew up in
Washington Heights on Manhattan Island listening to Red
Barber announce the Dodgers. Vin calls him "radio's first poet."

"Except for my mother," Vin wrote for a *Reader's Digest* tribune to
Barber, "he was the most influential person in my life. My father died
when I was not yet five, and Red became like a father to me."

Other kids wanted to grow up to be doctors or nurses or lawyers.
Vinnie always wanted to be a sportscaster.

"My family had one of those four-legged radio monsters that sat so
high off the floor, I could actually crawl under it," he recalled. "I'd lie
there for hours with a box of saltines and a carton of milk, mesmerized
by the play-by-play."

What he most admired about Barber's work, he said, was how he
made broadcasting an intimate conversation with the listener.

Vin went to Fordham Prep and then to Fordham University, inter-
rupting his education for a two-year stint in the navy. He studied speech
in college, played baseball—he was a good-fielding, weak-hitting outfielder—and worked for the radio station.

After graduating in 1949, he got a job as a summer replacement
announcer for WTOP, the CBS affiliate in Washington, D.C. That fall
he interviewed with CBS officials in New York and wound up talking
with their sports director—none other than Red Barber. Red didn't have
a job for him, but a week later, when he suddenly needed someone to
cover a backup game for the College Football Roundup, he remembered
Vinnie and gave him a shot.

His first assignment was Maryland vs. Boston University at Fenway
Park. Vin left his coat at the hotel, expecting a cozy press box. Instead,
he had to stand on the roof with only a headset, a microphone, a program, 50 yards of cable and a 60-watt light bulb on a pole.

He was supposed to supply 15-second updates every time he heard
Barber say, "And now up to Vince Scully in Boston." The game was close
all the way, and Notre Dame started routing North Carolina in the main
game, so Red kept switching the network coverage to Vinnie. The whole
country heard him as he fought off butterflies and frostbite.

Barber called a couple of weeks later and gave him another assignment, the Yale-Harvard game. Red had been impressed, he would say
later, not only by the quality of Vin's work but by the fact that the young
man never mentioned, let alone complained about, the raw conditions.

So another phone call soon followed, an invitation to come to spring training, on a trial basis, as the number three Dodger announcer.

"Oh, boy!" Vin recalled his reaction. "Here I was, 22, single, just out of college, and I'm asked if I'd like to go to spring training with the Dodgers!"

You can take that as a "yes."

Vin passed his trial and in 1950 became part of the Brooklyn Dodger announcing team.

Along with preparation and a conversational style, Barber taught his young protégé objectivity.

"Very early on, I found I was most accurate if I looked at things with my eyes instead of my heart," Vin noted.

When you turn on a Dodger game, you can't tell from his voice whether the Dodgers are ahead or behind. If a Dodger makes a great play, Vin says so. If a Dodger kicks the ball, Vin tells you that, too.

When his mentor turned down the job of announcing the World Series for Gillette in 1953 in a salary dispute, Gillette approached Vin with the job.

"Heartbroken, I asked Red what to do," he recalled.

"'Vin,' he said, 'if there's anyone in the world I'd want to take my place, it would be you.'" So Vin added the World Series to his resume.

When Barber was ready to hand the microphone over to Vin for his innings, he would often say a cheerful, "Okay, young fella. It's all yours."

In 1954, he handed the microphone over for good, moving over to Yankee Stadium to partner with Mel Allen. The Dodgers' number two man in the booth, Connie Desmond, was ailing. At age 26, Vin Scully became the lead Dodger announcer.

He moved west with the team in 1958, and he and wife, Joan, began raising their two boys, Mike and Kevin, in Brentwood.

For folks in southern California, Vin has always been *the* voice of the Dodgers, as much a part of the team as any player or manager—and perhaps more for many fans.

Vin also developed a national following, reporting the World Series until 1998, when CBS lost the franchise to ESPN and Vin turned down a spot on the radio team.

In 1992 he was inducted into the Hall of Fame. Among other honors, the Academy of Television Arts and Sciences hosted a "Tribute to Vin Scully" in 1997, and he was named Sportscaster of the Century.

While constantly in the public eye—or at least its ear—for five decades and counting, Vin has always shielded his private life, including his second marriage and his charitable work for causes like Saint John's Health Center's Neonatal Intensive Care Unit.

Even so, he's got friends all over town. True, most of those friends have never actually met him, probably never even laid eyes on him, except on television or perhaps from a distance in the Dodger broadcast booth, where he sits, left hand lightly touching his temple, eyes intent on the field. They know him by his voice, with its Irish lilt, its cadence and tone, and by his friendly invitation to "pull up a chair" and enjoy a game with him.

During "Fernando mania" in 1981, when a young pitcher named Fernando Valenzuela captivated Dodger fans with his biting screwball, his space-alien windup, and his obvious enthusiasm, Vin made this call when 'Nando hit a home run.

"There are no words to express what's going on here. The sounds of a cheering crowd tell it all. The Fernando Valenzuela magic is alive and well, and so are the spirits of 55,000 at Dodger Stadium…[W]ho is to say when it will end?"

When baseball at times rises to the level of high drama, and no words seem adequate to describe it, Vin Scully has always found the words, along with the eloquent silences, to make poetry of the moment.

CHAPTER 28

Unmasking Homophobia
Dave Pallone

"It is because of our faith that we continue to survive."
—Dave Pallone

"Kill him! Kill the umpire!" shouted someone in the stand;
And it's likely they'd have killed him had not Casey raised his hand.
—"Casey at the Bat" by Ernest Thayer

Name: Dave Pallone
Career: Umpire, 1979-1988

This time he was wearing a Houston uniform.

It was July 11, 1985, and Nolan Ryan was close to his 4,000th strikeout.

Nearly two decades earlier, as a 19-year-old Mets rookie, Ryan fanned the Braves Pat Jarvis for his first strikeout. Now, on a hot Houston night, he faced the team that had selected him in the 1965 free agent draft.

By the luck of the draw, Dave Pallone's crew was umpiring the Astros and Mets series at the Astrodome.

"There's no way I'm not gonna be behind the plate for Ryan's 4,000th strikeout," Dave Pallone said.

Despite smelling salts and a shattered cup, Dave didn't miss Nolan Ryan's party. It was Astros catcher Mark Bailey who didn't make it.

The Mets had a runner on third with less than two outs when Ryan delivered The Express.

"I didn't actually see the ball," Pallone joked, "but I knew it was a fastball because I saw its vapor trail—and also because the catcher missed it completely, and it hit me right in the cup."

A few innings later, Ryan fooled the Mets' Donnie Heep with a 0-2 curveball for number 4,000. True to his word, Pallone was still in there calling balls and strikes.

It was quite the night for both Ryan and Pallone. Ryan reached his lofty plateau, and Pallone became the first major league umpire to receive a Ryan-autographed cup.

A thousand Ryan strikeouts later, Dave Pallone was out of baseball. By the time Nolan nailed his 5,000th against the A's Ricky Henderson in August, 1989, Dave's reputation, his dream of working a World Series game, and his livelihood were all shattered.

The Men in Blue

Umpires compete for a scarce 68 major league umpiring jobs, cope with loneliness, incur the wrath of fans, players, and managers, and for an average of three hours per game labor under a giant microscope.

"The umpire is the most neglected, least appreciated, and most misunderstood participant in the National Pastime," Larry R. Gerlach wrote.

Dave Pallone faced an additional hurdle. He was gay in the super straight world of professional sports.

In December of 1988, Major League Baseball dismissed him, handing him four reasons. By the following March, he had accepted their settlement offer and walked away from the game he loved. His 10-year major league career as "one of the finest" was done.

It wasn't baseball's finest hour.

From Participant to Spectator

Saratoga Springs, New York, a city of 26,186, is famous for its thoroughbred racing, the summertime Philadelphia Orchestra, and two National Museum/Halls of Fames—racing and dance.

It's also where Dave Pallone was wrongly accused of having sex with teenage boys. In September 1988, the *New York Post* linked Dave to a Saratoga Springs criminal investigation. Major League Baseball got whiff of the scandal, and Dave's job hung in the balance.

Six weeks later, the district attorney dropped their investigation of Pallone and never filed charges. But the black cloud had quickly formed over him.

Besides his alleged involvement at Saratoga Springs, concerns about Dave's ability to perform under the adverse media pressure bubbled up. The league also referenced a Cincinnati bar rumor (another investigation found nothing) and his low 1988 rating.

"In 1987, I was rated among the top 10 umpires and worked the playoffs that year," Pallone said. "Then in 1988, after everything went public, I suddenly became the third worst umpire in the NL, and they said they wanted to let me go. I said, 'Fine, I'll quit. As soon as you fire the two who are allegedly worse than I am.' Well, they never fired anyone else."

Was Dave Pallone found guilty of being gay?

It sure looks that way.

"I was gay," Dave said. "And they didn't want the publicity surrounding that to tarnish baseball's macho image."

Dave took his loss hard.

"The baseball field used to be home, my refuge from reality, the one place in the world where I had some control," he said. "Now it was just a place to watch a game."

Yet he persevered despite a wave of ridicule, humiliation, innuendo, and distortion. Umpires uphold the integrity of the game. Dave kept his part of the bargain.

Switching on the Light

Dave Pallone may have lost the battle with Major League Baseball, but he didn't miss the lesson.

"Most gay and lesbian athletes remain silent," Johnny Diaz wrote, "because they fear unmasking themselves would stir a backlash among teammates and fans and cause the loss of lucrative contracts."

Dave took the opposite track—he went public, inviting the world in to glimpse the life of a professional umpire hiding his sexual orientation.

He wrote *Behind the Mask: My Double Life in Baseball* so readers could pull up a seat behind the plate and witness the nasty effects of fear, secrecy, and homophobia.

"Fear is something that most people don't associate with people who are gay/lesbian," Dave said. "When you have to hide who you truly are every day of your life to your family, friends, and coworkers, it makes your life miserable."

Umpire Dave Pallone was quite familiar with pressure and con-
frontation thanks to players and managers like Pete Rose, right.
So, instead of keeping his sexual orientation a secret, he boldly
authored a book about his battles with homophobia.

"The deepest, darkest closet is the locker room," Marcos Breton wrote. "Why? Because homophobia is accepted as part of the machismo of sports—accepted not only by the power structure of sports but by the sporting press and fans."

Dave opened the door and flipped on the light.

"I bring a different face to the reality of sexual orientation and especially a gay man," Dave says. "I first and foremost don't fit the stereotype of a gay man. I come from the world of professional sports, which most people don't think a gay man can be in. I bring a human face to a story that can affect most people if not all."

Dave's book and his story made a difference. Ask the 18 year old who wrote to Dave after he gave an interview promoting his book.

"I was sitting at home alone with a loaded gun," the letter said. "You convinced me not to take my life, and I hope someday to thank you."

Pallone deserves more than a few thank-yous. He has slowly begun to break down the barriers of homophobia.

"There are countless suicides every year by gay men and lesbians, particularly youth," Scott Bidstrup wrote, "which mental health professionals tell us are not the result of the victim's homosexuality, but actually the result of how the homosexual is treated by society."

Dave Pallone overcame that harsh treatment.

"I consider myself one of the lucky ones who was able to live two lives and survive. I have a strong will to never quit," Dave says. "I truly believe that my love for the game of baseball kept me from thinking too much about the loneliness and despair like so many others do every minute of every day."

The Path to Umpiring

Pallone's love of baseball was nurtured in Watertown, Massachusetts, less than 10 miles from Fenway Park.

His father, Carmine, was once offered a contract from the St. Louis Browns. It was during the depression, however, and Carmine turned down a promising pitching career to work.

Taking the cue from his father, Dave grew up on daily dosages of the Boston Red Sox.

He followed the team closely, listening to his team on the radio, and occasionally he made it to the Fenway bleachers with his dad.

He developed the knack, as *Boston Globe* columnist Brian McGrory wrote, of most Boston fans to "rue the bad, cherish the good, and always wait for their hearts to be broken, because it's all they've ever known."

In Dave's heart, though, he wanted to be more than a fan. Dave wanted to ump.

Red Sox broadcaster Curt Gowdy and former major league umpire Bill Kinnamon helped him on his way. During a Red Sox game in 1970, Dave heard a commercial about umpiring.

"All of a sudden Gowdy started reading an advertisement for the Umpire Development Program, a training school for prospective major league umpires," Dave said. "I'd never heard of it before, yet for some reason it caught my attention."

The classes didn't start until February, so Dave took a detour via the Ted Williams Baseball Camp in Lakeville, Massachusetts. There he hooked up with Kinnamon, a former American League umpire who had retired after nine years (1960-1969). Dave couldn't have found a better teacher.

"My contribution to baseball," Bill said, "has to be the number of kids who have gone through my school."

Dave aced the umpires' exam and was selected to attend school in February. (Of the 1,200 who applied, only 60 were selected, and of the 60, 30 got a minor league contract).

Dave spent eight years (1971-78) calling minor league games in sleepy towns like Thedford Mines, Quebec, and Geneva, New York. He quickly found out how tough umpiring could be.

"It is not easy to umpire," Kinnamon wrote. "It is very difficult thing to do well. But if you have the ability, umpiring is a great career. And if you have it, the majors will find you. You can't hide a good young umpire any more than you can hide a good young ballplayer—the really good ones stand out in every classification."

Answering the Call

Dave stood out—he knew the rules and exerted confidence. He defied the odds, getting his call in 1979 at age 27, thus becoming the third youngest umpire to make it to the big time. (The two youngest umpires—Billy Evans and Al Barlick—both reside in the National Baseball Hall of Fame.)

Dave's was a controversial call. He was one of the eight umpires hired by Major League Baseball during the 45-day strike at the start of the 1979 season. After many hours of soul searching, Dave decided to accept the two-year contract, knowing he would be the target of recriminations.

"Once I crossed the picket line," he wrote, "it was like taking the raft across the River Styx: One way, no return…I based my decision on the eight years I spent in the minors; it was time to take the step."

When the veterans returned, he was shunned and taunted. He accepted the abuse and moved on.

"I believe my will to survive was the key," he said. "And then having the friendship of Paul Runge as well as his mentorship (albeit four years after breaking in) made my career a success."

Eventually the strike-breaker stigma faded. Pallone was selected to umpire the 1983 50th Anniversary All-Star game in Chicago and worked the 1987 NLC playoff series between the St. Louis Cardinals and San Francisco Giants.

Day in and day out, for 10 years, he umpired close to 1,500 games, most routine, a few special.

He was at Riverfront Stadium in Cincinnati when Pete Rose singled off the Padre's Eric Show for his 4,192 career hit, surpassing the great Ty Cobb.

Three years later he met up with Rose again, this time at first base, on a much less joyous occasion, a Saturday Night Imbroglio, live at Riverfront Stadium.

Pete was managing the Reds against the Mets with the teams tied at 5-5 going into the ninth. With two outs and a runner on second, Mookie Wilson hit a routine grounder to Reds' shortshop Barry Larkin. Barry fielded it cleanly, but his throw pulled Esasky off the bag. As Esasky protested, the runner from second, Howard Johnson, steamed home.

Rose went ballistic, and the game nearly turned to a full-scale riot, with debris raining on the field.

Rose claimed that Pallone waited too long to make the safe call, and then the finger pointing and bumping started. Rose bumped Pallone twice and got the heave-ho. Rose later claimed that Dave scratched his cheek.

The *Cincinnati Enquirer* ranked it as one of the "100 greatest moments" at Riverfront. A more apt description might be "ugliest." When the dust settled, commissioner Bart Giamatti suspended Rose for a record 30 days.

What It Means to Be Human

Today, Dave Pallone lives in Colorado Springs, where he is a highly successful motivational speaker on diversity issues.

"In the course of the last 13 years that my book, *Behind the Mask*, has been written, there has been great progress," he said. "I have had the great fortune to start a different career in educating and enlightening young and old about sexual orientation. It has brought me to hundreds of college campuses and Fortune 500 companies."

Homophobia comes in many different guises, and Dave has seen and endured them all.

"Without my faith and prayer I truly don't believe I would have survived," he said. "Growing up I was raised a Catholic, and with that came a belief in heaven and hell. When my mom died so young, I believed that she went to heaven, so I prayed to her everyday. She was and still is whom I pray to, as I believe she will tell the higher being to watch over me. Each day I take time out to hike with my dogs, and that is where I say a prayer and thank the God I pray to for the blessing I have received."

Time has helped too.

"For me in my life now, I have no anger. However, when I was in professional baseball, my anger was on the baseball field a lot," he said. "I believe that whenever I was in an argument, my temper was greater because of my double life. And with my family, the anger was there because I had to lie to them all the time.

"So many people say to me that I have suffered a lot," he says. "Well, there isn't anyone who doesn't go through some sort of suffering in some way or another. But if we look at all the amazing things that happen to us in our lives, we will then realize how truly lucky we are.

"Until all Americans are protected under a federal law that they cannot be fired from their job because of who they are," Pallone said, "We will not reach equality.

"Respecting a person for who they are is so essential for harmony in our culture. There are, have been and will be people in professional sports who happen to be gay or lesbian. Please look at people who happen to be lesbian, gay, bisexual or transgender as human beings, not sexual beings."

CHAPTER 29

The Chicken Runs at Midnight
Rich Donnelly

"After Amy died, for weeks we would receive letters from people expressing their care and concern. Now I can return the favor."
—Rich Donnelly

Name: Rich Donnelly
Career: Coach, Texas Rangers, 1980, 1983-85; Pittsburgh Pirates, 1986-96; Florida Marlins, 1997-98; Colorado Rockies, 1999-2002; Milwaukee Brewers, 2003-present

Each time Rich Donnelly gazes at his 1997 World Series ring, he thinks of his daughter Amy. Rich was coaching for Jim Leyland's Marlins when Florida beat the Cleveland Indians in one of the most dramatic World Series endings ever. In Game 7, as the clock struck 12:00 at Pro Player Park in Miami, Craig Counsell touched home for the winning run on a Edgar Renteria base hit, and 67,204 Florida fans went crazy. Their Marlins had just become the first team to walk through the wildcard door to win the Series.

To some it might have seemed like a miracle, but the real miracle was occurring in Rich Donnelly's life.

Amy's Story

The story begins during the Pittsburgh Pirates spring training of 1992. Manager Jim Leyland, Donnelly, and the Pirates were hoping for another banner year. In 1991, they had come mighty close when Barry Bonds, Bobby Bonilla, and Doug Drabek took the Braves to Game 7 of the NLCS before John Smoltz shut them down. This year would be different.

For Rich Donnelly it surely was.

In late March, Amy, Donnelly's 17-year-old daughter, called him in Brandenton, Florida.

"Dad," she said. "There's something I have to tell you. Don't be mad."

Rich got nervous—maybe she was in a car accident or got herself in trouble. With her next words, Donnelly went numb.

"I've got a brain tumor," Amy said.

During a routine eye exam, the doctor detected an abnormality behind her left eye. The subsequent MRI found the tumor.

Rich rushed home to be with Amy and his family in Arlington, Texas. Within two weeks, Amy had brain surgery in Dallas.

After the operation, the surgeon didn't mince words. "Rich, it's malignant," he said. "The life expectancy for these tumors is nine months."

Donnelly went numb again.

A Season for Hope

During the summer, as Amy battled with her chemotherapy treatments, Rich resumed his third base coaching responsibilities. Life went on.

The Pirates ended the season in first place with a record of 96-66, nine full games ahead of the Montreal Expos. Pittsburgh led the National League in runs scored thanks to outfielders Barry Bonds and Andy Van Slyke. Couple that hitting with the pitching of Dave Drabek, Randy Tomlin and rookie knuckleballer Tim Wakefield, and you've got a team ready to avenge their 1991 loss to the Braves.

Amy knew how much her father wanted that World Series ring. So she was really excited when her father's friend arranged to fly her and her friend Cindy to watch the fifth game of the NLCS in Pittsburgh. Atlanta was marching along, leading the series 3-1, so the Pirates were one loss from a long winter vacation.

The vacation was placed on hold.

Perhaps Amy, wearing a baseball cap to hide her shaved head, brought the Pirates a wave of good luck. In the first inning, the Pirates ousted starter Steve Avery with four runs and won 7-1 on Bob Walk's three-hitter.

After the game, on the way back to the hotel, Amy asked her father a question that would supply the family with its rallying cry in the tough months to come.

"Hey, dad, " she asked, "when you yell to the players, what are you saying to them, 'The chicken runs at midnight' or what?"

"How did you come up with that?" Rich asked.

"I don't know. It just came to me out of the blue."

Rich laughed. Amy laughed. The saying became the family joke.

The Pirates came so very close to the World Series. In the seventh game, they entered the ninth leading 2-0. They needed just three outs. They got two.

With the bases loaded, pinch hitter Francisco Cabrera singled home David Justice and Sid Bream for a 3-2 Atlanta win. There would be no World Series ring this year.

The Donnellys gradually forgot about the Pirates' disappointing loss, but Amy's crazy saying caught on. For the next three months, that's all you heard around the house.

"The chicken runs at midnight" slogan was plastered throughout the Donnelly household. The kids would even end their letters with "The chicken runs at midnight."

The joke kept the family going.

During Christmas of 1992, however, Amy fell into a three-week coma.

Each day the family visited the hospital. Amy couldn't talk, but she could hear, so the Donnelly family placed a sign on her bed: "Be careful what you say—she can hear." Her mother arranged for a tape of *Cats*, Amy's favorite musical, to play for her.

Amy died on January 28, 1993.

Her tombstone read: THE CHICKEN RUNS AT MIDNIGHT.

The Miracle at Pro Player Park

When Leyland left the Pirates in 1997, he brought Donnelly with him to Florida. They brought 11 years of friendship, 995 wins and 863 losses, three National League East pennants, but no World Series ring.

When the Marlins won the '97 World Series in just their fifth year as a franchise, many considered it a miracle. But for Florida third base coach Rich Donnelly, the real miracle was the message of faith he received from his daughter, Amy.

When the Marlin's Craig Counsell crossed the plate in Game 7 against the Indians, Leyland and Donnelly finally achieved their lifelong goal. For Rich, though, the run had added meaning. When Counsell scored, the meaning of Amy's silly saying fell into place.

Fans poured onto the field. Leyland was running around the stadium shouting "Never give up!" Amid the panic, pandemonium, and pushing, Donnelly's son, Tim, who with brother Mike was a Marlin batboy, finally found his dad.

Crying, he embraced his dad, saying "Dad, Dad. Look. Look at the clock. Look at the clock!"

Rich did. It read exactly 12:00 midnight.

Counsell's nickname is "Chicken Wings." (If you ever watched him fluttering his bat before hitting, you would know why.)

Almost five years to the day later, Amy's silly saying finally made sense. The chicken really did run at midnight.

Rich was stunned.

"It was like I was hit with a punch to the stomach," he said.

At about two in the morning, sitting in the locker room littered with uncorked champagne bottles, he pulled out a letter from his briefcase that he had kept for five years. It was from Amy.

"Dad," she wrote, "'The chicken runs at midnight,' Love, Amy."

He read it again, and Amy was there, sharing the victory.

Call Him Coach

Rich Donnelly was born in Steubenville, Ohio, where he attended Catholic grammar and high school and then went on to Xavier College in Cincinnati.

As a kid, he remembers two things—going to daily Mass and playing ball.

His hero was his brother Romey, who pitched professionally. Romey told Rich that the quickest way to the major leagues was being a catcher. Rich took the brotherly advice, and right out of college he signed with the Minnesota Twins and played at St. Cloud. He was drafted in the winter by the Rangers and caught another three years for the Texas organization. He hit .230 with two homers and 115 RBIs and never made it up for his cup of coffee in the majors.

Instead, he became a Rangers minor league manager, toiling for 10 seasons and peaking at the AAA level.

Then he launched his coaching career, with stops in Texas, Pittsburgh, Florida, and Colorado, before coming to Ned Yost's Milwaukee Brewers in 2003. He has waved so many players around third base, he should be given a traffic light when he retires.

The Message

Rich had drifted away from his Catholic upbringing, but renewed faith helped get him through the tough times, giving meaning to his suffering. After the World Series miracle, God had his full attention.

He's calmer now, he says, not as impatient. He never hesitates to do things for people, whether it's getting a friend tickets to a Brewers game or flying back to Chicago to pitch to the Brewers' Richie Sexson in the All-Star Home Run Derby. He never misses an opportunity to help.

He spends a lot of time talking to Catholic youth groups. His message is simple: Don't be ashamed of your Catholic faith. He tells parents to spend time with their kids, because it means the world to them.

Rich Donnelly knows just how much it means to the parents, too.

Curtis Leskanic, then a pitcher for the Brewers, called Rich "one of the good guys."

We do, too.

Celebrate the Heroes of Baseball
in These Other Releases from Sports Publishing!

Fred Claire: My 30 Years in Dodger Blue
by Fred Claire
with Steve Springer

• 6 x 9 hardcover • 200 pages
• photos throughout • $24.95

The Great Rivalry: The Boston Red Sox vs. The New York Yankees
by Harvey & Frederic Frommer

• 8.5 x 11 hardcover
• 160 pages
• photos throughout
• $24.95

Big Stix: The Greatest Hitters in the History of the Major Leagues
by Rawlings
with Rob Rains

• 8.5 x 11 hardcover
• 160 pages
• color photos throughout
• $24.95

Larry Bowa: I Still Hate to Lose
by Larry Bowa
with Barry M. Bloom

• 6 x 9 hardcover
• 250 pages
• photos throughout
• $24.95

Bill Madden: My 25 Years
by Bill Madden
with the *New York Daily News*

• 6 x 9 hardcover
• 250 pages
• photos throughout
• $24.95

The Memoirs of Bing Devine
by Bing Devine
with Tom Wheatley

• 6 x 9 hardcover
• 225 pages
• photos throughout
• $24.95

Denny Matthews's Tales from the Royals Dugout
by Denny Matthews
with Matt Fulks

• 5.5 x 8.25 hardcover
• 200 pages
• photos throughout
• $19.95

Tales of the 1962 New York Mets
by Janet Paskin

• 5.5 x 8.25 hardcover
• 200 pages
• photos throughout
• $19.95

Good as Gold: Techniques for Fundamental Baseball
by Frank White with Matt Fulks

• 7 x 9.25 softcover
• 224 pages
• photos throughout
• $19.95

Yankees: Where Have You Gone?
by Maury Allen

• 6 x 9 hardcover
• 200 pages
• photos throughout
• $24.95